FISCAL FOLLIES

A Little Fun with Economics (and Economists)

BY DANIEL C. MUNSON

Keynote
BOOKS

Fiscal Follies: A Little Fun with Economics (Economists)

Keynote
BOOKS

ISBN-13: 978-1-963102-50-5 (Paperback)
ISBN-13: 978-1-963102-42-0 (eBook)
ISBN-13: 978-1-963102-43-7 (Hardcover)

Published by Keynote Books

Bulk orders of this book may be obtained by contacting Defiance Press & Publishing, LLC.

Public Relations Dept. – Defiance Press & Publishing, LLC
281-581-9300

Defiance Press & Publishing, LLC
281-581-9300

TABLE OF CONTENTS

PREFACE

Economics occupies an exalted place among the social sciences. Its practitioners have the ear of government leaders, Wall Street poohbahs, and corporate chieftains. When appointed to public office, the high priests of the economics profession have their every utterance taken down by scribes to be analyzed by armies of lesser mortals.

Surely such a profession should be able to handle a little criticism and a few good-natured jabs. That is what this book seeks to provide.

These pages concern themselves with the details of economic and financial history rather than—as with most such books—an author's conclusions regarding that history and/or predictions about the future. This is quite a different approach to the general topic, and I'll try to make the case that it is worth reading because of this.

Most books that review such history attempt to make some broad point regarding the blizzard of facts that comprise that history. This book takes a different approach: You get the facts, and you are left to process them. These facts come at you in a somewhat relentless manner, so I chose to give the reader a break and spice things up a little. I included some short diversions reviewing plots and characters in movies and plays, opera lyrics, etc. and connect those plots and characters and lyrics to this history in what I hope is a fun and engaging way.

Most of the history reviewed in this book is not the sort that the reader will encounter in a typical history class. There are reasons for this. Some of it, indeed quite a good deal of it, involves math and science and engineering, and while these subjects dominate much of our daily lives and explain so much of the material convenience we enjoy today, historians don't typically dwell on them. This may be because historians aren't very good at math and science and engineering, but there may be another reason as well.

Economic and financial history, when reviewed in detail, is sobering. Great political figures are encountered, but they are not central to this history. The actions of such prominent people are generally easy for most of us, including historians, to understand: the speeches, the wars, etc. Examined here is a world governed by powerful physical forces and mathematical inevitability. Most of us, including most historians and nearly all government leaders, prefer the idea that economic reality can be improved through government policy. The detailed review offered in these pages of such policies and the results obtained from implementing these policies does not leave one in the mood to champion more such policies.

Economic and financial historians who write of these matters, especially those with academic tenure, are quite rare. I suspect that the detailed factual and mechanical approach taken here, which tends to lead to a disdain for "new" or "transformative" government policy prescriptions, is not going to be attractive to most academics who are very often keenly interested in forming generalizations and guiding government policy around those generalizations.

The other type of book on this general subject might be described as the "Get Rich" variety. The authors of such books are often self-styled money managers who, oddly, prefer to write and try to sell books rather than simply apply their knowledge, something that—according to their own writings—would allow them to acquire much more wealth than could ever be garnered through selling books. The shop-worn adage that, "Those who talk don't know, and those who know don't talk" should always be kept in mind when perusing such books. The reader is hereby warned that this book contains no magic money-making schemes, although the study of the subject, and the skepticism and inquisitiveness I hope to engender in the reader, has in my own case not proved a good way to remain poor.

I therefore invite you to wade into these pages. You may not emerge spouting generalizations and platitudes about some form of economic injustice that only you can correct or insist that all within earshot learn from you how to "buy `um and sell `um." Instead, you will end up with a good deal of knowledge that may help you better process some of the economic and financial madness that surrounds us.

Chapter 1

INTRODUCTION: IS IT SCIENCE?

A few years ago, at a big, national meeting of professional economists, one of the economists in attendance is said to have created a period of uncomfortable silence when he asked the assembled throng to name an economic problem that the profession had actually solved.

It is a bit of a trick question, of course. Basic economics is really concerned less with solving problems than it is with structuring the discussion around questions a society and its citizens must constantly ask itself: What to produce? How to produce it? With what resources? How to distribute the produce? Et cetera.

The story, while perhaps apocryphal or exaggerated, is nevertheless interesting in that it exposes an uncomfortable truth. There are precious few widely accepted solutions to society's many economic problems. This lack of clear answers to straightforward economic problems has been a source of frustration for many decision-makers, up to and including officials at the highest levels of government. U.S. President Harry S. Truman, when asked what he could really use in his administration, famously said in exasperation, "Give me a one-handed economist! All my economists say 'On the one hand, on the other hand.'"

How could this be? How could a profession that sends at least one of its members to Scandinavia every year to receive a prize for achievement in the field of "Economic Science" grow silent when asked this question? After all, the Nobel laureates in other sciences such as physics and chemistry had specific achievements to tout, work that answered questions and was built on by others to produce real, tangible advancements and new products and technologies. How can a scientific field be bereft of tangible, permanent advancement?

One way to understand this uncomfortable silence is to look at the details behind the work done by some of those Nobel laureates. The Nobel Prize for Physics in 2017, for instance, went to a team of researchers who used extremely small distortions in space-time detected at the Interferometer Gravitational-Wave Observatory to observe—for the first time—the universe's gravitational waves, waves that in the particular case studied were generated over a billion years ago when two black holes collided. The detection method, the precision of the measurements, the underlying phenomena responsible are all a little abstruse, but the conclusions reached were clear, unambiguous, and repeatable.

In contrast, the Nobel Prize in Economics for 2002 went to an Israeli psychologist for work that showed how human behavior—economic and otherwise—was often irrational and driven by bias. His research methods involved not precise measurements but the use of surveys (!) that put subjects in situations designed to pinpoint this bias and irrationality.

Here was work that, unlike that of the physicists, was easy to understand. Irrationality in decision-making—who does not encounter this almost daily? The irony of giving the prize to a psychologist, not an economist, whose findings tended to undermine the certainty and repeatability of all the other work done in the field of economic science, was one that caused remarkably little comment.

Most of us don't understand the work done by these prize-winning physicists: It concerns solutions to problems whose relevance to our daily lives seems very small. We aren't particularly interested in the details either because they are both complicated and somewhat boring—a repulsive combination.

Conversely, a field of study interested in the many ways in which humans may behave in an irrational manner is a field of study that is accessible to all of us. Even when economists resort to using higher math, they deal with subject matter that is easy to grasp: markets, prices, supply and demand. We are familiar with these subjects because we confront them every day. They are also subjects concerning which members of the public can, and often do, have differing opinions and value judgments.

How might this familiarity and these different opinions be a barrier to the development of the "economic sciences"? Perhaps for the simple reason that if humans are behind the behavior that results in the observations made by economists, precision and reproducibility of results will become a problem, because when faced with the same or similar sets of circumstances, humans will not necessarily think or behave in the same, or in any consistently predictable way.

This lack of precision and reproducibility is an open, acknowledged issue in the "soft" sciences like biology and medicine. A recent survey of some 1,600 of these researchers indicated that 70 percent of them had failed in attempting to reproduce the work of others, and a whopping 50 percent of them had failed in reproducing their own work! (Physicists and chemists were more confident regarding the papers published in their field.)[1] Concern is utterly understandable in drug testing and in medicine and psychology testing, where humans are often the subjects of the experiment and where there are real human costs incurred when errors are made. Some 52 percent of these researchers considered this lack of reproducibility a "significant crisis." Social scientists are somewhat concerned, with one journal acknowledging the

---

1. *Nature*, May 25, 2016. See also "Why is Science Letting Us Down When We Need it Most" by psychiatric researcher Stuart Ritchie of Kings College, London, an editorial widely reprinted in American newspapers during August 2020.

problem and explaining that such social science studies are "difficult" to reproduce due to "culture" (because people are different) and "time period" (because people change).[2]

An example might illustrate what is a simple point. Metallurgists know that certain gold alloys are more flexible and more lustrous than pure, 24 karat gold. A gold alloy that is both strong and beautiful is a version of 14-karat gold obtained by blending gold, copper, and silver at a specific set of weight ratios—58.5/29/12.5. The results of heating and blending these elements in these precise ratios are utterly predictable: the luster, the density, the electrical conductivity, etc. Imagine taking a similar blend of humans—perhaps Chinese women, Scandinavian men, Sumatran men—and subjecting them to a test: a particular game of chance, a particular tax system, perhaps stranding them all on a desert island and observing how they organize themselves, etc. Would the results ever be as utterly predictable for the humans assembled in these ratios as would the metallurgical process? To ask the question is to answer it.

The hard sciences like physics and chemistry are simply different from these other fields of study. Lumping them together as different forms of science is to fail to make an extremely important distinction.

These differences can also be seen by reviewing a little scientific history, specifically the human behavior surrounding what may be the two greatest advancements ever made in physical science.

When Isaac Newton formulated his laws of motion and of gravity—oddly enough, by looking to the heavens and attempting to explain the mathematics of lunar and planetary motion—he did not run out and shout "Eureka!" In fact, he did not bother to publish the details at

---

2. "Social science reproducibility: Not great, but not as bad as reported?" *ARStechnica*, March 10, 2016.

all.[3] It was the seventeenth century; he had a secure job as a professor of mathematics at Cambridge University in England; and there was nobody looking at the problem in the purely mathematical way he was, and no professional need to "publish or perish." It was only years later, when rivals claimed to have reached some of the same conclusions, that Newton bothered to show the depth of his understanding by devoting two years to fully developing his views in Latin—the lingua franca of international scholarship at the time—in a compendious text he entitled the *Principia Mathematica*.[4] The book appeared in 1687, some twenty years after he had arrived at some of its central insights. His work set out both the laws of physical motion and of gravity and of the mathematical tools he had developed to explain it all, something we know today as calculus.

When Albert Einstein offered a slight modification to Newton's work a little over 200 years later, he knew that what he was advancing was counter-intuitive and not as readily demonstrable as Newton's laws of motion. He described his theory in a paper[5], but his development of the ideas and conclusions had been purely theoretical and mathematical rather than empirical or observational. In deference to the durability of Newton's work, and because of the abstruse nature of his own theory, Einstein set out three observable tests that would either confirm or refute his theory, what is now called the "General Theory of Relativity." If Einstein was correct, the results of the tests he proposed would be slightly different from those predicted by Newton's

---

3. *Newton's Gift* by D. Berlinski (New York, 2000), p. 23-59.

4. Ibid, p. 89-95.

5. Einstein formally presented the field equations that are central to the General Theory at a meeting of the Prussian Academy of Sciences on November 25, 1915. What we now call World War I was in progress, and such proceedings of the Academy were considered German state secrets. Copies of the paper, however, were smuggled out of Germany and reached Britain and the rest of the world during the war.

time-tested theories. If his new theory could not more accurately predict the results of these three tests, Einstein suggested Newton's work should stand unmodified. These tests later confirmed his theory, of course. Perhaps the most famous of these three tests will be discussed later in this book.

Let us consider these two advances, but not so much the science as the behavior of the scientists involved. Newton decided not to bother to publish his findings in the 1670s. Why? History has branded Mr. Newton a solitary and secretive sort, but this hardly puts him far from the temperamental mainstream of the scientific community. More important than his natural disposition, there was no professional or financial reason to do so. Perhaps most important of all, Newton *knew* he was right. There was simply no doubt in his mind that his equations worked. His math illustrating how a gravitational force proportional to the product of the masses involved and varying inversely with the square of distance from the sun explained the motion of the planets set down by Johannes Kepler earlier in the century—the elliptical orbits, the variations in planetary rotational speed—worked perfectly to explain Kepler's observations and equations. We know of once when he started to commit his thoughts to paper, but he never quite finished. There was no driving need to do so. Was he interested in the approbation or "constructive criticism" of his fellow scientists? Please! Further, what was the point of belaboring something that was so clear, so complete, especially because it would have entailed the tedious task of explaining the mathematical method he used, a method that was his own quirky creation?

Newton's intellectual and mathematical brilliance is worth a paragraph. Keeping in mind the rudimentary seventeenth century scientific knowledge that Newton had at his disposal, consider the following intellectual feat: Theorizing that the moon's circular orbit about the earth was a system that was similar to the elliptical orbiting of the planets about the sun, Newton used his mathematical ideas about the mechanics of circular motion and a gravitational force as well as the diameter of the earth and the moon's approximate distance from earth and combined it with the lunar cycle to define the moon's rotational speed. He then used this lunar speed and the moon's distance from the *center* of the earth to compute the acceleration of free-falling bodies at the *surface* of the earth, a value that Newton and a few of his contemporaries knew well: 32 feet per second per second. Sure enough, the motion of the moon and its distance from earth predicted with reasonable accuracy the acceleration of free-falling objects at the surface of the earth, proving to Newton that his theory and his math were correct and that the principle of gravity that he had invented and defined mathematically was universal and explained motion at the surface of the earth as well as the heavens. This leap of intellectual and mathematical wizardry, done using only these few skeletal facts, may simply have no peer.

ISAAC NEWTON

*He brought the motion of the planets
down to Earth—using math.*

Albert Einstein knew that Isaac Newton's math clearly worked to explain most of the physical world. A few specific tests could confirm Einstein's theory and permit him to modify Newton's work, tests that others were free to perform.[6]

The behavior of Newton and Einstein occurs every day at a far less interesting level in research laboratories throughout the world. Researchers and scientists work to solve technical problems, and the

---

6. The story is that Einstein was confronted by a reporter who asked about a new book entitled *Hundert Autoren Gegen Einstein* (100 Authors Against Einstein) critical of his theory of general relativity. "Why a Hundred?" asked Einstein in response. "If I were wrong, one would have been enough."

solutions are used to produce commercial products and potentially make money. Such advances are sometimes patented, but very often they go unpublished. The common law surrounding "trade secrets" has developed to protect property rights in such unpublished advances.

The idea of a social scientist, an economist perhaps, concluding something and keeping it to himself or herself is almost unthinkable, for any number of reasons. The whole point of the social sciences is to publish, ostensibly so that others can benefit from the conclusions. There are also extremely compelling monetary reasons for doing so, of course. Often the research is funded to generate and publish results. The social scientist could of course arrange a series of tests to confirm or refute the original finding, but this would often be prohibitively expensive and potentially wasteful in that the social scientist might have to concede that the original result was not reproducible and was, in fact, largely a matter of coincidence. It simply doesn't happen much.

Most social scientists approach any fact pattern with a theory that they use to view the facts. Their theory, furthermore, is not really a scientific theory. It is not a testable hypothesis. Social scientists deal not in testable, "falsifiable" hypotheses but in "world views," prisms through which facts are diffracted and filtered to generate a monochromatic light that illuminates the world in the tinted way in which the social scientist wishes to see it. To observe this, the social scientist discoursing upon their theory of "colonialism," or "imperialism," or "the flat tax" should be asked a simple Einsteinian question: What fact or fact pattern (past, present, or future) would cause them to reject their own theory? You and they will then discover that no such fact exists. If confronted by a fact that seems to contradict the theory, the good social scientist has a ready-made reason why it must be "filtered-out" or ignored due to some sort of bias or mistake they will insist was involved in its collection.

The intellectual legacy of the most influential social thinker of the last 200 years—for good or ill —makes this point. Karl Marx's social and economic theories yielded both a general "class-based" view of the world as well as an unambiguous economic prediction. Marx believed that these classes were intractably at odds with one another, and he, therefore, made a concrete prediction: Workers' wages would spiral ever downward as workers increased productivity, which he theorized would add to the supply of labor. "If one man does the work of 1-1/2 or 2 men, the supply of labor increases" is what he wrote—and additional supply of labor would, in turn, allow the capitalists to force down wage rates.[7] This prediction was a critical part of his worldview: Workers' wage declines would create desperate conditions that would lead to a revolution.

The ensuing decades, alas, would reveal Marx's prediction to be completely wrong. Wages in England, where Marx lived, increased in purchasing power by almost 60 percent over the last 30 years of his life—literally, before his very eyes.[8] No matter. Marx persisted in predicting his inevitable revolution even in the face of these realities, and his influence persists in the intellectual world because his nebulous, malleable theory about the class struggle–initially between the proletariat and the bourgeoisie, later the oppressed and the patriarchy–could be used to filter the light any way the viewer desired. The malleable "class theory" led Marx to make erroneous predictions, but if one ignored the errors and hoped others forgot them as well, the theory itself could continue to be useful, because his "class theory" wasn't a testable hypothesis in the scientific sense, and it remains vibrant among social scientists, if perhaps not most economists, to this day. More will be said of Mr. Marx later.

---

7. *Capital- Volume I* by K.Marx (1867, London 1990), p. 869.

8. Journal of the Royal Statistical Society, Vol. LXXII, Part I, p.102 (March 1909).

KARL MARX WALKS DOWN A LONDON STREET

*His theorizing was impervious to the
economic facts all around him.*

Some influential social scientists used to understand this. Prominent economist and social critic John Kenneth Galbraith made this lack of a corrective force in the social sciences a critical part of his wildly popular 1950s book, *The Affluent Society*. In discussing how conventional thinking develops and hinders the specific sort of Progress that Galbraith advocated, he posited that, "Because economic and social phenomena are so forbidding…and because they yield few hard tests of what exists and what does not, they afford to the individual a luxury not given to physical phenomena. Within a considerable range, he is permitted to believe what he pleases. He may hold whatever view of this world he finds most agreeable or otherwise to his taste."[9]

The more modern view taken by many contemporary social scientists is that objectivity and balance are morally suspect, and in explaining themselves, they illustrate their disdain for (or ignorance of) scientific reasoning. Howard Zinn, the popular writer of polemical histories, insisted in his most popular book that his slanted approach to history writing is justified, even required. "The historian's distortion… is ideological"[10] Zinn tells us, going on to illustrate that the "intent" of various historical figures leads him to abandon balance. In discussing the behavior of people like Christopher Columbus and other Europeans in conquering the New World, he asks rhetorically, "Was all this bloodshed a necessity for the human race to progress from savagery to civilization? …Perhaps a persuasive argument can be made—as it was made by Stalin when he killed peasants for industrial progress in the Soviet Union as it was made by Churchill explaining the bombings of Dresden and Hamburg, and Truman explaining Hiroshima."[11]

Zinn's logic, which is legalistic rather than scientific, is that if what Europeans intended in carving up the New World into private property as progress toward "civilization," that same intent to advance progress could be used to justify acts like mass bombings and Stalin's starving the Russian and Ukrainian peasantry.

Leaving aside the faulty parallelism involved in invoking the bombings of Dresden and Hamburg and Hiroshima, which were motivated not by a desire for progress but by a drive to end a terrible war as quickly as possible, Zinn claims the historian cannot distinguish

---

9. "The Affluent Society" by J.K. Galbraith (New York, 1958), p. 17.

10. "A People's History of the United States" by Howard Zinn (New York, 2005), p. 8.

11. Ibid, p.17

between what colonizers intended when driving native peoples off land to divide it into private property and what Stalin intended when dispossessing, starving, and killing millions of peasants. Unable to distinguish between these intentions on moral grounds, Zinn argues that none of them can be justified.

The application of scientific reasoning, which focuses almost exclusively on probabilities and detailed results and not intentions, cuts through Mr. Zinn's difficulty. Stalin's treatment of the Russian and Ukrainian peasantry was based on a new and novel theory—to wit, the entirely speculative notion that collective farming would increase farm output over land kept in private hands—that had never been tried on such a scale and that quickly proved a complete failure. The details of this failure will be discussed later. The Europeans who settled the Americas, on the other hand, in defining and placing in private hands land that had been used as hunting grounds, were applying methods that had proven successful in Europe for hundreds of years and that quickly met with success in America as well. By focusing on intentions—one speculative, the other time-tested—the social scientist is unable to distinguish them and falls back on tendentious criticism. Equipped with the ability to differentiate between speculation and likelihood, the physical scientist easily gets past such simplistic equivalencies.

A related difference between the hard sciences and the others, one that hinges on this difference in testable hypotheses, lies in the ease with which errors are exposed.

The "cold fusion" case from the late 1980s can serve as an example of the ease and speed with which errors in the hard sciences are laid bare. Early in 1989, two respected chemists reported that they had detected odd levels of heat energy in a calorimeter containing "heavy water" (i.e., D_2O) and a palladium cathode that were merely kept at room temperature and pressure. The chemists hypothesized that the deuterium nuclei in the heavy water were somehow interacting with the palladium catalyst and fusing with other deuterium nuclei nearby, and the "fusion" of these nuclei that results in the creation of a helium atom was producing the heat energy they were detecting with their calorimeter. If true, the energy produced in this way would be nothing short of a miracle in that it would be cheap and clean and plentiful because the energy released per fusion reaction is enormous. The results were widely reported, and the chemists behind the work were whisked off to testify before a Congressional committee. Alas, their results could not be replicated by others, and errors in their experimental methods and observations were quickly identified. Within a year, the excitement concerning the possibility of such a "cold fusion" reaction proceeding in this manner had completely dissipated.

If a physical scientist were to offer an alternative theory regarding the dependence of the gravitational force constant on distance and mass, perhaps through some correction of Isaac Newton's work, the theory could be tested in a matter of minutes. When a social scientist posits a new method of societal organization that will improve the lot of the average citizen, however, there is no way to test the theory short of imposing it on the public using the coercive power of government. As an example, when social scientists offer, as they often do, a new series of marginal income tax rates or tax tables that they claim will result in what they consider to be more equitable outcomes or greater economic growth, they start from a world view and simply imagine what will happen. The "data" used to buttress their theories are, by the standards of the physical sciences, imprecise and inadequate.[12] They have little scientific evidence to back up their claims–often because

_____

12. Dr. Sheldon Cooper, the physicist in the popular television comedy "The Big Bang Theory," uses the word "hokum" to characterize this imprecision. In one episode, he develops a detailed questionnaire to try to discover what his friends like about him, even though he concedes that "The social sciences are largely hokum."

such evidence is difficult and/or expensive to generate—and they have no scientific evidence that isn't confounded by dozens of facts.

Another difference between the hard sciences and everything else is more subtle and has to do with a principle called "the law of large numbers," a law that underpins the insurance trade as well as the precision of much of the hard sciences. This law can be summarized as "even the extremely improbable becomes predictable with enough data." An example: It was discovered in the 1940s that the half-life of an odd and radioactive isotope of carbon containing eight neutrons—carbon-14—was much longer than expected at about 5700 years. Following this, physicists gave birth to the idea of "carbon-dating." They proposed measuring the radioactivity of the skeletal remains of plant or animal life to determine how long ago the plant or animal died.

Carbon-14 is extremely rare. Only one in a trillion carbon atoms cycling through the atmosphere and through living plants and animals is a carbon-14 atom. Such carbon-14 atoms are created when cosmic rays hit the earth's atmosphere and convert a nitrogen atom into a carbon-14 atom. These exceedingly rare carbon-14 atoms react almost instantly with nearby oxygen molecules to become CO_2, diffuse down to earth and are there "fixed" (via photosynthesis) into living plants and then animals.[13] These one-in-a-trillion carbon-14 atoms are plenty, however, for the simple reason that every 12 grams of carbon atoms contains roughly a trillion-trillion atoms[14], meaning that those 12 grams of carbon atoms in a living plant or animal contain about a trillion carbon-14 atoms. This, in turn, means the age of the remains of a "once living" plant or animal can often be assessed with real accuracy

---

13. That's right: Cosmic rays contribute to atmospheric carbon. Not much, of course. The baseline level of CO_2 in the atmosphere is roughly 300 parts per million, 280 million times more than the carbon-14 level.

14. The precise number of atoms in 12 grams of carbon, 6.02×10^{23} or 602 billion trillion — "Avogadro's number" — quantifies the number of atoms in a gram-mole of such atoms.

even if the specimen contains only a few grams or even milligrams of carbon atoms because even if only one carbon atom in a trillion was a carbon-14 atom when the plant or animal died, there were still billions or even trillions of them in the specimen when it died, and their slow but predictable decay (back to a non-radioactive nitrogen atom) will allow the age of the specimen to be quantified because every 5730 years since the subject died, the number of such carbon-14 atoms declines by precisely 50 percent. Due to this rate of decay, the technique works best when the specimen died between 500 and 50,000 years ago.

This same law endows the hard sciences with incredible specificity. For example, the atomic weights of the lighter chemical elements listed in the Periodic Table of the Elements—those with atomic number less than 20 or so—are nearly always an integer multiple of the weight of a proton or neutron (which weigh approximately the same amount) because there are few isotopes and—like carbon-14—they're rare. An exception is chlorine, which displays an average weight of about 35.45 times the weight of a proton or neutron because about 3/4 of all chlorine atoms in nature are chlorine-35, and 1/4 chlorine-37. The odds of sampling even a microscopic sample of chlorine atoms—perhaps a trillion of them—and arriving at any average significantly different than 35.45 is basically zero. Why? The Law of Large Numbers, that's why. It may be possible to test a dozen chlorine atoms and get an average weight of 35, or 37, or any number in between other than that "true" average. A trillion chlorine atoms? Not a chance.

Do social scientists study trillions of subjects that behave in such a predictable manner to permit them to make such precise conclusions? Of course not.

Those social scientists with experience regarding the precision and reproducibility of the hard sciences would know that the conclusions they reach in their social studies should be properly modest regarding the reach and the finality of their conclusions. Such "hands-on" experience in the physical sciences is quite different, however, from simply passing a couple of science courses, and because of this, there are precious few such social scientists. Nearly all social scientists, therefore, do not realize that they are working in an *ersatz* scientific field, a hollow imitation of the real thing going on in the world's real laboratories.

Social scientists who work with economic data may appear—both to the public as well as to themselves—to be scientific and "data-driven" because the economic scorecards they toil over do seem very objective and precise. The financial figures generated by governments and corporations run to billions, even trillions, and the figures balance to the penny. Ledgers record tediously precise transactions; balance sheets show the equity account precisely equal to the difference between assets and liabilities.[15] Income statements are often misleading and later need adjustment, but the precision of the arithmetic leading to the income figure is unassailable. All of this lends a patina of precision that can mislead the observer because even with all this exactitude, the doors of the fiscal world cannot be opened tomorrow without considerable uncertainty as to what the new day will bring.

The social sciences are simply not science in the same sense as the physical sciences. The studies they undertake in attempting to understand the past to better predict the future might be said to be "arithmetically systematic," but that does not necessarily make them science. The conclusions they draw are often made using data and "correlation coefficients" that would make physical scientists giggle.[16]

---

15. This is largely a matter of definition, of course: what you own minus what you owe is your equity.

16. See "Noise" by Kahneman, Sibony, and Sunstein (New York, 2021), p. 151: "An extensive review of research in social psychology, covering 25,000 studies and involving 8 million subjects over one hundred years, concluded that 'social psychology effects typically yield a value of r [correlation coefficient] equal to 0.21.'" The engineering term to describe a correlation coefficient of 0.21 is "useless."

Social scientists and medical/biological scientists are often heard discoursing on a "model" they use to analyze a situation, and their work is often the subject of press releases that involve "associations" — e.g., greater use of laxatives was recently "associated" with dementia. The hard sciences do not use such terms—they use "equations."

By starting from the presumption that the social sciences are a science in the same sense as the hard sciences, the intellectual world makes a dreadful mistake. This book is a compilation of some of these mistakes, chosen not merely to criticize but also to get us to laugh a little at the folly that is human endeavor. "Error," as the old saw goes, "is what comes of getting out of bed in the morning."

If the social science of economics is not science in the same sense that the hard sciences are, what is it? If the higher math that developed around the physical sciences should not be applied to economic and social problems, at least not with the hope of the same precision and certainty, what sort of imaginative constructions should be used to inform such disciplines?

This book argues that this social world can be better understood through the facts of economic history as well as works of fiction—plays, movies, opera lyrics—with all the fun that such understanding might allow. Articles developing these ideas and presented here appeared in national magazines and journals and websites devoted to economic and financial issues, and the comments generated suggested that readers found them interesting and fun.

This approach will no doubt impress some among the stern, hard-boiled, non-fiction element of the reading public as silly and non-serious. In defense of this approach, I can only say that—unlike the economic theorists whose work I discuss—I am not trying to solve an economic problem with finality. If one's thesis is that the study of the economic world is not a scientific process leading to the development of precise economic solutions, it would be sillier still to begin announcing such solutions.

The writing here is not entirely devoid of the scientific method, however. The work of social thinkers is reviewed not by looking just at their ideas and intentions but by looking at their results, contrasting those results with the theories and predictions they used to justify the policies that produced those results. Economists have devoted precious little time to this approach, although they seem to have the time to study just about everything else.[17] Errors made by economists and their cousins in the business world in approaching the general economic problem of scarcity have been huge and sometimes so disastrous that the reader might take this approach seriously.

Mistakes can be funny, but perhaps not as they are being made. Mark Twain famously told us that, "Humor is tragedy, plus time." The social sciences produced bouts of almost unimaginable tragedy in the last few hundred years, but with the advantage of hindsight, we can look back and analyze some of the mistakes and have a chuckle or two, something that would have been much more difficult when those tragedies were occurring. Similar mistakes are with us today if we are willing to look. That is what I've tried to do in this book.

---

17. e.g., "Freakonomics" by S. Levitt and S. Dubner (New York, 2006). This popular book discussed the work of economists that included – among other things – a study of the wage hierarchy of drug dealers and an analysis of Japanese sumo wrestling results.

Chapter 2

A DIFFERENT KIND OF DISMAL

The reputation that economics has for being the "dismal science" is well-earned. The term was given to this field of study by a nineteenth-century Scottish historian and philosopher, Thomas Carlyle. He was a Victorian, and he might be forgiven for taking a dim view of matters economic. Mid-nineteenth-century Scotland was probably the sort of time and place where such matters and the associated working conditions could easily rouse the melancholy sensibilities: Six-day work weeks involving often back-breaking labor done much of the year in cold, damp, drafty conditions.

If the difficult working conditions of the early Industrial Age were not bad enough, the economic thinkers who surrounded Carlyle were as bleak in outlook as were the conditions in many workplaces. The nineteenth century got off to a morbid intellectual start with the writings of English pastor Thomas Malthus. The Reverend Malthus fancied himself a mathematician of sorts, and he argued that humanity was doomed to live on the edge of starvation because whenever a society figured a way to generate food in plentiful amounts, the citizenry would begin to copulate more frequently and multiply to the point where the plenty would quickly become a shortage, and a fresh bout of starvation would ensue.[18] A little later, another Englishman named David Ricardo seemed to explain quite a lot when he concluded that any increase in the productivity and wages of the average citizen would merely cause

---

18. "An Essay on the Principle of Population" by T.R. Malthus (1798). Needless to say, the ensuing 200 years have proven Mr. Malthus completely wrong.

landlords and the landowning gentry to raise rents and food prices and vacuum up all the benefits for themselves.[19] A reader of the economic philosophers of the time, someone like Carlyle, could hardly fail to get a little depressed.

Readers of fiction could not escape this general dirge. Charles Dickens began his 1854 novel *Hard Times* with an exhortation by a hard-boiled, unlikable character: "In this life, we want nothing but Facts, sir; nothing but Facts!" The story takes place in and around a benighted, soot-covered industrial midlands city that Mr. Dickens called Coketown. Dickens dedicated *Hard Times* to Thomas Carlyle.

Things improved during the nineteenth century, but slowly. Dismal conditions could still be found for those late-nineteenth century investigators eager to find them, although wages and working conditions in the aggregate showed improvement. The early years of the twentieth century saw the development of large numbers of less onerous, white-collar jobs around designing and monitoring the rapid production and repairing of tremendous labor-saving wonders like automobiles and telephones. Millions of people began to enjoy what later became known as leisure time, which created the phenomenon of citizen Babe Ruth, who made more money than President Hoover because he was good at hitting a pitched ball with a wooden bat.[20]

---

19. "On the Principles of Political Economy and Taxation" by D. Ricardo (1817). Ricardo defined rent very expansively to include the rental value of farmland, and those who owned the most productive farmland would be the real beneficiaries of all human progress. The plausibility of Mr. Ricardo's theory survived for about fifty years, or until the industrial revolution changed everything.

20. The story is told that when Babe was informed that his 1931 salary demand was for more money than President Hoover received, he asked rhetorically "What the hell has Hoover got to do with this? Anyway, I had a better year than he did."

BABE RUTH

"What the hell has Hoover got to do with this?
Anyway, I had a better year than he did."

Around this time, as dismal was being driven from some of the work-a-day world, a new kind of dismal was developing.

Some people have always had the time and inclination to consider broadly the operation of the entire mass of economic activity, and to imagine how the whole thing might be summarized, or quantified, or improved upon. Societal classes (upper, middle, and lower) and work classes (blue- and white-collar, bourgeoisie and proletariat) were defined by such people, and the relationship between different types of workers was generalized: labor and management, exploited and exploiting, etc. On the arithmetical front, techniques were developed to measure such economic aggregates as gross national product, and those inclined began to study how such abstract quantities might be influenced by controllable factors, like tax policy. It was the work of an intellectual minute to theorize how changes to the controllable factors might improve or retard the prospects of certain classes or increase these aggregate quantities.

Such work was, like the many white-collar jobs developed around the same time, not physically difficult. It became a popular vocation. An American economics and sociology professor of the early twentieth century penned a slightly scandalous book entitled *The Theory of the Leisure Class* in which he coined the term "conspicuous consumption" to describe the tendency among the many newly rich Americans of the time to spend their money in as ostentatious, or "conspicuous," a way as possible.[21] Later in that century, a mischievous member of this same tenured group, in an attempt to describe his lifestyle and that of his work colleagues, flipped the words around to come up with, "The Leisure of the Theory Class."

If the eighteenth century belonged to the political philosopher, the nineteenth to the engineer, then certainly the twentieth century ushered in the golden age of the "worldly" theoretician. Such theoreticians combined the best of both those earlier worlds: They concerned themselves with weighty matters that, unlike those of the earlier philosophers, were of practical moment. Even better, they dealt with such matters at an abstract enough level that they remained above gritty practical details. Better still, unlike the engineers, the theories they advanced could not be quickly proven wrong.

Such people would have remained harmless had they confined their

---

21. "The Theory of the Leisure Class" by T. Veblen (New York, 1899)

theorizing to their campuses and their think tanks. The application of their ideas to economics and politics, however, gave their theories some practical importance, and this practicality permitted them to escape their natural habitat. When economic and political conditions at certain times and places throughout the century caused many in the public to wring their hands in frustration and confusion, these theoreticians often emerged from their chrysalis to foist their theories as to what should be done next on an innocent public.

Some of these theories required no societal re-organization to implement and were thus blessedly innocuous in practice. The early days of the Franklin Roosevelt administration, for instance, were plagued by a rare twentieth century malady—price deflation—which caused an obscure agricultural economist from upstate New York to emerge from his cocoon. Professor George F. Warren had studied farm prices for many years, and he noticed that they varied with the price of gold.[22] President Roosevelt was interested in getting farm prices up any way he could because farmers in the United States simply could not make money and re-pay their bank loans at the dreadfully low agricultural prices prevailing in 1932-1933. Professor Warren was the man with the plan, or at least the theory the President wanted to believe in.

The President watched agricultural prices closely through the late summer and early fall of 1933 and noticed that, indeed, they seemed to vary up and down with the price of gold. This George Warren fellow was on to something, he felt. Roosevelt conferenced with Warren, to the consternation of the few establishment bankers in the President's inner circle. By mid-October, things had come to such a pass that Roosevelt decided to try out Warren's theory.

---

22. "Prices" by G.F. Warren and F.A. Pearson (New York, 1933). See Figure 7, where British commodity prices in British pounds and gold appear to track one another. Prices expressed in gold coins, however, vary inversely with the trading price of gold.

The details of this experiment will be explored more fully later in this book, but in summary, the idea was that when these government purchases of gold set the trading price of gold up in U.S. dollars, agricultural prices would go up in U.S. dollars as well. That was how President Roosevelt interpreted Professor Warren's theory.

All concerned were mesmerized and confused by a correlation that led them to infer causation: i.e., if two things go up and down together, the change in one must be causing the other to change. However, two things may move in tandem because both are being influenced by a third variable. This is a chronic problem in the social sciences because their world is filled with so many variables.

In the case involving President Roosevelt and Professor Warren, agricultural prices and gold can be observed varying together not necessarily because one changes the other, but because they are both influenced by a third variable, namely the market assessment or the value of the currency in which they are both priced or in the governmental rate of exchange between gold and currency, so that as the assessment of the value of that currency goes down, the prices of things go up, and vice versa. Buying up gold could not induce a decline in the value of the currency, because the increase in gold and commodity prices was the result, not the cause, of the currency devaluation. The experiment failed: The U.S. government could increase the gold price, but as it did so, agricultural prices refused to budge. The experiment was abandoned in favor of a simple devaluing of the dollar versus gold in early 1934[23], and Professor Warren receded into a well-deserved obscurity.

---

23. The Thomas Amendment to the Agricultural Adjustment Act was adopted in January 1934, mandating a 59% reduction in the government's exchange value of the dollar versus gold — from $20.67 down to $35 an ounce. (By increasing the number of dollars exchangeable for an ounce of gold you decrease the value of the dollar.) The important and lasting effect of this legislation, however, was the power it gave the Federal Reserve Bank to buy and sell government securities, not the re-valuing of the dollar vs. gold.

Events furnished other twentieth-century social theorists a much tighter and prolonged grip on governmental power, with disastrous results. At about the same time that Professor Warren was bending President Roosevelt's ear regarding farm prices, the economic theories of Karl Marx and Vladimir Lenin regarding the benefits of communal ownership were being applied in the Soviet Union by collectivizing agricultural land. This communal approach, in the words of Mr. Lenin himself, was grounded in science: "Modern socialist consciousness can arise," he wrote, quoting an Austrian socialist named Karl Kautsky, "only through profound scientific knowledge."[24] The scientific theory being applied predicted that farming "collectives" would produce more food than the same land owned and farmed by short-sighted individuals. Lenin's loyal acolyte and successor, Joseph Stalin, put it thus: "… we must do our utmost to develop in the countryside large farms of the type of the collective farms and state farms and try to convert them into grain factories for the country organized on a modern scientific basis."[25]

The Russian countryside in the 1920s, however, was being farmed by millions of peasants acting individually, simple people who knew little or nothing of socialist science or these supposed benefits of collectivism. Stalin needed their land and crops, however, and he referred to the process of conscripting crops and land from these peasants as "procurement."[26] Farmers who expressed their misunderstanding of the

24. "Lenin, Collected Works", Volume V, page 383. Expanding on this point regarding the connection between socialism and science and who among us can appreciate the connection, Lenin quotes Kautsky further: "The vehicle of science is not the proletariat but the bourgeois intelligentsia."

25. Stalin, Collected Works, Volume XI (1954), p. 44-45.

26. Ibid, p. 49-51. Stalin's remarks concerning "the measures we took to increase grain procurements" were delivered at an April 1928 meeting in Moscow of the Central Committee. Stalin announced the new policy and concluded by saying "Whoever thinks of conducting a policy in the countryside that will please everyone, rich and poor alike, is not a Marxist, but a fool, because such a policy does not exist in nature, comrades." There was much laughter

theory by refusing to turn over their land or crops to the new communist government were labeled "capitalist elements" or "counter-revolutionaries" and were very often shot dead.[27] The crops thus conscripted or produced by these collectives became property of the state, and as such they were very often sent back to Moscow or exported abroad to generate hard currency for the government. Millions in rural areas were in this scientific manner left without food and starved to death.[28]

Rather than increasing agricultural output as the theory had predicted, this collectivization caused it to decline by frightening, monstrous amounts—some 30 to 40 percent by various estimates.[29] The theoreticians behind this disaster decided to reinterpret this decline as part of a painful transition to a new and more perfect world that their theories would eventually bring about. The poor citizens of the Soviet Union spent most of the rest of the twentieth century waiting in vain for this more perfect world to appear.

These sorts of results in the Soviet Union were not bad enough to discourage others, however. Like-minded political leaders and their theoreticians did much the same "scientific" collectivizing elsewhere, in places like China and Cambodia most notably. The results obtained there were much like those obtained in the Soviet Union.[30]

---

and applause at this point in the speech, according to the Soviet editors (p. 52). To read these pages concerning "procurement" now—a beastly, murderous policy—and then considering the laughter and applause that greeted these words is truly revolting.

27. "Evaluation of Unnatural Deaths in the Population of the USSR 1927-1958", an article that appeared in *Cahiers du monde russe et sovietique*, March 1977. The estimation method used arrived at a figure of roughly 10 million people who unaccountably disappeared.

28. "The Great Terror: Stalin's Purge of the Thirties" by R. Conquest (1969), p. 22: "...perhaps the only case in history of a purely man-made famine."

29. "Istorii a SSSR", No. 5 (1964), p.6. Figures listed here show livestock production in 1933 was only 65% of the level in 1913, and that total draught power was lower in 1935 — tractors included — than it was in 1928, when there were fewer tractors.

30. The land reforms in Mao Zedong's communist China in the 1950s and 1960s resulted in many executions of "counterrevolutionaries." An accurate figure for the number of such executions, arrived at by French General and China scholar Jacques Guillermaz, military attache

Carlyle's "dismal science" phrase was originally meant to convey the idea that the study of economics concerned itself with the drudgery of the mid-nineteenth century working world. By the mid-twentieth century, it was becoming clear that dismal was more properly a modifier describing the type of science being done by some of its practitioners.

The late twentieth century marked the dawning of the "computer age" in the advanced western countries, and this age placed vast amounts of low-cost computing power in the hands of scientists and even ordinary citizens. An hour's work on a huge 1950s supercomputer could be done with a few deft keystrokes on a modest 1990s-era home computer. The modern social scientist and theoretician, anxious to keep up with these tremendous technological developments, has used this awesome new computing power to spawn new and interesting forms of fallacy.

Some simple mistakes of elementary statistics were made fast and facile by this new computing power. Such mistakes were at the heart of the recent 2007-2009 financial crisis, one that spun downward around the market for single-family housing in the United States.

The market for such housing is controlled to a large extent by those people and institutions who extend mortgage credit. These lenders are understandably interested in estimating the potential "downside" in making a loan, and in the case of a home mortgage loan this downside is limited by the price the lender can get on re-selling a foreclosed home. If the borrower doesn't make the required payments and the

---

in Beijing from 1937-1949 and 1964-1966, is between 1 million and 3 million. "La Chine Populaire" by J. Guillermaz (3rd ed., Paris 1964), p. 47. The starvation that resulted from these "reforms" is believed to have resulted in millions more deaths.

In Cambodia, the agrarian socialism of the Khmer Rouge regime deliberately killed over 1 million people during its forced labor initiative in 1976-1979, according to the Yale Cambodian Genocide Program. Over 1 million more are estimated to have died of starvation and disease. "Counting Hell: The Death Toll of the Khmer Rouge Regime in Cambodia" by B. Sharpe (Mekong. net, 2008).

loan is foreclosed upon, the price the house commands on re-sale is the critical variable that determines the loss the lender will take on the loan. It is a messy process, full of angst all around, but the financial damage done is limited by this simple metric.

Tasked with estimating the risks involved in this re-selling process, the statistician uses the hammer he has at hand. In the years leading up to the crisis, data was compiled of nationwide home price changes going back a few decades, and those roughly thirty years of year-over-year price appreciation and depreciation data gave the statistician a couple of statistics: There was, on average, a 5-6 percent per year average increase in housing prices across the country over this period of time, and a distribution of price changes above and below this average.

One simple way to estimate probabilities given such a data set, involves making an assumption about the nature of the variability that allows the statistician to completely flesh out a mathematically continuous probability distribution. Once such a distribution is established using a theory regarding the nature of the variability, the probabilities of different year-over-year house price changes are completely defined. This is most easily done by assuming that the underlying distribution of outcomes will be "Gaussian," a distribution defined in the eighteenth century by the prolific mathematician Georg Friedrich Gauss and known to all modern-day statistics students as "the bell curve." The mathematical model generated from this statistic is known as a Monte Carlo simulation.[31]

Other modeling was done attempting to correlate the risk of default with the creditworthiness of the borrower. This is normally a sound

---

31. "Odds-on Imperfection: Monte Carlo Simulation", Wall Street Journal, May 2, 2009: "These models were supposed to help quantify and manage the risks of mortgage-backed securities, credit-default swaps and other complex instruments. But given the events of the past couple of years, it appears that the models often gave big institutional, as well as small investors, a false sense of security."

practice: Reams of data are available concerning the creditworthiness of borrowers. Such data has been used successfully for many years to predict loan default rates, and the credit-ratings of borrowers are designed to conform to this bell curve.

There were a few huge problems with these models, however. There is no reason to think the true distribution of year-over-year home price changes will follow the bell curve, because the assumption underlying the bell curve is that there is a symmetrical randomness to the data. The process for making ball bearings produces a random distribution of ball bearing weights and diameters; there is no reason to believe home prices would produce a similar sort of randomness, if for no other reason than that humans are involved in trying to guess these quantities as they are produced. The business of estimating the true variability in the process, or "standard deviation," is also tricky, and thirty random data points is considered the bare statistical minimum for the estimate to be acceptable for such engineering purposes.

The business of predicting mortgage default rates from credit histories and income data is also difficult, clouded not by the data around creditworthiness but by the legal structure surrounding mortgages. Nearly all mortgages in the United States are "non-recourse" loans in the sense that the lender has no legal recourse against the assets of the borrower in the event the borrower defaults. The loan is secured only by the property itself, meaning that in the event of default, the only legal recourse the lender has is re-possession of the property.

There were even bigger problems with these models. This was not exactly a random thirty-year period, either. These were the thirty years following the U.S. government's decision in 1971 to disavow any promise to exchange gold for the U.S. dollar, a period during which interest rates gyrated wildly, the purchasing power of the U.S. dollar declined sharply, and the single-family home gradually became one of the few savings vehicles the citizenry could rely upon. It was, in general, a good thirty-year period for single-family housing prices. A random thirty-year period, then? Perhaps not, but it was the only thirty-year period the U.S. mortgage bankers' statisticians had, so they used it.

The statistical analysis done around this data set, a remarkably limited analysis, concluded that the chance of a nationwide decline in single-family house prices was minimal: The bell curve told them there was only a small chance of a decline. Mortgage bankers could thus blithely approve loans to questionable borrowers because the statistical model told them that in the event of foreclosure, the lender could be sure to get a decent price when re-selling the house that was used as the collateral for the loan. From this assumption, any number of loans that might have been considered foolish could be approved.[32]

We all know what happened. Housing prices declined in 2006-2010 by amounts that the bell curve thought not only very unlikely, but close to impossible—the sort of chances we associate with winning a multi-state lottery. Rather than the modest increase the model thought most likely, national housing prices declined by something over 20 percent, and in certain very populous areas by roughly 50 percent.

When wealthy, credit-worthy borrowers watched the value of their million-dollar houses on which they had placed a $900,000 mortgage decline in value to $700,000, their creditworthiness did not keep them from sending the keys back to the mortgage-holder—in many cases even though they could still afford the mortgage payments.[33] The math-

---

32. The issuing of mortgages was, of course, the goal in the first place, because the initiating and securitizing of these mortgages and the managing of these mortgage securities was an almost obscenely profitable business.

33. The defaulting mortgagees could expect their credit rating to decline. When weighed against the chance to relieve themselves of a big liability, however, the option of defaulting and moving elsewhere was often very appealing.

ematical models associating default risk with credit rating did not work: The correlation was based on conventional recourse loans and on the gradually increasing house prices of the preceding decades. It simply failed when applied to the serious 2006-2010 bear market in housing prices, when millions of mortgage balances suddenly exceeded the value of the property by large amounts.

The nation's mortgage bankers learned the hard way that the production of average national housing price data is not the same as the production of ball bearings.

The effects of these little miscalculations were enormous. Trillions in losses were taken in mortgage finance; hundreds of billions more related to mispriced insurance policies taken out to insure against such losses. The government's mortgage purchasing entities had to be formally absorbed by the government and their loans guaranteed, and all the major banks were given government money in return for issuing preferred stock to the government so they could be kept solvent. A steep recession resulted.

Economists rode to the rescue.

The idea these economists advanced, the theory, was that a certain additional amount of government spending, roughly $800 billion worth, spent in a particular way dictated by economic science, would sluice through the economy in a predictable manner that would result in economic activity that would not otherwise occur. Such activity, they asserted, would keep the unemployment rate from going over 8 percent and would have the effect of setting the U.S. economy back on an upward path.[34]

There were those out in Flyover Land who must have read the details and wondered exactly how the whole thing would work as planned.

---

34. "The Signal and the Noise" by N. Silver (New York, 2012), p. 40-41.

Much of the spending touted by the bill's proponents was going to be for "infrastructure" projects—roads and bridges—but those with any granular knowledge of the construction trades had to wonder how this was going to work. The planning and constructing of roads and bridges is work done by engineers and skilled tradespersons, many of whom are seldom currently sitting on their hands and can't instantly plan and execute such projects. Materials must be ordered, and skilled workmen scheduled. Before this work can even begin, however, the precise plans must be vetted by the local communities. Studies must be done on the effect such plans would have on local water tables and wildlife. Lawsuits are often brought to challenge the proposed plans.

The timing and the breakdown of the total amount of "stimulus" spending into different types of spending was critical to the effect it would have on the economy. The economic models insist that different sorts of spending have different economic effects, depending on the nature of the spending. For example, "infrastructure" spending would result in a predictable increase in the demand for concrete and asphalt. Unless the spending could be targeted properly, the economic effect would not be quite as predicted.

The mistakes were legion. Sure enough, only about $30 billion of the $800+ billion found its way into infrastructure projects, for some of the reasons mentioned.[35] Much of the rest was directed elsewhere: payroll tax reductions rather than spending, and aid to state and municipal governments to keep those governments from having to lay off quite so many employees, neither of which would necessarily result in increased demand for asphalt and concrete. Worse yet, the spending that did result was not nearly as effective as the economic models had predicted. In economist parlance, the "multiplier effect" of some of

---

35. "Finding Infrastructure in the Stimulus Plan" by P.K. Howard, The Huffington Post, Feb.18, 2014.

the spending—an economic metric that will be discussed later—was not nearly as strong as estimated. The economy did not respond as planned: The U.S. government's "unemployment rate" raced through 8 percent on the way to over 10 percent. The red ink spilled by the U.S. government broke all records.

The twentieth-century experience of applying economic theory and planning to the real world had the economic theorists prepared, though. The flood of red ink was deftly and quietly mopped up, and the low-interest rates mandated by another arm of the government allowed the whole sordid affair to be politely ignored. All things considered and by the standards established by experience, the economic scientists concluded it wasn't all that bad. It was merely another perfectly good theory shot down by reality.

Economic policymakers often escape blame for such errors by pointing out that the economy is complicated, or by blaming bankers, or by pointing to other factors that cloud simple cause-and-effect connections.

Sometimes, however, they are caught red-handed.

Sri Lanka's government leaders recently illustrated this by taking upon themselves the job of managing the business of their country's farmers. Sri Lanka's economic and political leaders worried, as many such leaders do, about the country's balance of payments, and they focused specifically on the amount of money their farmers were spending on fossil-fuel-derived fertilizers and pesticides. It was a lot of money in Sri Lanka: $400 million per year. The nation's president was a man of action, and he acted: On May 6, 2021, he banned the importation of such fertilizers and pesticides.[36] Problem solved.

The nation's farmers objected to the ban, but whatever decibel

---

36. U.S. Department of Agriculture Report, Foreign Agriculture Service, June 3, 2021.

level their objections could reach were drowned out by the adulation that rained down on the prime minister and his ministers from the world's nongovernmental organizations—NGOs—and the people who advance the principles of environmental, social, and governance—ESG—standards. Fertilizers and pesticides derived from fossil-fuels can, they insisted, harm people. The ban would stick.

It only took a half dozen months, or roughly one harvest season, to expose the problem with the government's management of the nation's farms. Crop yields collapsed.[37] The agricultural minister tried to assure farmers that direct payments would compensate them for their losses, but that didn't increase the amount of food. The country's food export business largely vanished—the government instead had to borrow money to import rice as crops were used by the Sri Lankans themselves to prevent their starvation, something that can also hurt people. Food inflation soared. Everyone knew why. The president had to flee the presidential palace "in his stockinged feet." He fled the country, needless to say, using a fossil-fueled airplane to do so.

There have been many other such economic fiascos, but responsibility for them cannot be placed squarely at the feet of the economic scientists. Such theorists were encouraged by the political process, and the need to find an economic theory or a scientific study to justify what political leaders wanted to do in the first place. If the twentieth century was the age of the theorist, it was also that of the specious pile of facts and figures dumped onto the political process as a substitute for reasoned argument.

Early twentieth-century American president Woodrow Wilson laid the groundwork for this new approach to government when he was a

---

37. Reuters New Service, March 3, 2022, report by Uditha Jayasinghe and Devjyot Ghoshai. One rice farmer profiled in the article saw his yields plummet from 60- to 10-bags over a two acre plot.

young professor at a small college. He argued in an 1887 essay entitled "The Study of Administration"[38] that the millions of average voters were "selfish, ignorant, timid, stubborn, or foolish." To be governed by such people through a purely democratic process was, in Wilson's view, unacceptable. What was needed was rule by those "hundreds who are wise." These hundreds would staff the administrative state, that operational part of the government that is not supervised by the whims of the voting public. "This is why there should be a science of administration which shall seek to straighten the paths of government," he wrote.

That word again: Science. Who can argue against the idea of matters of public concern being decided upon a "scientific" basis? From this little kernel of consensus, any number of foolish theories can grow, provided they sound scientific. Mr. Wilson had provided the theorists with their marching orders, their reason for being, and for so much of the "scientific" insanity that plagued the twentieth and now the twenty-first century.

---

38. *Political Science Quarterly*, July 1887.

Chapter 3

"SOPHISTICATED" BUSINESS

Politicians like to wax rhapsodic upon the difficulties—the "hard work"—involved in the process of passing laws. They sometimes do this while contrasting this work with what they see as the comparatively simple process of running a business, where—as they see it—the sole purpose is simply to make a profit. California Governor Jerry Brown put it this way in an interview conducted during the 2016 Democratic National Convention in Philadelphia: "When you're in business, you have only one variable; it's called revenue over cost. Money. That's one. It's a one variable operation. In politics, you're dealing with psychology, you're dealing with religion, you're dealing with feelings, you're dealing with power relationships. It's very sophisticated. And you can't come from a one variable world into a multi-variable universe and expect to have the skill, the confidence, the know-how, to not make catastrophic mistakes [i.e., in politics]."

The governor went on to speak at the convention, telling the assembled throng that, "Combating climate change, the existential threat of our time, will take heroic efforts on the part of many people and many nations."

This is as good a distillation of the politician's worldview as one is likely to encounter. The process of legislating and commandeering the votes needed to pass a law, perhaps one to combat climate change, is the world of politics.

There are other differences between business and politics, of course, things a man who has spent his entire adult life in and around politics would scarcely be aware of, much less credit. The ability to sell a manufactured item for more than it costs to make often requires skills not enumerated in Governor Brown's list of "dealings." The folks at the Chevron Corporation who extract oil from the ground and then convert it into useful products—using billions of dollars of specialized equipment they purchased and then installed and often modified themselves—do so using skills not mentioned by Mr. Brown. It is perhaps true that they produce these products while giving little thought to psychology, religion, feelings, and power relationships. They attempt to make up for these shortcomings by giving some thought to geology, physics, chemistry, and thermodynamics.

Governor Brown's educational background does equip him for these dealings with political power relationships. He is the son of a California governor, and he is a law school graduate. Fine things, of course, for one intent on spending one's life dealing with "power relationships." He seems to feel, however, that this training allows him to deduce as fact the idea that carbon emissions must be curbed to prevent catastrophic climate change, and he has policy proposals that will curb such emissions. One searches in vain for any evidence in the governor's education or work history that equips him to reach such conclusions on his own. He can read the conclusions of scientists, of course, but he is like most of us in that he cannot process and grade the information outside of his area of expertise. He does not appear qualified to critique the specific scientific inferences underlying such conclusions: the precise dependence of global temperatures on the concentration of carbon dioxide in the atmosphere, etc. Governor Brown is doing what so many of us do in this age of specialization: He is taking the word of scientists and climatologists he feels he can trust, thus turning the scientific question into one involving the psychology, religion, feelings, and power relationships that he is comfortable with.

One other little difference between the "one variable" operation of a business and this "multi-variable universe" of politics is that the politician does not make monetary bets that have a monetary consequence to him or herself. The politician lives in a deal-oriented world, but one in which the appearance of the deal is more important than the wisdom implicit in the details. After a time devoted to the deal-making world of passing and enforcing laws, the politician goes on to a public-funded pension life; the body politic is left with the long run details. When the ribbon-cutting ceremony for the new publicly-funded bank of solar panels is held—the smiling politician front and center—and the images have been used for whatever political benefit they give the politician, the citizenry is left to operate the solar panels with a fifty-year payback period and a thirty-year useful life.

Such is not the case in the "unsophisticated" world of the "one variable operation." The long-run viability of an industrial business depends on a successful cycle of investment, then production, then selling and then reinvestment, each of which is carried out using some specialized knowledge. The different parts of the cycle act as checks and balances against the others. If shortcuts are taken in production, the product often cannot be produced at a quality level that will generate the profits that might have been expected. In the 1980s, General Motors demonstrated how to make profits disappear in this way with production shortcuts and simplifications taken to employ their "X-Car" manufacturing platform. If the processes and the raw materials required exceed the sales price the market will bear, there will be no money left for re-investment and–absent a friendly banker or government subsidies or a credulous stock market–the business will grind to a natural halt. American solar panel manufacturers showed us how this is done very recently, even with government support.

Businesses that have been around a long time illustrate this constant error-sensing, self-correcting process, a process filled with hard-earned lessons that politicians can choose to ignore and details that are much more interesting than the abstract accounting summaries mentioned by Governor Brown.

The tangible details behind many businesses are often fascinating—the new technology, the mathematical insights, the new design features and product offerings and labor-saving innovations, etc. This is the world the professional politician does not often see, the world of slow and steady improvements and of "unsophisticated" technical and financial competence. The old saw that, "Science owes more to the steam engine than the steam engine owes to Science" is close to a truism to those familiar with the history of technology.

Examples abound of technical advances developed by business-people. One example I enjoy is the t-tables used extensively by statisticians. These were first published in English early in the twentieth century by an Irishman who simply signed his published work "Student" and whose statistical mathematics are still known as the "Student's t-distribution." This "student," William Gosset, was an employee at the Guinness Brewery in Dublin engaged in the important business of brewing beer. His statistical work grew out of his need to grade input raw materials such as barley with as few data points as possible, because—as every businessperson knows—data acquisition takes time which equals expense which equals money.

The business of writing insurance policies is another example. When it was discovered a couple of centuries ago that over long periods of time, the frequencies of certain unfortunate events such as deaths, shipwrecks and fires could be estimated with some precision, the business of insuring against these events was born. The business was initially very profitable and then later–not coincidentally—more competitive and less profitable. Mathematical experts called "actuaries" improved the estimates of the frequencies of the deaths and wrecks and fires and the amount of money that had to be collected and invested at certain rates-of-return to pay the benefits when due. It was what we today might call a "fintech" advance. Insurance company leaders who ignored the mathematical advice of their actuaries often paid dearly for doing so.

When the sophisticated politician decides to try his/her hand at writing such policies, however, it can lead to 'catastrophic … existential … mistakes.'

The Missing Battle

What kind of insurance company lets the salesmen run everything? A government nonprofit insurance company. [39]

Over the past dozen years, the U.S. government's finances have become increasingly debt-ridden. About 30 percent of federal spending last year was borrowed. Total federal debt is growing at almost 10 percent per year.

Recent attempts to address the deficits that swell the debt were criticized as too painful, but in reality they were too small. The tax increases were tiny in comparison with annual deficits, and the spending cuts called "sequestration" applied only to part of the federal budget.

Most experts agree that the long-term problem lies in the part of the deficit that was not cut: the social-insurance programs. Social security runs pension and disability insurance; Medicare and Medicaid are enormous medical-insurance plans for the aged and the poor. These huge programs are out of balance, with projected benefits far beyond intended payments. Demographic trends are making things much worse.

---

39. "The Missing Battle" appeared in the March 18, 2013 issue of *Barron's Financial Weekly*.

Hundreds of American businesses operate similar insurance plans without running huge losses. Why is government insurance so different? Government insurance is not for profit, but insolvency and bankrupting the country aren't the idea, either.

We could look for a solution to this mystery not in life but in art—specifically, the best movie ever made about the insurance business (and yes, there have been blessedly few such movies): The 1944 film-noir classic, *Double Indemnity*. The plot involves a young insurance salesman, played by Fred MacMurray, who agrees to hasten the end of one of his recently insured lives, at the request of the insured's fetching wife and beneficiary, Barbara Stanwyck.

This is standard Hollywood fare. The more important part for us is the portrayal of the tension within an insurance company, played out between this young salesman and the company claims manager played by Edward G. Robinson. The claims manager spots the young salesman's brains (if not his morals), considers those brains wasted in the sales game, and hopes to recruit him for the claims department.

What does this have to do with these insolvent government insurance programs? Let's listen to Robinson's claims manager explain to the salesman what is so challenging about working in the claims department, with help from screenwriters Billy Wilder and Raymond Chandler.

"It's the company. The way they do things. The way they don't do things. The way they'll write anything just to get it down on the sales sheet. And I'm the guy that has to sit here up to my neck in phony claims so they won't throw more money out of the window than they take in at the door...I get darn sick of picking up after a gang of fast-talking salesmen."

There's a constant battle within an insurance company among the actuaries who set the policy terms, the salesmen who hunt for acceptable clients, and the tough guys who investigate and settle the claims. The healthy tension between people with different skills and temperaments keeps the firm solvent.

Robinson's insurance company, like any company, must try to control its fast-talking salesmen. All salespeople know that the merchandise would move a little faster, and their lives would be much easier, if the home office would give them a little more flexibility—lower prices, looser qualifications for customers, and a little more generosity in paying claims and refunds. The flexibility they seek, alas, invariably eats up the company's profit margins and threatens its long run survival.

Government-run social-insurance programs are dysfunctional because the sales force—the elected officials—have the flexibility that successful private companies would never give them. They get themselves elected with what Robinson, the claims manager, calls "a smooth line of monkey talk," promising their voters low premiums and big benefits. There is no home office to stop them.

In the U.S., the Constitution grants taxing and spending powers to the Congress, but the Founding Fathers never dreamed that Congress would turn the federal government into an insurance company with the representatives and senators acting as the sales force.

Our elected officials have written and sold policies that will "throw more money out the window than they take in at the door," as the movie claims manager says.

The salesmen in Congress hear testimony concerning the solvency of Social Security and Medicare from nonelected, powerless trustees and actuaries, and they are told point-blank that these programs are fiscal disasters. They hear that average Medicare recipients will receive over $100,000 more in benefits than they paid for. But the lawmakers don't have to heed the warnings. They don't have to change the policy terms to promote solvency. Recently, they awarded cost-of-living increases to recipients when none were required and lowered the payroll-tax premiums to promote economic growth. Congress runs the actuarial department as well as the sales department.

When frustrated claimants complain, however, home-state legislators and their staffs swing into action to make sure their constituents get every benefit they're entitled to, and more. Legislation is passed to make sure certain claims are never denied again: for example, the 1960 change allowing people under 50 to claim disability, and the 2005 change providing prescription-drug coverage. Congress runs the claims department, too.

In *Double Indemnity*, the death of the husband raises the claims manager's suspicions: The facts are improbable, as is the idea that it was suicide. The young salesman is very anxious to learn what the police think, and the claims manager tells him the police figure that the husband "got tangled up in his crutches and fell off the train. They're satisfied," he says dismissively. "It's not their dough."

Politicians could defer to experts in writing and policing these government insurance plans, so that they do not bankrupt the country. Politicians, however, know that same important fact: It's not their dough.

Chapter 4

WALL STREET PAY: NICE WORK, BUT "GOD'S WORK"?

What, precisely, do those folks on Wall Street do to deserve the lavish pay they receive? Are they doing God's Work?[40] We know that they raise the capital for "capitalism," so they do perform a function in the larger scheme of things, but this is a fairly routine business that would not seem to automatically dictate that its practitioners receive such high pay.

40. Goldman Sachs CEO Lloyd Blankfein was quoted by The Times of London in 2009 to the effect that he and his fellow Goldman Sachs investment bankers were "doing God's work."

Most of the very well-paid folks we are aware of in our daily lives have skills or talents or blessings that we can understand. The millions raked in by some—movie stars, corporate chieftains, utility infielders—are at least explicable in that these folks have demonstrated some rare talent or ability. Now the ability to be physically alluring enough in movies or on television to get millions of us to buy tickets or to hold our attention until the next set of commercials is aired doesn't seem all that important, but we must concede that it is a rare ability, and that it is economically profitable.

The reasons for high pay on Wall Street are much more difficult to understand. When Intel Corp. decides to raise money to open a new factory, all sorts of people are willing and able to lend to them or help them in some other way to acquire the money for the factory. Intel is a "good credit," so it is not difficult to find buyers for any bonds it might issue. Often the government where the Intel factory is to be located practically begs Intel to take money in the form of tax breaks and to improve the roads and the sewer service at or near the prospective plant location using municipal bond proceeds, etc. The job of selling additional shares of Intel common stock to raise money seems to be easy work as well, given that tens of millions of shares of Intel common stock trade every day. The normal rule in business is that when large numbers of people are willing and able to provide a service, the wages connected with providing that service are not high.

All of this misses the real reason that Wall Street wages are so healthy because the real reasons are not explained by classical economics. The people in lower Manhattan, and its satellite locations in places like San Francisco and Chicago, are very good at charging the rest of us in unobtrusive ways and for work of dubious value that sounds complicated. That's it. They are simply good at billing us.

This would normally be difficult to impossible to pull off in a world whose thrifty investor class is generally full of prudent people. Wall Streeters are so well-paid not merely because they have the gall to charge high fees, but because they are extremely good at assessing these fees without their customers noticing.

In the non-fiction bestseller *Liar's Poker*, author Michael Lewis described the trading in mortgage-backed securities that developed at the firm where he worked in the 1980s, Salomon Brothers. The firm dealt and traded with bank presidents at the nation's Savings and Loans, a group of people you would think had a little on the ball. The traders at Salomon Brothers, however, made hundreds of millions of dollars off them. "Why, you might wonder, did thrift [i.e., S&L] presidents tolerate Salomon's huge profit margins [associated with the trades]?" Lewis posed. "Well, for a start, they didn't know any better. Salomon's margins were invisible."[41]

In those cases where the fees are technically visible, a different dynamic can develop. Many of the prudent people in the investor class can read their fund statements. The management fees assessed them, typically 1-2 percent per year of assets under management, doesn't seem awfully high. They weren't that high, either, back in the 1960s and 1970s when the fee structure was arrived at and the funds being managed were in the millions. Many of these funds now count their assets in the tens of billions, however. The economies of scale resulting from this increase in funds under management would seem to dictate that these 1-2 percent management fees should be much lower now. Fund management, in other words, should benefit from an "economy of scale." The fund companies themselves disagree, and they spend considerable efforts not in assessing the appeal that lower fees might

---

41. *Liar's Poker* by Michael Lewis (New York, 1989, 2014), p. 143.

have to investors, but in scouring the investing world for more assets to manage.

The fees charged by hedge funds are an egregious example: 2 percent of assets and 20 percent of any profits, but at least these hedge fund managers are up-front about it. These fees are often paid by institutions, not people, institutions who simply want to be seen to be doing something pro-active, and the hedge funds are very good at touting their very aggressive strategies that promise specialized and perhaps outsized returns. Occasionally, such hedge fund managers are even successful in providing such returns.

The fees charged by unleveraged, open-end mutual funds are more difficult to explain. They don't quite charge hedge fund-level fees, but they don't promise to do much that is out of the ordinary, either. The article below, "Too Many Choices," describes one such charging process in grisly detail, as well as the way in which some of the difficult work of money management has been removed from the investment manager and deftly handed over to the customer. Those interested in organizing or performing such work must keep this need for fee structure opacity firmly in mind.

Too Many Choices

Why do we pay mutual-fund managers if not
to make investment decisions?[42]

The financial pages have been filled lately with tales of self-serving mutual-fund companies. It seems some of them were being run for their benefit and not for their shareholders' benefit! Cozy deals with brokers allowing excessive commission charges, big clients allowed to trade at stale prices, etc. It all adds up to another in the series of

---

42. "Too Many Choices" appeared in the July 12, 2004 issue of *Barron's Financial Weekly*.

pathetically predictable "Dog Bites Man" stories in the history of commerce, wherein the unwitting customer has been gouged for a few bills when it has seemed expedient.

Another more distressing trend in the mutual-fund industry goes largely unnoticed, however. The recent growth of the mutual-fund industry has been accomplished in such a way that the customers have been put in charge of portfolio management, although they must still pay fund-company management fees.

Twenty or thirty years ago, fund managers looked over the entire universe of securities as possible investments. Peter Lynch ran the Fidelity Magellan Fund 26 years ago in a way that is almost unheard of today. The choices he made show someone unconcerned with growth, value, style boxes or capitalization issues.

In his 1994 book, *Beating the Street*, Lynch describes the securities he was buying in 1983: Jan Bell Marketing, Costco, Chrysler, Volvo, and Ford, and more than 100 savings and loan institutions. He explained that although "Magellan was continually described as a growth fund, it was the flexibility to buy any sort of stock that enabled me to take advantage of opportunities."

This sort of "flexible" money management in which professionals choose between all the various securities and between broader asset classes, is what most small investors would like to sign up for when we invest in mutual funds. But such funds are much more difficult to find today.

For this dubious development, we can thank the mutual-fund marketing and legal departments. The industry has decided—perhaps under pressure from its customers, perhaps not—to slice and dice the investment universe into pieces so small that most discretion has been removed. When certain classes of stock are "hot," the fund-company's marketers can promote the gaudy numbers the funds they have invested in these "hot" classes of stock will show. In the event a certain sector does poorly, the lawyers need not worry, for the poor performance of a sector fund clearly can't be ascribed to management incompetence.

This change can be sensed by counting modifiers: Generic fund-company "Stock Funds" have given way to various Small-, Mid- and Large-Cap Growth and Value funds. We now have "Multimedia" and "Net-Infrastructure" funds, "Social Equity" funds and funds for every good-sized continent and most good-sized countries around the world.

Each modifier creates constraints. A "Multimedia" fund can't decide to own Altria or Exxon, regardless of how compellingly low they might trade. A "Net-Infrastructure Fund" can't put significant money in Intel bonds pending the identification of an attractively priced "net-infrastructure" common stock.

Grim experience teaches that the effects of ignoring the effects of this trend are not small. I have invested for my children with results that make these points.

My oldest child has had his money socked away in a plain-vanilla large-cap growth fund for his dozen years. I was feeling more adventurous with the money set aside for our second child, however, and I put his in a more aggressive growth fund. During the nineties both funds appreciated smartly.

In late 1999, however, the aggressive growth fund began shooting up wildly, and I made the one and only change I ever needed to with these accounts, trading out of the aggressive fund into a small-cap value fund.

I am certainly no mutual-fund expert. My years of experience as a customer however, taught me one thing: The fund managers at the aggressive growth fund were not allowed to have an opinion regarding the wisdom of continuing to invest in the speculative New Economy common stocks that dominated their holdings. Or if they had an unfavorable opinion of these stocks as a class, they were certainly not to allow it to influence their management of the fund. Their job was to take all the money at their disposal and continue to buy these stocks. If every simple valuation metric suggested this class of stock was over-valued, it was my job, not theirs, to do something about it.

The results since realized in the two accounts have been very differ-ent. The large-cap growth fund has steadily lost value, and still stands more than 30 percent below where it was in early 2000. The small-cap value fund has steadily appreciated at more than 10 percent per year since the bubble burst.

What's truly surprising is how these funds rank in performance for the last three or four years. Amazingly enough, the large-cap fund, which has steadily declined in value, ranks quite high for three-year performance: second quartile among funds of its type. The small-cap value fund that has allowed my younger son's capital to continue to compound at 10 percent-plus a year is at the bottom of the barrel, the fifth quintile among funds of its type.

Large-cap growth funds that have managed to lose money only gradually over these years are stellar performers, while small-cap value funds need to have done more than 15 percent a year over that stretch to be above average. With results like these, scholars and many investors have concluded that choice of management matters much less.

The fund industry has responded and lets us know that the modern idea is to own a number of funds from each of the various classes and style boxes. They want us to pay attention to "allocation," and to consider routinely "rebalancing."

This is hardly the ideal situation. Many investors would like to hire a professional to do this work for them, to get them in and out of these stock classes and style boxes as conditions dictate. We know that this cannot be done unerringly—but we don't demand perfection, just attention.

Lacking such attention, we ought to be asking why we pay 1 percent to 2 percent a year to professionals who refrain from actually applying important financial acumen.

★ ★ ★

Postscript: Things have changed since "Too Many Choices" was published in 2004. The world of overpriced open-end mutual funds has contracted somewhat, and much of that shrinkage occurred in the specialized funds described in "Too Many Choices." These funds were replaced in many cases by something called Exchange Traded Funds, or ETFs. These ETFs are often quite specialized, but they are much lower in costs and management fees than the old open-end mutual funds.

Wall Street has gotten even with us, though. The old, specialized open-end mutual fund was high in cost to the investor, but at least there were humans involved in making investment decisions. The new, specialized ETFs charge lower fees, but they are basically index funds run by computers. In other words, the old system involved Wall Street receiving high pay for doing work, and it has now been replaced by Wall Street receiving somewhat lower pay in return for doing no work at all.

A system such as this would appear to leave the investing public with a little more of its own money due to these lower fees, but to regard this happy thought as the end of a happy story would be to underestimate the creativity of the financial industry. The industry confesses to its customers that these computer-run index funds behave like automatons and therefore require watching, and as a result, the industry has developed an asset watcher they call the financial planner, a salesman who spends most of his time hunting up clients very much in the manner of the old mutual fund salesman. This financial planner is a professional-looking type who is often employed by the same firms that minted those many actively managed mutual funds that charged 1-2 percent per year. What does this financial planner charge for watching and re-balancing those low-cost computer-run funds? You guessed it: that same 1-2 percent of assets managed.

★ ★ ★

The Fine Art of Borrowing Your Watch to Tell You the Time

Until the twentieth century, the study of the business world was not considered a matter of true scholarship. Real scholars studied and translated ancient manuscripts, developed mathematical techniques, explored and categorized the natural world. They did not study business. When Harvard University founded a business school in 1908 as part of the humanities school, most of the rest of the academy turned up its collective nose. Old European liberal arts institutions such as Oxford University eschew such a school of business even today, and faculty members at such institutions often refer to the subject matter taught at such schools as "mere cant." Even right-leaning intellectuals in the New World occasionally express skepticism concerning the academic rigor of such business schools, calling such study a "pseudo-discipline."[43]

Business schools, like law schools, employ the "case study" method, wherein students familiarize themselves with a business situation and consider ways in which the business might make changes or improve itself. There is a crucial difference, however. Law school students read cases and struggle to apply the prevailing black-letter

43. e.g., *12 Rules for Life* by Jordan Peterson (Random House Canada, 2018), page 312: "I think the science of management is a pseudo-discipline." Mr. Peterson is a clinical psychologist and professor of Psychology.

law. Business schools do no such thing for the simple reason that there are few such laws involved, and if there is a legal issue, the company lawyers are put in charge. The idea that certain useful business practices will emerge from a close study of other business situations is largely a matter of faith. The idea that the hurly-burly of the business world, with its constant technological, market, and legal changes, is not amenable to such study is given little space in the modern businessperson's consciousness.

Nevertheless, the professional businessperson has become a fixture of modern life. Certain of their maxims have found their way into everyday parlance: "out-sourcing," "human capital," "exceeding expectations," "lean forward," "down-sizing." The list of such phrases is irredeemably long and tedious.

The highest form this new creature assumes, the professional businessperson, is that of the business "consultant." Sometimes, such people are useful; their task is one that truly needs doing: the assembling of a specific organizational structure to avoid unnecessary taxes, the implementation of computer control systems, etc. Often such consultants go much further, however, offering to provide the client, the company, a new "vision" that will help them manage their business in a new way or sell certain businesses in favor of other businesses. This requires them to acquire detailed knowledge about the company's operations, knowledge many company employees already possess. This is exasperating for the regular employees, of course, because the nature of the problems the current business faces may have been painfully obvious to those employees for some time. "They borrow your watch to tell you the time," is the lament of company employees who watch these consulting firms come and go.

The never-ending, recurring problem in the business world is capital allocation: Where to invest? Where to divest? These questions are increasingly answered by the ranks of these new professional business-people. If such questions are increasingly addressed by people who have studied the same cases and drawn the same conclusions, then these capital allocation decisions might be made in the same general way. The possibility that the business schools who crank out these managers and consultants may be dispensing the same advice, advice that then results in the nation's companies making the same or similar decisions—that possibility seems to be a distinct possibility that is seldom explored.

What happens when capital (i.e., supply) crowds into certain industries and away from others? The general rules of economics, that thorny thicket of time-worn truisms much older than the oldest business school, suggest the returns realized on the capital thus allocated won't be quite the same as that which might have been predicted.

The General Electric Corporation might serve to illustrate what 'could' happen. General Electric common stock was a darling of the investing world in the late twentieth century, and its top executives were considered the finest in America. The top managerial talent at GE was often coaxed away from GE by other corporations desperate to learn from the best by acquiring this top managerial talent. GE's managerial techniques emphasized the objective, or at least the highly arithmetical, view. All these managers using similar arithmetical techniques to make similar decisions across the country—what could possibly go wrong? GE's stock price currently stands at about 1/5th its level of the late 1990s, and its profits have stagnated. Perhaps that is what might go wrong.

GE and "The Great White Way"

How to Succeed in Business Without Really Trying was a big Broadway musical hit in 1962 and later a Hollywood movie. The lead character is a young, ambitious fellow named J. Pierrepont Finch. When the curtain rises, he is washing the windows of a company office tower. Young Finch is ambitious, however, and he has a self-help book the author assures him will be his guide to business success.

The book teaches young Finch that he must find the right company to work for. "It is essential that the company be a big one," the book instructs. "It should be at least large enough so that nobody knows exactly what anyone else is doing." Finch goes inside the office tower and finds a certain amount of chaos, which he finds encouraging. In the movie version, he hears a distressed middle-manager shout to others that, "Denver has run out of wickets! Have 50,000 two-toned wickets sent at once!" He's certain that he has found the right company when one of them turns to his fellow managers to inquire "What the hell's a wicket?"

Portrayals of the large business conglomerate have been a rich source of fiction, both comedic and dramatic. As with all such sources, the richness owes to a simple fact: Most contain more than a grain of truth.

The business schools that crank out executives to staff the conglomerate world are the wellspring of this fiction, because it is they who teach the doctrine of the "wicket." For wicket one can substitute any commercial product: engine oil, aspirin, television comedies. Business schools don't dwell on how the wicket came into existence. That is the lowly job of creative people like chemists and screenplay writers. The business school teaches its acolytes how to manage the wickets—whatever they are—once created.

The General Electric Corporation is certainly run by such executives, and its record over the past quarter century bears the unmistakable fingerprints of this top-down, wicket-counting approach. The folks who invented and commercialized the light bulb, the diesel locomotive, the jet engine, the medical imaging devices that were the making of GE are long gone from the halls of GE headquarters. It is worth a moment's thought to consider what is lost in this natural process.

Such advances are hard-won, and those who were there when they were being made know just how hard-won. These employees have detailed knowledge of the advance, but also a sense of whether the business will be easy to replicate—i.e., whether this new business has a certain 'creative moat' around it. Business schools seek to drum any such sense out of their charges, and the conglomerates they create inevitably favor abstract accounting metrics like returns-on-equity and discounted cash flow estimates when judging and comparing various businesses.

GE jettisoned its plastics and silicones businesses about a decade ago. The specialty chemical business is not appealing to the metric-minded executive. It's messy, both literally and arithmetically. The advances made by chemical engineers often lie fallow for years until some new commercial problem surfaces that requires the advance. Such companies often have little control over when and how these problems arise, and how large the business of solving the problem will be—hardly the sort of situation conducive to mathematical modeling. This lack of predictability frustrates even great investors like Warren Buffett, who, when asked why he never invested in a prominent Midwestern chemical products company explained, "I never know what [they] are going to come up with next, and neither do they." GE certainly found it unacceptable: Plastics and silicones had to go.

Financial services, on the other hand—there is a business with some appeal to those who like predictability! A good credit like the General

Electric of the late twentieth century could easily borrow at rates much lower than it could lend, so why shouldn't it? "Borrow at 3[%], lend at 6, and be on the golf course by 3 goes the old banking saw, and the executive who cannot do the math on *that* business plan has no business being in business! GE Capital found that certain home mortgages and re-insurance contracts could earn potentially higher rates. What could possibly go wrong? Some two decades later, the GE Capital business was sold off (under the "GE Capital Exit Plan") in small bite-sized pieces—perhaps to prevent indigestion—but only after much damage had been done to the GE balance sheet.

The wicket-minded executive, however, rankles at the idea that it is strictly about the numbers. When asked to define the 'mission' of their company, a CEO often becomes almost poetic when discussing his or her 'vision,' because working 50+ hours a week tallying and cataloging wickets sounds a touch tedious.

General Electric tells us they are a "global digital industrial company transforming industry with software-defined machines and solutions that are connected, responsive, and predictive," a statement of mission that probably wows the gang in the business school faculty lounge. GE sales, cash flow, and profits, however, are substantially lower than they were a decade ago, and the stock price has been cut by over two thirds. Meanwhile, the people at the Momentive Chemical Company, the poor Neanderthals who now run the hopelessly non-digital silicone chemicals business formerly owned by GE, watched their stock price double and then triple on receiving a buy-out offer.

J. Pierrepont Finch does indeed find the perfect company to work for and to apply the principles of his self-help book. He rises quickly. His most successful tactic involves getting the people on the rung above him fired or re-located to Venezuela. He eventually becomes Chairman of the Board—and without really trying, just as his book had promised. His tactic for 'climbing the ladder'—the backstabbing of his superiors—also has blessedly little effect on the company's operations. The happy ending to the story finds him chairman of a company very similar to the one he washed windows for. GE shareholders should have been so lucky!

Chapter 5

DEATH AND MATH

New York literary figure Fran Lebowitz can capture the world of the cloistered Manhattanite as well as anyone. She has described the great outdoors as, "what you must pass through in order to get from your apartment into a taxicab," and that, "When you leave New York, you are astonished at how clean the rest of the world is. Clean is not enough." Of actual intellectual matters, she perfectly captured this secluded, self-satisfied worldview by writing that, "In real life, I assure you, there is no such thing as algebra."

Readers who share Ms. Lebowitz's somewhat limited mathematical imagination are a core part of her target audience, and many undoubtedly concur with her views on things algebraic. "When," they might have asked rhetorically at some point during their school years, their tone one of exasperation, "will I ever use this differential calculus stuff?"

Our elected leaders have made a good living off these limitations.

One of the recurring subjects in American political debate has to do with whether certain income groups in this prosperous society "pay their fair share" in taxes. The operative word in this discussion, and the reason that any political discussion concerning this topic can cycle like an old vinyl record, is 'fair.' The statistics on taxes paid by income group are a simple matter of public record, as are the tax rate schedules by income bracket. Whether the whole system is fair or not is, of course, a matter of opinion and not fact.

There is, nonetheless, a sense among the public that these arid statistics don't tell the whole story. Many citizens hold the view that the system is 'rigged' and therefore could use more 'fairness.' Even among those few citizens who don't like to resort to the use of such a nebulous term as 'fairness,' there is a nagging sense that these income and tax rate schedules are missing something.

Beneath this storm of forms, there is algebra.

They are. The United States tax system has been subjected to so many 'credits' and 'phase-outs' and 'revenue neutralizing offsets' that the true rates paid by tens of millions of middle-class people are a good deal higher than the tax rate tables suggest.[44] In this way, the

---

44. For those confused on the mathematical analogy, tax rates can be thought of as the slope of a line (a.k.a. the first derivative) plotting total taxable income on the x-axis and total tax on the y-axis.

government is a little like Wall Street in that they are good at charging us, in this case more than they tell us they are going to charge us. By way of explaining how this little corner of governmental obfuscation came about, and how to cut through the mathematical thickets and make some sense of it all, the plight of those millions is explained in "Wandering Through Phase-Out Land."

"Phase-Out Land" is a little legal bourn where millions of Americans reside without knowing it. These folks, who report yearly income to the taxing authorities of somewhere between $100,000 and $500,000, are in many ways a group to be envied. They spend most of their days in climate-controlled surroundings; they seldom miss meals; they can very often pay their bills as they come due; and they can look forward to a retirement of relative physical comfort. This life of sunny ease is marred for most of them by the tiniest of dark clouds of algebraic ignorance: They simply don't fully grasp their marginal income tax rate.

Wandering Through Phase-Out Land

This article appeared in 2007.[45]

A lot of hot air has been ventilated in Washington over the past few years about whether to extend the Bush tax cuts beyond the end of the decade.[46] Much of it concerns the way in which such cuts benefit the rich through lower marginal tax rates on income, stock dividends, and long-term capital gains. Opponents of extension say the lower rates provide nothing to those of modest means and cost the government sorely needed money. Defenders counter that the lower rates stimulate economic productivity, cause more such income to be realized in the

---

45. "Wandering Through Phase-Out Land" appeared in the February 12, 2007 issue of *Barron's Financial Weekly*.

46. The specific tax cuts in question in this article were the 2001 and 2003 tax cuts, but the same general political debate follows every election.

near term, and may even bring in more tax revenue in the long run.

Although the debate is interesting, and both sides are passionate, it misses an important point.

For many upper-middle-income taxpayers, the structure of the tax laws neutralizes most of the supposedly beneficial effects of the cuts being discussed. Above $100,000 of income, many of the credits, deductions, and exemptions that lower-income taxpayers enjoy are phased out. The child tax credit begins to shrink; personal exemptions must be recalculated downward; itemized deductions begin to shrink, and, finally, the alternative minimum tax, or AMT, must be paid.

The result of all these phase-outs is a more steeply progressive tax code in Phase-Out Land than is generally understood from reading the tax-rate tables published by the United States Treasury.

The road to this particular hell was paved with good intentions. Most Americans have agreed that the rich should pay some income taxes. This 40-year-old nod to common sense brought us the AMT.

Congress didn't bother to index the definition of 'rich' for inflation, however, so it is now possible for a hard-working nurse or firefighter with a big home mortgage and lives in a high-tax state, to pay this tax meant for "the rich."[47]

Americans also have agreed that it isn't fair for the rich to take big deductions for all the mortgage interest and property taxes they pay on their mansions, so their itemized deductions are gradually reduced, based on their income.

But the income level at which we begin this phasing-out process causes many to begin losing these deductions at income levels that rule out owning any mansion at all.

The child tax credit and two different college tuition credits were

---

47. The Trump tax cuts of 2017 eliminated this problem for this hypothetical nurse and/or firefighter.

designed for the child-rearing middle-class folks who were getting 'squeezed'—not the rich. The child credit begins to be reduced at $110,000 of income for joint filers, however, a family in a high-cost state can still feel quite a bit of financial pressure. The Hope college tuition credit starts to phase-out at $82,000 of joint income, and the Lifetime Learning tax credit starts its phase-out at $87,000.

The unintended effect of all these good intentions has been a more complex tax environment and higher marginal tax rates. If for every $100 of extra income, you lose deductions that would otherwise reduce your taxes; then the real marginal tax rate on that $100 isn't the rate in the tax tables, but a somewhat higher rate. Since most of these phase-outs occur over the same range of income—roughly $100,000 to $400,000 for joint filers—the marginal rates paid by those in this range of income are a good deal higher than advertised.

Suppose a family of four with some $130,000 to $140,000 in wage income reads the usual descriptions of tax rates and provisions and decides to avail itself of the 15 percent maximum federal tax rate on stock dividends by selling some municipal bonds and buying dividend producing stocks. When tax time rolls around, they will find that they aren't paying 15 percent federal income tax on these common stock dividends and any capital gains they might realize, but instead they are paying 20 to 23 percent, depending on their investment income.

The additional income will cause this family to lose child tax credits and then their itemized deductions and personal exemptions. Then, they might begin paying the alternative minimum tax. If they do begin paying the AMT, they will quickly lose the full AMT exemption because it starts to be phased out at income levels over $150,000. This is a little trick that makes the AMT rates a good deal higher than the supposed rates of 15 percent, 26 percent, and 28 percent—at least for the great majority of upper-middle-class taxpayers who recently have begun paying it. This also causes the highest marginal alternative tax rates to be paid not by the rich, but by the residents of Phase-Out Land.

When the family begins paying the AMT, they will lose their deduction for state taxes, raising the total tax rate for taxpayers in many states to roughly 30 percent on such stock "income."

Suppose our family of four relied on the tax-rate tables to decide for a spouse to go to work or take a better-paying job. The federal tax tables would tell them that an additional $80,000 in wage income would be taxed, first at 25 percent, and then at 28 percent. In practice, however, they would find that the additional federal income taxes would amount to 29-30 percent of the additional income, not the 25 percent or even 28 percent. The reason, of course, would be the phasing out of most of the credits, deductions, and exemptions that the family had been entitled to take.

The situation for such filers would be worse if Congress hadn't also decided to freeze the impact of the AMT at the same time it extended the Bush tax cuts on dividend income. Without this limited and temporary fix, this family would see a dramatic rise in their alternative minimum tax assessment, and marginal rates on this income of well over 30 percent.

People subject to phase-outs are generally not without resources. Many have computer software or accountants to help them with tax planning, and money to pay the extra tax. But the lack of public discussion and awareness regarding the effective marginal rates being paid by the residents of Phase-Out Land distorts the whole income-tax debate and leaves the impression that many people are paying income taxes at lower rates than they actually are.

Discussions as to what rate on what income is fair or unfair ought to hinge on the real differences in these incomes and rates.

★ ★ ★

Indifference to matters mathematical is not confined to New York literary figures and their followers. It is practically a pandemic ...

Innumeracy: The Scourge of the Computer Age

There was something vaguely disquieting about an image I was confronted with almost every day during the height of the home-refinance era of the 2000s. A shapely female silhouette gyrated wildly at the edge of the computer page I had downloaded. She was hard to ignore, and she was clearly excited about something. Below her silhouette, you could read why: She was exhorting people to re-finance their mortgages (as perhaps she had just done) at terms that seemed, well, suspicious: A $500,000 mortgage in return for a monthly payment of only $999-per-month?[48]

The image itself was one thing, but what has also stuck with me since is that these pathetic appeals were being displayed on personal computers. Computers. The devices that are designed to empower regular folks to quickly perform arithmetical calculations.

This confluence of successful yet mathematically impossible sales appeals on the same device with the ability to check and refute them is a central contradiction of the era. Never have there been more people making a good living off the innumeracy of others, and never has the vast populace been given such wonderful tools to use to defend themselves. Do you doubt it? Let us look around us. This same wonderful contradiction shows up everywhere you look.

Some folks may remember being forwarded the e-mail from the person who was outraged by the 'bailout' of AIG during the deep, dark

---

48. The mortgage rates that prevailed at the time were not remotely low enough to make this possible.

days of the last recession. The author of the email argued that the $85 billion that was thrown at AIG could have been given to individual Americans to the tune of $285,000 apiece, and the author suggested that in so doing many of the problems at the root of AIG's mortgage-related problems could have been solved. The problem was the arithmetic: $85 billion split 300 million ways is roughly $285 per American, not $285,000.

The people who give us the news on television have certainly not gotten any better at checking simple math using the devices plopped down in front of them. When financial-information magnate Mike Bloomberg dropped out of the presidential race in 2020 after spending some $500 million on television advertisements and other campaign efforts, certain news people told us in exasperated tones that Mr. Bloomberg could have done more for the everyday American by simply giving every American a million dollars instead of spending as he had on campaigning. Perhaps it was the number of digits involved, but these national news people were wrong by a factor of a million: $500 million divided by 330 million people is $1.50 or thereabouts for every American, not $1 million.

The larger problem with the AIG email and the campaign 'tweet' concerning candidate Bloomberg's spending was not so much the arithmetical errors. At least the authors involved had tried to do some arithmetic. The problem was the number of times the errors were forwarded and reported before being debunked.

The twenty-first century home computer, we must concede, is now used much more as a television than a computing device. Television— whether of the phone, laptop, or flat-screen variety—now dominates public conversation in the advanced world to such an extent that we have conveniently forgotten the ridicule with which it was greeted when it was rolled into the stores in the late 1940s. "The idiot box" it was called, and "the boob tube," often by resentful radio personalities who instantly recognized the passive, credulous and idiotic trance it induced in the viewer. It was a trance, however, that proved difficult to break, and the hypnotic state thus induced gradually swallowed up most of society. Television emphasizes that which can be made graphic and visual, of course. Certain subjects that can't be easily communicated or made simple using images or simple conclusory words and phrases were quickly recognized as unacceptable subjects for television, and they were then treated like so much rancid meat by the high priests of the medium. Central among these 'unmentionables' was, alas, arithmetic.

Our politicians have only gradually adapted to this reality. Many of them still feel compelled to point to the arithmetic underlying their various policy proposals, poor devils, and the high priests of television occasionally find it necessary to steer them back to television reality.

During the 2000 presidential debates, one of the candidates attempted to make a mathematical point concerning the effective marginal tax rates facing people of modest means for whom additional taxable income will cause them to lose governmental cash assistance. "If you're a single mother making $22,000 a year and you have two children," the candidate argued, "under this tax code, for every additional dollar you make, you pay a higher marginal rate on that dollar than someone making more than $200,000 a year, and that is not right. My plan drops the rate from 15 percent to 10 percent and increases the child credit from $500 to $1,000 to make the code fair for everybody..."[49]

The candidate was making an important point relevant to tens of millions of citizens. The moderator, a television personality from the relatively high-brow precincts of public television, could not permit

---

49. This argument was offered by candidate George W. Bush on October 3, 2000 in Boston, Massachusetts in a debate moderated by Jim Lehrer.

such a mind-numbing arithmetical argument to go on, however. This was a political debate aired without commercials, but this was still television, dammit! When the candidate finally paused, satisfied perhaps with having gotten his arithmetical facts right, the moderator quickly changed the subject. "Having cleared that up," he interjected, perhaps a little exasperated at the television naivete of the candidate, "we're going to a new question …"

One of the more profound societal changes of the last couple of decades has been the public embrace of government-sanctioned gambling. Our leaders of fifty years ago would have found it morally deplorable, but governments now use gambling to generate revenue, and hoteliers and Native Americans use it to make money, too. And make money they certainly do, as vast numbers queue up to pull slot machines and buy lottery tickets. The odds against the lottery players are almost unimaginably long. Even worse, the game and the tax laws are also rigged against them. The multi-state "Powerball" lottery keeps roughly 70 cents of every dollar wagered when you combine the charitable 'take' with the predictable income tax effects. The math is quite simple, as after-tax income on the part of the millions of ticket buyers is magically transformed into before-tax jackpots that are highly taxed. This is a little steep. Our grandparents would have called it "exploitative," but our modern leaders appear untroubled, and the third estate that believes in "afflicting the comfortable and comforting the afflicted" doesn't seem too interested in pointing out just how steep. Perhaps the editors know that the advertising departments that tout these lottery tickets have big ad budgets, and they buy acres of ad space, or the editors feel nobody really cares, or that the subject is complicated, or that after all it is called 'charitable' gambling.

When the last recession hit, the State of California suddenly found itself in very tough fiscal shape. A state capable of attracting the best and brightest from around the world was in financial straits. How could this happen? This is a big surprise, right? Well, for years California has gradually shifted its income tax burden to the wealthy. It is easy to do when 'fairness' is the stated goal, while simultaneously growing its expenditures in line with revenues and then bumping them up with generous yearly increases. Government outlays are nearly all wage related. If you grow your expenses very steadily with yearly employee raises including healthcare and other benefits, then the occasional hic-cup in the fortunes of those wealthy people—as occurred during the recent "great recession"—makes for some serious government budget shortfalls. It is as predictable as next summer's blockbuster sequel. When the next recession hits, many Californians will perhaps again be shocked, shocked[50] by the state's resulting fiscal problems.

The general recovery from the "Great Recession" of 2007-2009 was agonizingly slow. Long after the 'recovery' was underway, aver-age Americans of all stripes pondered: When will this steep recession really, truly end? The economists told us that it had already ended, and millions could not quite understand how they could make this asser-tion. The problem is math, and the way economists and regular people interpret the question differently, and the economists need to interpret the question mathematically. The hope held by millions of regular people posing this question was that this current economic problem would at some point be 'fixed,' and when it was, we could all walk out of that horror movie of a recession and everything would be like it was before. In other words, it was another problem of math versus imagery.

In the fourth quarter of 2008, U.S. economic activity was about 6 percent below where it had been during most of 2007. Economists tell us that a recession is over when further declines stop occurring,

---

50. A reference to that wonderful bit of dialogue uttered by Captain Renault in that California-made movie of 1942, *Casablanca.*

not when everything is returned to the way it was. When a recession bottoms out at 94 percent of earlier 'baseline' economic activity, that means when it bumps back up to only 95 percent of those earlier levels the economists tell us that the recession is over. It did not feel as though it was over to most of us, though, because economic activity was still well below the levels of 2006-2007.

A similarly confusing mathematical puzzle surfaced again when the nation's economy was set reeling by the corona virus pandemic of 2020. The April-June quarter of that year saw a steep 32 percent drop (when annualized) in GDP (gross domestic product), followed by a sharp economic recovery in the July-September quarter of that same 32 percent figure, a startling recovery and a startling increase. The citizenry did not feel as though everything was fine in October, however, and they should not have: A 32 percent drop followed by a 32 percent rise leaves the October economy 10+percent below where it had been in March[51], because you can't simply add the percentages. The problem, the reason for the confusion, was again the math.

★ ★ ★

"Let me tell you about the very rich. They are different from you and me." This was one of the many pithy, social observations put to paper by early twentieth century American author F. Scott Fitzgerald. He may have been right. He was certainly correct that the rich are different when it comes to managing their money. No matter how they may have amassed their pile, when the rich have put it together, they are very different from the rest of us in that they can hire the best, the most mathematically sophisticated money management advice available.

The federal income tax that got us started on the general subject of

---

51. $0.68 \times 1.32 = 0.8976$, or 10.24% below.

mathematics is a good example of their ability to use such advice.

Tariffs had been the central method of federal revenue generation into the early twentieth century, but when the force of events caused the federal government to ramp up its need for revenue, it was the income tax that was sent to go get it. Exactly how to extract money from the sort of people who are themselves good at accumulating and holding on to it—i.e., the very rich—turned out to be a more difficult problem than our elected leaders may have first thought. Those initial stabs at high income taxation were only partially successful because those elected leaders hadn't quite reckoned with the brains they were up against.

Treasury Truisms

Reviewing America's First Experience with a Steeply Progressive Income Tax[52]

("Treasury Truisms" appeared in the Spring 2022 issue of *Financial History* magazine, a quarterly published by the Museum of American Finance.)

Critics of the scholarly pursuit of historical truths—and it must be conceded that such persons do exist—often lament that history seems like "just one damn thing after another." In response, those of us who value history often quote the philosopher George Santayana, who said that, "those who cannot learn from history are doomed to repeat it," but our warnings often fall on deaf ears.

Financial historians should perhaps admit that perfect historical parallels that can be relied upon for guidance are quite rare. "If past history was all that is needed to play the game of money," legendary investor

---

52. "Treasury Truisms" appeared in the Spring 2022 issue of *Financial History* magazine, a quarterly published by the Museum of American Finance.

Warren Buffett famously told us, "the richest people would be librarians."

A good line, although an inveterate reader like Mr. Buffett would have to admit that librarians are paid to catalog history, not to think (much less act) on it. Nevertheless, historians must grant that Human Progress, while generally a good thing, tends to make comparisons with the past necessarily imperfect. Those of us who find history informative might modify Santayana and rely instead on the old Mark Twain-ism that, "History doesn't repeat itself, but it often rhymes."

Nowhere can we see these historical rhymes more easily than in the income tax laws, and in the debates concerning what system or series of tax rates is best. It is a recurring subject of spirited give-and-take, a 'Golden Oldie.'

In such matters the drive for tax fairness is always balanced with the practical concern for economic efficiency. This balancing act was famously expressed over 200 years ago by French economist Turgot when he wrote that the art of taxation involves, "procuring feathers from a goose with the least amount of hissing." Thus, if high rates on certain high incomes are considered by some to be 'fair,' the rates may be counter-productive if they discourage the activity that produced the income to be taxed at those high rates.

The French also gave us that priceless bit of wisdom that, "The more things change, the more they stay the same." Conditions change, but human nature does not, so the historian struggles on, mining the records in search of those gems that rhyme with today's very different conditions.

The present U.S. income tax system got its start in 1913, and it had a tumultuous first ten years. The system started modestly but was quickly called on to help finance the country's World War I effort. Top marginal rates escalated dramatically to try to keep up with the war spending: From 7 percent on income over $500,000 (huge money in

1913), the top rate went to 15 percent in 1916, then jumped dramatically to 67 percent in 1917 (the year the United States entered the war) and finally to 77 percent in 1918 (the year of the armistice).

These martial matters are easily forgotten by the financially minded. One thoroughly modern French economist recently asserted that it was growing income inequality that drove the adoption of the income tax in the United States all those years ago. "Between 1880 and 1910," he wrote, "while the concentration of industrial and financial wealth was gaining momentum in the United States and the country was threatening to become almost as unequal as old Europe, a powerful political movement in favor of an improved distribution in wealth was developing. This led to the creation of a federal tax on income in 1913 and on inheritances in 1916."[53]

Not exactly. The 1913 income tax—at roughly 1 percent for most high-income people and increasing to a mere 7 percent only on very, very high incomes—wasn't very re-distributional. Additionally, the inheritance tax of 1916 was not new, and the version passed in 1898 to finance the Spanish-American War was arguably stiffer.

Most important of all, the real drive to institute the 1913 income tax stemmed not from a desire to re-distribute income but to simply make up the revenue lost from a reduction in tariff rates. Wilson scholar Kendrick Clements states flatly that, "Tariff reduction was Wilson's first concern."[54] Wilson had campaigned in 1912 on the idea that tariffs had been "a method of fostering special privilege" and needed to be trimmed back or even eliminated. Wilson believed that import tariffs favored certain commercial interests—American sugar and wool producers were very visible beneficiaries—and corrupted members of Congress while unfairly raising prices to all American consumers.

---

53. "A Tax on Wealth is Long Overdue" by T. Piketty, The Boston Globe, Feb. 11, 2019.
54. *The Presidency of Woodrow Wilson* by K. Clements (Kansas, 1992), p. 35.

Wilson succeeded, and tariff rates were reduced from roughly 40 percent to around 25 percent. The drop in tariff revenue was recouped with a modest income tax. Under the new income tax law passed in early October 1913, a single taxpayer making $5000/year—a very comfortable income in 1913—was asked to pay a 1 percent tax on their income exceeding a $3000 personal exemption, or a mere $20 that year.

It was the Revenue Act of 1917, passed in October of 1917 as the U.S. government found itself spending money hand-over-fist in prosecuting a war it had joined the previous April, that sent rates on higher incomes rocketing upwards: from 15 percent to as high as 67 percent. The increase was so dramatic that one tax expert worried at the time that taxpayers were "not yet psychologically prepared to pay what they should."[55] Politicians later figured out that 'their fair share' sounded better than "what they should." The shock was greatest on high income earners, but even our $5000/year taxpayer would be asked to pay $240—a 6 percent rate on their income above a reduced $1000 personal exemption—or a twelve-fold increase on the amount owed in 1913.

Another central fact of those years was the general inflation fueled by the war spending, which resulted in an increase in wages for most workers. This rise in wages is clearly visible in the treasury data: In 1913, our "$5K taxpayer" would have been one of only about 400,000 American 'households' required to file a return because not many Americans had yearly income greater than the personal exemptions of $3000 for single people and $4000 for what we today call 'joint filers.' By 1918, however, the number of such 'households' required to file had increased over ten-fold to over 4 million. Our comfortable $5000/year taxpayer of 1913 would probably have been disappointed to earn

---

55. "The War Revenue Act of 1917" by R. Blakey, American Economic Review (December 1917), p. 811

no more in 1918 than in 1913. Had their income grown to $8000 in 1918, their income tax would have risen to $630—about 30 times their 1913 bill. Such a hypothetical may more accurately reflect the extent to which the burden of paying for the war was shared in ways not captured by the tax rate tables.

These same years reveal quite dramatically a little kernel of taxing wisdom that is with us, both substantively and rhetorically, to this day. It is seen in the behavior of those very wealthy taxpayers who were suddenly faced in October 1917 with 60+ percent marginal rates and whose income derived principally from investments and not from wages. The capital of these very wealthy taxpayers was somewhat mobile, and their income was therefore somewhat flexible as to how it was generated, and in their behavior, we see for the first time in U.S. history the difficulty, the 'goose-hissing,' of taxing income at extremely high marginal rates.

They were indeed high marginal rates: By 1918, the income of single persons exceeded $100,000/year and was taxed at 64 percent, and income over $300,000/year was taxed at 75 percent.

People subject to these 60+ percent rates were undeniably wealthy. Legendary 1920s baseball player Babe Ruth made headlines when his wage income increased from $52,000 to $80,000/year, a salary that readers of the sports pages in those days found almost stratospheric.

Instituting these extremely high marginal rates, however, resulted in a sharp drop in the number of returns declaring income subject to these rates. For example, some 1,296 tax returns declared income of over $300,000 in 1916 when such income was taxed at 15 percent. In 1918, when such income was taxed at 71-77 percent (depending on filing status), the number of such taxpayers declined by over half, to 627.[56]

---

56. "The Revenue Act of 1921" by R. Blakey, American Economic Review (March 1922), data from Senate Report, no. 275, 67 Cong., 1 Sess., p. 5.

The income tax was only five years old in 1918; these very high rates were newer still, so it is quite stunning to observe the speed with which the wealthy and their advisors reacted to these changes. Whether it was because they were not "psychologically prepared to pay" or some other reason, it is clear they acted quickly. Consider that these high rates became law only in October 1917, and within a few months, over half of the $300,000+ earners of 1916 simply disappeared from the rolls of such earners of 1918.

Such a decline in the number of those returns is impossible to place at the foot of the economy: During the years 1916-1918 the number of people filing returns and reporting higher wage incomes escalated dramatically, and these were years when progressives accused rich industrialists of "war-profiteering."

This drop in very high-income returns did not reflect illegal tax evasion; rather, these very wealthy citizens were engaged in the legal process of tax avoidance. A popular method of legal tax avoidance, one familiar to many readers of this journal, is redirection of investment capital into state or municipal bonds, the income from which is free of federal tax. The extremely wealthy and/or their advisors clearly figured this out very quickly. There was a sharp stock market decline in that fourth quarter of 1917 following passage of the Revenue Act of 1917. With those dramatically higher rates, the drop perhaps was traceable to the selling of shares to raise the money to pay a big tax bill and re-direction of capital towards municipal bonds.

The popularity of this method of tax avoidance was such that three years later it dominated the debates over the Revenue Act of 1921, debates that concerned not whether but how much to reduce these high marginal rates. These debates witnessed U.S. senators reviewing calculations (calculations!) aimed at pinpointing exactly how much these top marginal rates would have to decline to reduce the incentive for wealthy taxpayers to invest in "Munis." Senator Reed Smoot of Utah approached the question using "a mathematical calculation" and arrived at a maximum marginal tax rate of 32 percent. "The reason," he explained, "is because 32 percent is the difference between the income from a tax-exempt security and one that is taxable on the basis of today's money market." One taxation scholar of the time summarized the money market situation underlying these debates as follows: "... no one paying 73 percent or even 58 percent ... will invest in 6 percent or even 10 percent taxable railroad or industrial securities so long as 5 percent state and municipal tax-exempt bond may be purchased at par or thereabouts."[57]

The 'rhyme' in this fact pattern is that these same calculations are done exactly this way today, albeit with different bond interest and marginal tax rates. "Muni bonds are often a good investment for people with high incomes living in states with high income taxes, such as California"[58] advises the Investopedia website. Tax advisors have also formulated other methods of tax avoidance in response to other tax law changes. The 80+percent marginal rates of the mid-twentieth century instituted to try to pay for World War II inspired a veritable cottage industry of other 'rhyming' schemes: passive loss real estate investments, hobby farms, etc. Our modern-day tax advisor is not a lazy stiff.

A defense of these high rates on high incomes was raised a century ago, just as it is today. A century ago, the argument was made that although collections on income above $300,000 had declined, total tax receipts from the wealthy had increased. The ranking minority member of the House Ways and Means Committee asserted back in 1921 "... that for each year since 1916...there has been a gradual increase of

57. Blakey, p. 81.

58. "Are Municipal Bonds a Good Investment?" by D. Moskowitz, Investopedia, January 19, 2020.

millions in collection of taxes from income from $50,000 upward. In 1919...were collected...$586 million more than in 1916." He went on to defend a system that encouraged investment in municipal bonds, asking rhetorically, "Are not the people of the states and counties and municipalities thereby benefitted by getting a higher price for such bonds, and do not the proceeds from these state and municipal bonds go more directly for the benefit of the people than the taxes of the federal government?"[59]

The choice by the ranking minority member of $50,000 for comparison was no accident. Income tax rates on the first $50,000 of taxable income were much lower during those years than they were on income around $300,000. The marginal rate on income of the dollar over $50,000 was 36 percent, but a single payer with $50,000 of taxable income in 1918 was assessed $11,690 in taxes, or only 23 percent of their income because of the lower rates prevailing on the income below $50,000. Such well-heeled taxpayers were therefore positioned to justify investment in taxable industrial bonds at 8 percent rather than state or municipal bonds at 5 percent, and therefore willingly declared such amounts of taxable income.

As with so many other maddeningly complex and seemingly contradictory mathematical facts, both these debating points were true: Collections on extremely high incomes of over $300,000/year were decidedly down and probably for the reasons enumerated, but at the same time collections on somewhat lower but still very high incomes were up strongly, due to these tax law and economic (and inflationary) effects. It is only when the inducements to investment at each of these precise income levels are examined closely—and mathematically--that it becomes clear why both facts could be true.

---

59. Blakey, p. 83.

The translation of these specific historical facts to the present day is necessarily imperfect. Things have changed. Marginal rates do not escalate as rapidly and to the levels they did back then. Large numbers of 'middle-class' Americans now have wage incomes that cause them to be taxed at fairly high rates on their wage income—especially when their federal tax levy is combined with the state and social insurance taxes they now must pay—and such wage income leaves them few alternatives to reduce their tax burden. Humans have not changed, however, and what may have been glaringly true to policymakers a century ago is probably true today: Marginal tax rates of over 50 percent will cause taxpayers subject to those rates to look for alternatives, and alternatives they will find, regardless of whether the passage of time reveals these alternatives to be financially rewarding.

Chapter 6

1 PERCENT INSPIRATION 99 PERCENT PERSPIRATION

This interesting and oft-repeated quote regarding the components of what we call 'genius' is attributed to the world-renowned inventor Thomas Edison. He was often called a genius, so he knew in his own case of what he spoke. Edison's early days involved wiring offices in the Wall Street area in the 1880s. His system required nearby power stations because over longer distances, the power losses were too great. In those early days, such small 'micro-grid' networks required constant monitoring of the power station output, the insulating and burying of the wires extending from a nearby power station through conduit piping, connectors, fuses, etc. into offices and to incandescent lights of dubious reliability—all to make sure the wires and bulbs worked consistently and did not set the neighborhood ablaze.

This approach, needless to say, required improvements. Nobody wanted to live close to a power station with the noise and the belching coal smoke required to produce the steam pressure that turned the turbines to generate the electricity. To be practical, electrification of offices and households also could not increase the chances of fire. The idea was Edison's baby, though, so he and his myriad companies hoped to make the many required improvements that would make the idea of mass electrification less dangerous and easier to live around.

Alas, when the most important electrical power project of his life was scoped out and contracts awarded, Edison looked on as the precocious young Croatian-born inventor, Nikola Tesla, provided the required spark of genius that paved the way for the tremendous electrically powered world we enjoy today.

Tesla's genius was still not enough, however. Considerable work—i.e., perspiration—was required to develop and commercialize this huge hydroelectric project: money raising, blasting, excavating, equipment fabricating and installing, miles of power poles to support the high-voltage wires, transformer stations, etc. The details behind this great achievement are worth reviewing, if only to remind us that Mr. Edison's pithy aphorism proved true in the end.

An Investment Banker Lights the World[60]

("An Investment Banker Lights the World" appeared in the
Winter 2024 issue of *Financial History* magazine.)

Investment banking is often thought of today as the simple raising of money through the issuance and marketing of securities. In the nineteenth and early twentieth centuries, however, when managerial and engineering expertise were scarce resources, competent investment banking sometimes required organizing the technical and industrial effort involved.

J.P. Morgan, Sr. understood this. Morgan was the most important investment banker of his time, and many new ideas for industrial development crossed his desk. He knew from dint of experience that what separated good ideas from bad was not his assessment of the technology – he would have been the first to admit he was not a technologist – but the managerial and engineering competence of the people organizing the technical effort.

One such idea was the large-scale generation and transmission

---

60. "An Investment Banker Lights the World" appeared in the Winter 2024 issue of *Financial History* magazine.

of power using natural water flow. The idea was compelling for New Yorkers: Niagara Falls, one of the world's largest waterfalls, was located at the western edge of the state, and the potential energy released as the water cascaded downward was massive. "As a site for the development of water-power," wrote one promoter, "the falls of Niagara stand without rival in all the world" and occupy "a truly strategic position upon one of the great trade routes of the continent."[61]

NIAGARA FALLS

Mr. Morgan was optimistic about the general idea. He and his fellow residents of lower Manhattan had been using electric lights since the 1880s powered by coal-fired steam turbines at the nearby Pearl Street Power Station, but the nearest large city to Niagara Falls was Buffalo some 25 miles away, and the technical problems surrounding

61. "Niagara Power" compiled by E.D. Adams (New York, 1927), Vol. 1, p.14.

longer-range power transmission were filled with uncertainties.

One of these ideas for harnessing and transmitting the hydro power at Niagara Falls was pitched to Mr. Morgan in the late 1880s. The prominent financier was enthusiastic, but monetarily non-committal. When asked about the source of his reticence, Morgan said, "Your scheme is all right, but you have no man to run it."

"Whom would you suggest?" asked the ardent promoter.

"Well, there is Adams. If you can get him, I'll join you."[62]

Edward Dean Adams was a small, meticulous, and cultured man working as an attorney and banker on Wall Street. A distant relative of two American presidents, Adams was unusual among Wall Streeters of the time in that he was an MIT-educated technologist, a practical and pragmatic man "who knew how to make things happen and get things done."[63] Years later, *Time* magazine described Adams' reputation at the time in this way: "...he had already established among the more flamboyant New Yorkers a quiet reputation as a thorough investigator and sound organizer of the projects into which men put money."[64] Such a man was known to Mr. Morgan through Morgan's many railroad reorganizations, and such a man could be expected to make things happen and get things done—i.e., 'to run it.'

The promoters approached Mr. Adams who agreed to a six-month contract to "see what could be done." He consulted mechanical engineers, including a man he would depend on for the project, Dr. Coleman Sellers of Philadelphia. Adams also cabled Thomas Edison, who at the time was in Paris: "Has power transmission reached such development that in your judgment scheme practicable?" he asked the world-famous Mr. Edison.

---

62. "Empires of Light" by J. Jonnes (New York, 2003), p. 281.

63. Ibid

64. *Time Magazine*, May 27, 1929.

Edison replied: "No difficulty transferring unlimited power. Will assist."[65]

A company was organized, the Cataract Construction Company, in early 1890. Adams was put in charge of it, and when news of this got around, the company was quickly capitalized at the then lavish sum of $2.63 million.

The core mechanical principle was compelling and thoroughly understood. By diverting the river flow from a point above the falls and channeling the flow downwards using large diameter pipes called "penstocks," the tremendous hydrostatic pressure unleashed at the bottom of the vertical column of water could be used to spin turbines. The motion of those turbines would then spin long, vertical shafts that could be used to generate power.

The work to channel the flow was daunting and began before fully answering the question of how to use the energy of the spinning turbines. The work was brutal: dynamiting and excavating a tunnel first alongside, then downward some 150 feet through bedrock near the falls, then sloping down gradually through a 1+ mile long tunnel—the 'tailrace tunnel'—to an exit, the 'tunnel portal,' that channeled the water back into the Niagara River downstream of the falls. Thirteen hundred men worked day and night blasting and excavating 600,000 tons of rock, and 28 of them would die in the process.[66]

The central technical issue to be resolved was the transmission of the power generated. To merely send power to the 2500 people in the nearby town of Niagara would not justify the tremendous expense. The challenge was to transmit power to the 250,000 people in the bustling port city of Buffalo.

The uncertainties led to fractious technical disputes. George

---

65. *Time Magazine*, May 27, 1929.
66. *Empires of Light*, p. 286.

Westinghouse, known now as one of engineering's towering figures, was so skeptical in 1890 of the idea of long-distance electricity transmission that he originally suggested using compressed air to transmit the power to Buffalo. Mr. Westinghouse, it may be recalled, had invented the railroad air brake. "Today it is almost impossible," Edward Adams wrote years later of the technical uncertainties, "to realize the situation at the earlier date [i.e., in 1890]."[67]

Technology, however, was moving fast. Long-distance transmission using alternating electric current—i.e., 'AC'—was demonstrated in 1891 in Germany over a 100-mile span, with a power loss of less than 25 percent[68] That same year, at the Gold King Mine in Colorado, Westinghouse engineers sent AC current thousands of feet above the waterwheel hydro power source to energize a Nikola Tesla-designed AC-motor near the mine to drive a stamp mill. It was proof-of-concept, but the power transmitted was modest.

Vexing details remained in the translation of Niagara's spinning turbine power into electricity. A professor from Scotland was brought over to design a few critical parts of the translating system, but the Westinghouse engineers found his low frequency design completely unworkable. It was left to Adams to work out a technical compromise using the skills he had developed in getting railroad managers and financiers to cooperate.

Much has been written about these technical details; it is a pivotal point in the history of electrical engineering. The contestants were some of the titans of technological history: Thomas Edison and General Electric on one side of the debate, Nikola Tesla and the Westinghouse Corp. on the other. These matters boiled down to a question of whether to use alternating or direct current—AC vs. DC—to transmit power to

---

67. "Niagara Power," Vol. II, p. 269.

68. *The Merchant of Power* by John F. Wasik (New York, 2006), p.50.

Buffalo. Edward Adams was in the middle of this technical tussle, and it was Adams who would make the final decision.

These matters, while interesting, can easily distract us from an equally important but largely forgotten story. This issue, one that occupied Mr. Adams just as much as the technical matter, was how to arrange the financing of the project in such a way that the company would generate cash flows sufficient to produce a return on the capital raised. Adams knew as well as anyone that for all of Thomas Edison's technical successes, Edison's companies in the 1880s were routinely in financial difficulty as they struggled to cover their development costs.[69]

The financial issue weighed on the technical issue. Tesla wrote to Adams during the critical decision year of 1893 that "what my [AC] system has offered was to do away with the commutator and brushes in the generator and the motor...This renders the system simpler." Tesla went on to critique the idea of DC power, asserting, "The power you would furnish with such machines would be unavailable for many uses, for instance, electric lighting."[70] This little passage, added towards the end of a long letter, may have caught Mr. Adams attention because lighting was the feature that would induce the citizens of Buffalo to willingly pay the utility bills that would allow the project to work financially.

The water flow to be diverted and the vertical drop through the penstocks and turbines created potential power that was a quantum leap above that produced by the power stations then in operation—and all without the noxious coal smoke associated with conventional steam power. Ten huge 5000-horsepower generators were planned for Niagara, potential electrical power far greater than any other single power plant in the United States. George Westinghouse commented

69. Ibid, p. 22-26.
70. *Tesla* by W.B. Carlson (Princeton, 2013), p. 171.

that the size of the generators was "far beyond all precedent" and as such that "nearly every device used differs from what has hitherto been our standard practice."[71]

The uses to be made of such power by the citizens of Buffalo were potentially vast, but the price the citizens would be willing to pay was uncertain and would undoubtedly be politically contentious. The Cataract Company therefore directed some of their capital to the purchase of some 1500 acres of land near the falls for an industrial park, promising any interested industrialists access to cheap electrical power.

The Cataract Company was building a potentially better mousetrap, or at least a bigger mousetrap, and the world indeed "beat a path to their door." The embryonic industry of producing aluminum from bauxite required large amounts of electrical power—aluminum is sometimes described as "congealed electricity"—and the ambitious people in Pittsburgh running what would become Alcoa contacted Adams with a plan to place a factory right in Niagara and the request for all the electrical power Adams and his Cataract Company could provide. The manufacture of 'carborundum'—i.e., silicon carbide—a mineral used for cutting tools, abrasives, and gem polishing, required electrical furnaces capable of producing 4000F temperatures, and the Carborundum Company of Monongahela, Pennsylvania was eager to move operations to Niagara to access this abundant electrical power source.

The fortuitous nature of these parallel developments was not lost on Edward Dean Adams. "How often it happens," he wrote, "that two movements, unknown to each other and widely separated...plod along slowly...until they seemingly just happen to meet at the exact moment when each needs the aid of the other!"[72]

---

71. *A Life of George Westinghouse* by H.G. Prout (New York, 1926), p. 152-153
72. *Niagara Power*, Vol. II, p. 312

Some of the project's dependence on the technical uncertainty of long-distance power transmission to Buffalo was relieved by these corporate customers. For these corporations, the electric power was well worth the price. When the first of the turbines was set spinning in mid-summer 1895, Alcoa and the Carborundum Company began receiving power.

The way in which the profits gushing from new technologies can grease the financial gears to hasten broader societal change is a recurring theme in financial history. For instance, the lucrative spice trade stimulated a good deal of ship building in Elizabethan England, later permitting a group of religious separatists without much money to charter a couple of older merchant vessels, the *Mayflower* and the *Speedwell*, for a pilgrimage to the New World. The British East India Company passed on using the *Mayflower* years earlier.[73] Similarly, the discovery of gold in 1849, a few dozen miles from Sacramento, led a few years later to the lavish capitalizing of a railroad, the Sacramento Valley Railroad, whose sole purpose was to ship gold and supplies between the mines in the foothills of the Sierra Nevada range and Sacramento. Fifteen years later that line served as the western terminus of the Transcontinental Railroad.[74]

The turbines were spinning, and aluminum and carborundum production was proceeding while the city of Buffalo wrestled with how to organize and regulate the proposed electrical utility. Buffalo's Common Council, later its Board of Public Works, could not agree on issues like the right to revoke terms and rates and whether they should have the power to mandate burying the wires underground. These questions, while important, weighed on the financials of the project, where the timing of the cash flow is most important.

---

73. *The Anarchy* by W. Dalrymple (New York, 2019), p. 10.
74. *Nothing Like it in the World* by S. Ambrose (New York, 2000), p. 55.

The project's capitalization was significant: Additional offerings brought the total to roughly $6 million when the 25+ miles of transmission lines sending alternating current to Buffalo were completed and transformers were in place. Power was first sent to Buffalo in the early minutes of November 16, 1896 and immediately began powering the city's streetcars–ironically, only after being transformed to direct current.

Eight weeks later Buffalo's burghers decided to celebrate. They packed the top floor dining room of the ten-story Ellicott Square Building for a banquet—an AC-powered, electrically lit banquet—organized by the Cataract Power and Conduit Company. Adams and the capitalists traveled from New York City along with the world-renowned Mr. Tesla in a private railcar, and they visited the powerhouse on the way to the banquet. Mr. Tesla was to be the keynote speaker, but New York moneyman Francis Stetson spoke first and took some of the air out of what was to be a festive evening by complaining about his company's lack of profits as of that date. He and his fellow investors, he lectured, had shelled out over $6 million to build the great power station. He made a point of quoting the precise amount "without thus far receiving one penny of profits or dividends or interest."[75]

The audience was in too good a mood to be put out for very long by this self-interested rant. Mr. Tesla's speech followed, and he focused instead on the 'type of man' responsible for this great engineering feat, one "whose chief aim and enjoyment is the acquisition and spread of knowledge, men who look far above earthly things, whose banner is Excelsior!"

---

75. *Empires of Light*, p. 333.

Nikola Tesla statue alongside Niagara Falls

The crowd roared. Buffalo's citizens were proud of their city's new and growing power grid. It had started modestly, but it would escalate rapidly: By May 1900, all ten turbines connected to power-house #1 were spinning and generating 50,000-horsepower (37 million watts).

Buffalo's merchants were so enchanted by the illumination of their business district that they financed an Exposition, a World's Fair, in 1901 that would highlight this new electric age. They were intent on outdoing the Chicago World's Fair of 1893, the one that had first hinted at the tremendous technical capabilities of electricity. And it was a success, although it is known to history now largely as the site of President William McKinley's assassination in September 1901.

The technical achievement of those Niagara engineers and work-men is easily forgotten. A large 1950s era dam project increased power generation at the site and left few remnants of their 1890s work. The pioneering engineers were too busy to spend much time tout-ing or documenting their Niagara achievement. Their leader, George Westinghouse, was famously non-reflective[76], and Nikola Tesla was quickly absorbed with other projects. The electric age had begun, and they were at the vanguard.

One man did not forget. Edward Dean Adams quietly kept the doc-uments and tracked the project's tremendous influence on the world. In 1927, he produced a beautiful two-volume history of the project, *Niagara Power*, and sent copies to libraries around the country. He compiled statistics showing how influential the Niagara project was on the nation's total electrical power output: Niagara Power initially accounted for a substantial fraction of the total electric power produced in the country, but by the 1920s, long distance AC transmission from coal-powered plants had grown so fast that Niagara's share of the nation's total electric power generation was much reduced. Adams and his advisors cautioned, however, that coal was a finite resource, while hydro power was renewable and sourced (via evaporation) from the sun.[77]

Adams also made a detailed accounting of the value of the metal-lurgical and chemical products made possible by Niagara power. "The value of the products dependent upon Niagara power is reckoned in billions of dollars annually," he wrote, "whereas the gross earnings of the Niagara Falls Power Company from the largest and finest hydro-electric development in the world was $8,549,269.83 in 1926. The [Company's] tax budget for 1926 was $1,508,794.94, thus making the

---

76. *Empires of Light*, p. 337.

77. *Niagara Power*, Vol. II, p. 447.

Niagara Falls Power Company not only one of the real conservers of natural resources (its power-houses operate at an efficiency of 90 per cent) but a source of income to the state and a benefaction to the industries and citizenry of the nation."[78]

---

78. *Niagara Power*, Vol. II, p. 371-372.

Chapter 7

THE DIRTY, SLIMY, OILY, AND INCONVENIENT TRUTH ABOUT ENERGY

The scientific realities underlying electrical power generation are the stuff of college engineering courses. Students who have successfully completed the required first year coursework in mathematics, physics, and chemistry then apply these learnings to the various mechanical and chemical processes used to generate electrical energy. The general principles are inviolate, the calculations exacting and unambiguous. The student who takes on this coursework hoping to change the world through 'renewable' energy sources such as wind and solar often emerges somewhat dispirited by these calculations.

Politicians are not so easily discouraged, often for the simple reason that they didn't complete such coursework. Thus liberated, they often advance new ideas regarding the use of these renewable sources to accomplish what they regard as public spirited goals. They sometimes make the mistake, however, of asking engineering questions of their engineering experts, and the answers they receive sometimes cause them to lapse into a stern silence that is the ignorant version of the student's dispiritedness.

The Midwestern Governors Association illustrated this recently when they innocently asked a midwestern power company to make some electrical power cost estimates connected with different blends of conventional and renewable sources. The governor acting as chairperson had set a goal for the association to "focus on creating a more secure and modern electric grid in the Midwest," so the information request was consistent with her policy goal. A laudable goal, but one that probably should not have been boiled down into a series of engineering questions for power company engineers to answer publicly before the governors were given a hint as to what those answers would be. Perhaps the governors had gotten a little complacent: If you give the same stump speech for years extolling the "clean energy future" you plan to bring about, and your followers don't stop you to ask you detailed questions, you may actually begin to believe your own rhetoric.

The sober reality was laid bare for the governors in one slide. The power company technicians were asked to compare their current renewable/conventional power mix with three alternatives: 50/50, 80/20, and 100/0. The cost curve went up a small amount in going to 50/50, increased over eight-fold in going to 80/20 (i.e., 80 percent renewable), and then shot out of sight to over 30 times the current cost in going to 100 percent renewable.[79]

The slide was not widely discussed. The governors certainly did not dwell on it, and they were not asked much about it by members of the press. This should not dissuade the curious like you and me, my dear reader, because a more than thirty-fold increase in electrical power prices is—ahem—statistically significant and should be made sense of.

One obvious cost associated with increasing reliance on wind and solar is a cost that conventional energy sources do not incur: storage (i.e., batteries). The wind does not blow reliably; the sun sets, and these two events often occur concurrently with an increase in electricity demand as people arrive home from work at dusk and proceed to turn on lights and televisions and ovens. Energy storage using batteries is therefore required with wind and solar power generation, *lots* of

---

79. *Thinking Minnesota* magazine, Winter 2020 issue, p. 7

storage, to accumulate for later use the energy that is generated when the wind blows and the sun shines.

The State of California illustrates this now because state mandates have increased the use of wind and solar by their utility companies and the shuttering of coal-fired and nuclear power sources. (California's grid is currently at about 36 percent renewables.) When increased electricity demand occurs during periods when air conditioning demand is up, but the wind is down and/or the sun has set—as can happen—blackouts occur. The state's governor was forced to concede recently that the resulting electricity blackouts were traceable to the fact that storage (i.e., battery) technology must be "substantially improved." As reliance on wind and solar approaches 100 percent, the use of these storage technologies in need of substantial improvement increases dramatically, and with it the unreliability as well as the costs.

"Still," we hear the alternative energy advocates argue, "the wind and the sunshine are free." This is true, and it would be the end of the discussion but for another uncomfortable fact known to business and engineering students the world over as 'cost accounting.' Wind and sun energy are free, but the wind turbines and the solar panels required to capture that energy and transform it into electricity are decidedly un-free. Furthermore, those turbines and panels require maintenance and wear out, meaning that another dirty word must enter the discussion: 'depreciation.' Wind turbines are good for only 20-25 years at the most. The turbines in a large wind farm near me in northern Iowa are being replaced less than 20 years after installation. Solar panels are good for about 30 years at the most, and batteries much less than that. The lithium batteries that are so *au courant* are impractically expensive and they are fire hazards. Meanwhile, the nuclear and coal-fired plants near me are closing in on 50 years of service. The upshot of all these uncomfortable 'accounting' facts is that wind and solar as sources of electrical energy are quite pricey.

Another fact was left out of the above discussion, and yet it is extremely relevant to those interested in bringing about a clean energy "carbon- and nuclear-free" future. The energy these various sources produce per unit area here on Earth is limited, and space here is limited.

Most advanced economies like those in the United States and Europe use energy of one sort or another—nearly all of it generated by burning fossil fuels that then produce carbon dioxide—at a predictable rate of roughly 1 Watt per square meter of land.[80] The wind farms we see driving through rural areas generate energy at only about 2 watts per square meter; solar panels generate energy at only about 5-10 watts per square meter.

The implications of these facts, played out on a large scale, are almost cartoonish. Roughly 50 percent of the land area of Europe and/ or the United States would have to be covered by wind farms if wind were asked to generate all the power (i.e., grid plus transportation plus heating/cooling systems) required in those places. Solar panels do slightly better, but only slightly: 10-20 percent of the land area would have to be devoted to solar panels if they were depended on for all the power currently required. Nobody likes living near these wind and solar farms, however, so transmission costs would eat into these efficiencies if such farms were to generate all the energy currently required. A plan to use both wind and solar would require covering 20-40 percent of the land mass of a country such as the United States with such turbines or panels and batteries and replacing them all every 15-30 years. Talk about a recycling problem!

It is all very dispiriting.

An important question arises from all this, one that truly needs to be asked but seldom is and, oddly enough, can easily be answered: Why

---

80. A good review of the energy used per unit of land area in different countries is provided in a TED Talk given by Dr. David MacKay in 2014.

are these renewable sources so difficult to justify? Or alternatively: How is it that these old-fashioned conventional sources produce power that the high-tech renewable sources have such trouble matching?

A conventional source like nuclear power is easily understood: In a more concentrated form, after all, it is the stuff of nuclear bombs. Nuclear power plants generate power at about 1000 watts per square meter of the large area normally reserved for them, or 200-500 times more than wind and solar on this per-unit-area basis. Most of us might have guessed this, and we have all come to our own conclusions regarding the wisdom of using nuclear power.

The fascinating question left unasked and unanswered is why these renewables fail to match the old-fashioned hydrocarbon sources like coal and natural gas and heating oil and unleaded gasoline that dominate the American power grid, because the power contained in these hydrocarbon sources—given the controversial nature of nuclear power—is the real barrier to the use of these renewable sources.

Let us boil the question down to the thermodynamic details of an item of commerce that we are all familiar with. The 'fossil fuel' used to power the Volkswagen Jetta that I drive contains a typical four-cylinder engine that has a peppy little turbo feature but is in no sense a 'muscle car.' Yet if asked to perform at full throttle, this small 1.5-liter engine can generate 145 horsepower of purely mechanical energy. The V8 engine in the latest Ford Mustang, a true 'muscle car,' can generate 750 horsepower. The Jetta engine itself occupies roughly 1/2 square meter of land area (a little less, really), and because there are 746 watts in one unit of horsepower, this is an available mechanical energy output of 210,000 Watts/m2—some 20,000-100,000x more power-per-unit-area than wind and solar and over 100x that of a nuclear power plant. (Nuclear plant reactors are usually surrounded by large amounts of non-energy producing land, thus limiting their energy-per-unit-area capacity.) Therefore, a single 4-cylinder VW engine set up to turn turbines rather than tires can generate the same amount of electric power as a 25-acre wind farm or 7 acres of solar panels. By extrapolation, that Ford Mustang engine can generate power equal to a 70-acre wind farm or 22+ acres of solar panels. In addition, these automobile engines also generate some frictional heat energy that is transferred to the coolant that courses through the engine block to keep it from overheating, a feature that allows for heating of the car's passengers in winter.

The dirty little secret behind this nineteenth century power source is something our grandparents understood perfectly well but one that we have taken for granted or ignored or chosen not to confront: Hydrocarbons are incredible.

The key is in the name itself: hydrocarbon. All these carbon-emitting sources—coal, natural gas, heating oil, gasoline—have one extremely powerful chemical fact in common: hydrogen-carbon chemical bonds. Lots of them. An incredible number of them. The density of these chemical bonds in the gasoline used by the engine in my Volkswagen is fascinating to a chemical engineer. For example, octane—the stuff of gasoline—is a molecule with a modest molecular weight twice that of table salt. Yet while two molecules of table salt contain two chemical bonds, the octane molecule of comparable weight contains fully twenty-five chemical bonds: eighteen carbon-hydrogen bonds and seven carbon-carbon bonds. Each of these twenty-five chemical bonds are very reactive in the presence of heat and oxygen, and the reaction that occurs to produce carbon dioxide and water liberates energy, *lots* of energy.

The source of this tremendous energy has to do with the nature of the bonds in the reactants and products. Those twenty-five bonds in octane react with thirteen oxygen molecules (each containing an oxygen-oxygen bond) and are transformed into nine water (H_2O) and eight carbon dioxide (CO_2) molecules. The chemical bonds in water and carbon dioxide are, in the parlance of thermodynamics, 'inert, low energy' bonds. Carbon dioxide is one of the lowest energy molecules known. The rule in thermodynamics is that if the reactants contain 'high energy' bonds such as hydrogen-carbon bonds and the products of the reaction are 'low energy' carbon-oxygen and hydrogen-oxygen bonds, then: 1. The reaction goes very decidedly in one direction (i.e., water and carbon dioxide never react to produce octane) and 2. The tremendous difference in energy between the reactants and the products appears in the form of heat. In conclusion: The breaking of a single hydrogen-carbon bond or a single carbon-carbon bond in the presence of oxygen liberates a good deal of energy, and there are twenty-five such bonds in each molecule of octane, a relatively small molecule. Therefore, the energy produced in 'combusting' gasoline, per unit of weight and per molecule, is tremendous.

There is nothing else on Earth quite so potentially powerful and at the same time so plentiful and portable as these hydrocarbons. These powerful and plentiful relics of earlier plant and animal life have been wreaking havoc across the industrial world for well over a century. They currently act as a barrier to change—a change to a more renewable energy future.

When this power was first identified and unleashed, however, it hastened rather than prevented change. In those days, the hydrocarbons extracted from coal and crude oil acted as an angry bull in the delicate china shop of existing industrial arrangements.

The Battle Over the "Midnight Oil"

(This article appeared in the Winter 2021 issue
of *Financial History* magazine. [81])

Wee spend our mid-day sweat, or mid-night oil;
Wee tyre the night in thought; the day in toyle.[82]

That quaint seventeenth century rhyme takes us back to a world that vanished only recently. Electric lighting is about the same age as the automobile, and the world it extinguished was quite different from the incandescing, fluorescing, diode-emitting world we inhabit today.

Re-visiting that world can be done by financial historians through the mid-nineteenth century commercial tussle over the fluid used to 'burn the midnight oil.' Tree extracts, lards, and oils from animals and distillates of crude oil contended for market share. Perhaps inspired by those thinkers who worked long hours by oil or candlelight, modern economic theorists have devoted pages and pages to this battle.

Some subscribe to the 'invisible hand' school of economic thought and argue that the whaling that depleted whale populations in the 1850s produced market conditions that 'incentivized' the discovery of crude oil in Ontario and western Pennsylvania.[83] Others who prefer the 'corruption' school of human affairs to explain economic history point to the Civil War-era tax on ethyl alcohol, the ingredient common to so many adult beverages, that was also a key ingredient in a popular tree extract-based lighting fluid and constituted, they assert,

---

81. "The Battle Over the 'Midnight Oil'" appeared in the Winter 2021 issue of *Financial History* magazine.

82. *Emblames* by F. Quarles (England, 1635)

83. *The PBS Newshour Whale Oil Myth* by A. May, wattsupwiththat.com, April 24, 2018.

the first corrupt government subsidy to the oil industry.[84]

This theorizing is all very laughable to an old chemical engineer and presents the opportunity to impart a little edification to those whose devotion to any single school of economic thought may leave them somewhat myopic. Shakespeare hinted at this myopia in composing the part of Hamlet, who tells his good friend that, "There are more things in heaven and earth, Horatio, than are dreamt of in your philosophy."[85]

In the year 1850, the market for 'midnight oil' offered customers whale oil, sperm whale oil (not quite the same thing), lard oil from slaughterhouse waste (you can imagine the smell), coal oil liquid residues, as well as a blend of tree extracts dissolved in alcohol called 'camphene.'

Price and value govern markets, so the costs incurred in producing these fluids were important to their market position. These costs are sometimes ignored by theorists for the simple reason that producers only grudgingly divulge such cost information to preserve their pricing flexibility.

'Midnight oil' customers in 1850 therefore had an interesting and diverse group of options and costs.

Camphene—sometimes 'camphine'—was a blend of camphor oil from camphor trees and turpentine from pine sap dissolved in ethyl alcohol, a mixture that burned with a somewhat pleasant smell. In use, it was a fire hazard, but camphene was a low-cost option and the volume leader. The alcohol was the low-cost component, but if the blend contained too much alcohol and not enough camphor or turpentine, it

---

84. *The Whale Oil Myth* by B. Kovarik, pbs.org, Aug. 20, 2008: "The fact is that kerosene did not simply replace whale oil. In 1860, the government determined which technology would be the best way to get light at night. The oil industry was the favorite, and in effect, it was born with the competition swept neatly away and the silver spoon of subsidy lodged firmly in its teeth."

85. *Hamlet* by W. Shakespeare, Act I, Scene 5 (England, 1600)

didn't produce much actual illumination, so camphene producers could not skimp on the tree extracts.

Whale oil was slightly more expensive than camphene. It was extracted from whale blubber renderings, and like lard oil and coal oil, it was a mish mash of oils and fibrous bits. The variegated nature of these oils often became painfully obvious in use as the ingredients sent forth a black, acrid plume that could leave the purchaser to reflect that any money saved at the point of purchase was somehow paid out later.

Sperm whales, those gargantuan beasts with the long, flat row of teeth and broad foreheads, hold oil of a much more chemically consistent quality. Such oil burned bright and clean and sold for 2-3x the price of generic whale oil.

The extraction of 'midnight oil' from sperm whales is familiar to those who have enjoyed Herman Melville's excellent novel, *Moby Dick*, published during the height of this competition in 1851. Melville's readers were taught how to locate and harvest these valuable fluids from the sperm whale carcass. He wrote of the "Heidelburgh Tun" of the sperm whale—an allusion to a giant wine barrel stored in the cellar of a large castle in Heidelberg, Germany—where "the most precious of all his oily vintages," namely the sperm whale's oil and spermaceti, reside in the large snout-like area above the sperm whale's long row of teeth.[86]

---

86. *Moby Dick* by H. Melville (New York, 1851), Chapter 77

Whaling: Tougher than oil drilling

Melville's description of the harvesting of spermaceti from the sperm whale carcass is riveting prose, but it should be remembered that spermaceti and oil are different. The spermaceti that fascinated Melville is a soft, wax-like substance in the whale that hardens with exposure to air and worked perfectly as candle wax.

The spermaceti lay at the top of the whale's snout, in the 'Case,' in what Melville describes as an "absolutely pure, limpid, and odoriferous state." Melville estimated that "a large whale's Case generally yields about five hundred gallons of spermaceti, though from unavoidable circumstances, considerable of it is spilled, leaks, and dribbles away, or is otherwise irrevocably lost in the ticklish business of securing what you can."

The sperm whale oil is located between the Case and the whale's large mouth, in—to use Melville's words—"one immense honeycomb of oil, formed by the crossing and re-crossing, into ten thousand infiltrated cells, of tough elastic white fibres." When drained from within this honeycomb, however, this oil was of consistent quality. The spermaceti and the oil could be harvested together on whaling ships and separated later by cooling, a process the whalers called 'wintering.'

Whaling ships such as the *Pequod* captained by Melville's Ahab were often out for years at a time. The Pequod sailed southeast from Nantucket to the Azores, then south and around the Cape of Good Hope and east to the typhoon-plagued waters off Japan to hunt the prized sperm whale. By modern standards, whaling was an almost impossibly difficult way to make a living, and yet Melville makes clear that the crew relished the immense physical challenge it presented.

Shortly after *Moby Dick* was published, crude oil changed everything.

Crude oil was initially a nuisance encountered in drilling for salt water. An enterprising Pennsylvanian named Samuel Kier realized he could burn the crude to illuminate his salt works, but the raw crude burned in a smelly, smoky manner. He had it chemically analyzed and was told that a certain fraction of it would burn much cleaner than raw crude if it were distilled, so he distilled and marketed this liquid.[87] A simpler evaporation + filtration process had been used on coal since the 1820s to produce a flammable gas—what we today call 'natural gas'—that was pressurized and piped into street lamps and upscale housing for 'gaslight' chandeliers and sconces. At about the same time that Kier began producing his liquid lighting fluid from crude oil, Canadian Abraham Gesner was perfecting a similar process using coal and shale oil to produce a similar liquid he called '*kerosene*.'[88]

Kier was lucky: A crude oil well was developed near him in August

---

87. *Samuel Kier: Medicine Man and Refiner* by J.A. Harper (Pennsylvania, 1995)
88. Abraham Gesner by L.S. Russell, Dictionary of Canadian Biography

1859 in Titusville, Pennsylvania. Within a few years, dozens of oil refiners in Pittsburgh were making lighting fluid.

Crude oil is a blend of hydrocarbon 'molecules' of various weights—i.e., heaviness. The lightest-weight components, those that evaporate readily, could not be used as lighting fluid for lamps. Those that were not gases like those piped to the street lamps were simply too light, too 'volatile,' to keep from quickly drying up in a table lamp. They were boiled off and discarded. The next to evaporate, what Gesner called kerosene, evolved at slightly higher temperatures and had just the right weight and vapor pressure to work in the lamps. Kerosene was slightly heavier than the modern day 'octane' gasoline used in automobiles and could be safely stored and then would evaporate at just the right temperature in lamps.

The kerosene-from-crude-oil process was wasteful; only a small fraction of the crude was extracted and used. It was pumped from these shallow wells at little cost, however. Compared to whaling, it was low in cost and required no long sailing voyages and years of provisions. In fact, it was almost immediately cost competitive with camphene.

Kerosene was destined to prevail, but historical events have clouded the vision of the economic theorists and led them astray.

John D. Rockefeller became the world's wealthiest man in thirty short years in the late nineteenth century because of his appreciation of the commercial potential of crude oil refining. He was a ruthless competitor, employing business practices that would later be outlawed. His cut-throat methods captured the headlines, but it was the chemical nature of crude oil—initially its bright kerosene flame, later its tremendous energy density that permitted myriad other profitable uses—that was his most powerful asset.

Whale populations may have been somewhat dented by the brisk trade in whale oils during the first half of the nineteenth century, but the data on this point is cloudy at best. It is clear that the pursuit of whales went from expensive in the 1850s to pointless by the mid-1860s when confronted by this new low-cost competitor.

Melville's intrepid whalers were doomed. Even had the *Pequod* survived its encounter with the great white whale Moby Dick, Captain Ahab, first mate Starbuck, harpooners Queequeg, Daggoo, Fedallah, and Tashtego—those conquerors of the oceans and subjugators of the world's largest creatures—would have been impotent against the commercial power of 'black gold.'

Camphene was cost-competitive with kerosene until the Civil War. The Union's need for money to finance the war led the federal government to pass the Revenue Act of 1862, which placed a tax on liquor that was collected from the distillers and applied to the ethyl alcohol used in camphene as well. The tax quickly became significant. Initially it was only 20 cents per proof gallon (i.e., 20 cents per gallon of 100 proof, or 50 percent alcohol, solution), but price escalated dramatically to $2/gallon by war's end. As with so much government activity, the consequences of the tax were not quite what was intended. These "high tax rates of the Civil War had less of an effect on its consumption as a beverage than on its non-beverage uses," according to one taxation historian. "Its use as a fuel for illumination ceased."[89]

This surprising cessation can hardly be classed as a deliberate subsidy to the fossil fuel industry—which was then just the tiny kerosene industry—of the early 1860s. The drafters of the Act were clearly more interested in financing a war by taxing liquor sales than they were in favoring crude oil by taxing camphene.

It was the cost structure of kerosene that made this cessation permanent. Growing kerosene volumes permitted scale economies, and

---

89. *Federal Excise Taxes on Alcohol Beverages: A Summary of Present Law and a Brief History* by T.B Ripy (1999)

other uses would be found for the crude oil 'waste' that spread the refining costs more thinly. Crude oil began to be used in heating and electrical generating systems. Some twenty-five years after kerosene was first sold, German engineers designed a simple combustion engine to power their new-fangled automobiles. The crude oil cut that was a bit lighter than kerosene, something then called 'ligroin' and what we today call octane, worked perfectly in the combustion chamber and created a new market that spread refining costs still thinner. By the late-1890s, the price of kerosene had declined by over 80 percent from the levels of the 1860s.

Electrical engineers commercialized arc lighting and then incandescent lighting in the late-nineteenth century, setting in motion events that would eliminate the need for lighting fluid of any variety. Crude oil producers and refiners were not distressed by this development: The dawning markets for gasoline, heating systems, power generators, and engine lubricants offered sales potentials that dwarfed the kerosene market. The engines later required to power airplanes needed a slightly heavier fuel than that used to power automobiles; kerosene fit the bill perfectly, and the kerosene portion of crude oil is used in jet fuel today.

Crude oil has been a juggernaut, its many uses often surprising and unexpected. Crude derivatives would displace other tree-extracted chemicals in markets where shortages and regulations played no role. The adhesives used to make masking and packaging tapes, for example, were originally made by blending natural rubber with rosins culled from pine sap. The 'catalytic cracking' process used in oil refineries to make ethylene for polyethylene and other plastics also produced a heavier distillate that appeared to be useless but was later found, in resinous form, to blend perfectly with the rubber to make those same adhesives sticky. This refinery by-product, called 'piperylene,' was much cheaper to produce than tree rosins, and its chemical purity made it more resistant to yellowing. Initially a waste product, piperylene took over a market involving tens of millions of pounds a year in a few short years in the 1960s and `70s without the aid of a shortage or war or government subsidy.

"The capitalists," Soviet leader Lenin is said to have predicted, "will sell us the rope with which we will hang them." Such a trans-action never actually occurred, but financial historians must concede that the cynicism dripping from such a prediction was not completely baseless. The commercial world is driven by profits often realized in an extemporaneous manner. These many uses of crude oil, for example, were often driven less by market needs or government policy than by serendipity. Theorists should probably tread lightly when attempting to generalize concerning financial and economic events. There are any number of ways to make a profit. Businesspeople try to look at all of them, and most do so without the slightest regard for philosophical consistency.

Chapter 8

THE BANKER GETS A MAKEOVER

The financing of a single-family house has historically never fascinated the ambitious banker very much. There are many reasons for this. The most important of these is probably that the single loan to finance the building or purchase of a single house was usually not a big loan. Your typical banker is like most of us in that they have their dignity, and they like to think their calling should play out on a slightly larger stage, and such a stage requires a larger loan amount. This was especially true years ago when single-family houses were rare and built at irregular intervals. The banker of a century ago saw the financing of such a house as 'small beer.' By contrast, the project that required a much larger loan amount would interest the banker. For example, a new country club site where the banker should be able to get a tee time. And he might be interested in a new department store, or a large industrial complex. It is there that the banker can operate on a scale that permits the demonstration of real banking vision.

Because of this, and because in making a home loan the banker was forced to rely on the continued prosperity and employment prospects of the home buyer, the banker of days gone by generally required a hefty down payment and short terms. The borrower might be able to get the banker to extend the loan for only five or ten years, with a large payment due at the end of the term that might require the borrower to find a different lender to finance the remaining balance. It was an emotionally difficult business, filled with a good deal of *Sturm und Drang* in the event things did not go smoothly. As far as many bankers were concerned, the whole thing wasn't worth the hassle.

This is the sort of attitude, this indifference to the material dreams of the average citizen, that has—throughout history—seldom failed to garner the banker bad publicity. The banker of literature, for example, was very often portrayed as a tight-fisted, single-minded character alive to his own interests and little else. Shakespeare's Shylock was nobody's idea of a benevolent and public-spirited citizen, and Charles Dickens' tedious Tellson's bankers in *A Tale of Two* Cities worked around the Parisian tumbrils and guillotines without a peep of protest.

The modern banker strives to improve his image, to little effect. To all appearances, our modern-day banker is no longer the weary and wizened old white man, but in movies and folklore, he or she is still a self-interested and greedy Gus or Ginny, although perhaps now he or she is better dressed.

It is not for lack of trying. The modern banker has gone to great lengths to improve his/her image and the appeal and access of the merchandise. A mortgage loan secured by a single-family house is now approved by the modern banker with nothing short of alacrity. At one point during the early years of the twenty-first century, bankers were advertising their willing-ness to issue second mortgages on any remaining equity the homeowner might have. When housing prices declined sharply last decade, the citizen's lament came full circle from the pre-World War II grouse, "I can't believe they won't give me a loan" to the twenty-first century post housing crash grumble that, "I can't believe they gave me this loan."

The process of transforming the bankers' wares, if not their image, was slow and painstaking. An interesting point in this process is cap-tured in glistening black-and-white celluloid by the 1946 Hollywood movie, *It's a Wonderful Life*, in which this tug-of-war between bank-ers old and new is seen in the little commercial kerfuffle between the old-line banker Henry Potter and young George Bailey and his Bailey Savings and Loan.

A Glimpse of Pottersville

The old man of the movie knew a thing or two[90]

The 1946 movie *It's A Wonderful Life* has become a holiday favorite for many Americans. The heart-rending story of George Bailey (played by Jimmy Stewart) who, in his hour of despair is vouchsafed a glimpse of what the world would be like if he'd never been born. The plot holds great meaning for many Americans. So does the drama played out between George and his father, Peter, and their professional nemesis, rich, old banker Henry Potter (Lionel Barrymore). It provides a vivid look at the dramatic changes in American finance that had taken place in the years leading up to the time the movie was made.

The recent problems in the mortgage market bring the story and its characters to life once again. The Baileys and Old Man Potter disagreed about any number of things, but principally about the credit worthiness of what Potter calls the 'the riff-raff,' the average citizen in their home-town of Bedford Falls. The Baileys believe they are creditworthy, and Potter generally does not.

---

90. "A Glimpse of Pottersville" appeared in the December 3, 2007 issue of *Barron's Financial Weekly.*

Lionel Barrymore plays Old Man Potter in
the 1946 movie *It's a Wonderful Life*

Potter remembers the recent past when lenders made the rules, insisting on repayment in gold coin or its equivalent, on big down payments and short terms. Most important for middle-class folks, Potter sees residential real estate as illiquid, mediocre collateral. George and Peter Bailey and their Building & Loan envision a future of suburban development, of small down payments and decades to pay. When George looks at the world had he never been born and sees a vacant field instead of the Bailey Park housing development financed by the Bailey Building & Loan, he is looking at what would have been Pottersville.

Too Much Reality

History, and director Frank Capra, were with the Baileys. Yet it is instructive to reflect that Old Man Potter wasn't irrationally mean and closed-minded—although his concealing the Bailey's missing $8,000 was reprehensible.

The world that Potter knew was simply different from the world George Bailey was bringing about. Potter's experience, and that of most bankers of his time, taught that you couldn't expect a working man to be employed continuously enough to repay a mortgage loan in monthly installments over 30 years. Business conditions waxed and waned significantly in Potter's time, and a workman's life was often cut short.

The banker also couldn't rely on a house being easily foreclosed upon and sold. It was when times were tough that he had to repossess and sell real estate—the very point at which it was most difficult to sell. Minimum down payments were a large chunk of the purchase price, and terms were short to save lenders from taking too big a bath on the occasional foreclosure.

Times changed. Workers lived longer and worked more consistently, often in safer and less physically demanding jobs. Residential real estate became more plentiful, fungible, and easier to sell. The continual decline in value of the U.S. dollar also helped by reducing the true value of the principal balance. What were thought to be shaky loans to shaky borrowers could be paid off in full, a process that made the more liberal loan officer appear prescient.

Too Much Fantasy

Fast forward to the twenty-first century. Real estate is now a staple on the balance sheet of the modern American bank, often in the form of mortgage-backed securities and collateralized debt obligations.

Touted as being almost as liquid as Treasury securities and more diversified than single mortgages, these gradually came to be judged good banking assets. Demand for such securities created supply, and in recent years, George Bailey's ingenious successors became more liberal with terms and with income qualifications. They created the "30-year, Zero Down, No Documentation Option ARM," a product that would have given Old Man Potter apoplexy.

The problems that have recently surfaced in the mortgage industry are a result of this liberalization. This same trend helped create the boom that preceded it. Although the interest rate for subprime and 'Alt-A' applicants may have been inched upwards to compensate lenders for the additional risk, clearly many of these higher-risk applicants were going to remain solvent only under the most favorable of housing market conditions. There is no way so many of these loans could have gone bad so quickly after only a mild house-price decline and a moderate increase in short rates without these liberal terms and income qualifications.

The Real Cost of Easy Credit

The potential for a full-blown real-estate bust is what we have before us, perhaps the first on a national scale since the 1930s. We've had short regional slumps before, but the inflation of the 1960s and 1970s and then the gradual lowering of interest rates over the past twenty-five years have cushioned the blows. If we learn, as Old Man Potter knew, that real estate is not a great investment, retirement-planning tool, inflation hedge and status totem, we could be in for some protracted financial pain. The single-family home may resume the role it played in the popular imagination during the first half of the twentieth century, a black hole into which self-indulgent homeowners throw their money until foreclosure. Old Man Potter would have understood. He knew why the rules were written. He knew why you didn't lend people the money for the down payment.

Real-estate finance, however, is not going to go back to the way things were in the 1930s. Terms won't be limited to five years, and 30 percent down payments will not become mandatory. Too many things have changed, and inflation is too thoroughly infused in American economics and politics.

Yet a large group of potential home buyers have now been revealed to be non-creditworthy, and the value of the collateral underlying their loans may continue to decline.

"Experience is the name everyone gives to their mistakes," Oscar Wilde said. In loan offices and boardrooms across the country, the experiences of Old Man Potter may overshadow the joy of *It's a Wonderful Life* for a few years. George Bailey is in trouble and is still looking for his guardian angel.

Chapter 9

YOU SAY INFLATION. I SAY DEFLATION. LET'S CALL THE WHOLE THING OFF! [91]

"There is nothing new under the sun[92]" goes that ancient snippet of Holy Writ, and people who think the Bible is humbug repeat it daily. The Bible is more a spiritual than a temporal guide to life, of course, and our modern world generates dilemmas the Bible and the world-weary ancients cannot now help us with: Mac vs. IBM, Roth vs. Conventional IRA, etc. Another dilemma that modern-day economists have created for which the ancients provide no guidance is whether inflation or deflation is preferable for an economy. The ancient world had a difficult enough time organizing and policing the money supply—they didn't give much thought to the question.

We moderns have developed the ability to create paper money and electronic funds on demand, meaning that we can now choose between inflation and deflation. In choosing, our political leaders feel compelled to justify the choice they have made.

There may be some innocent souls out there reading this who retain the belief that the inflation figures produced by the world's governments are newsworthy, sometimes surprising, and largely a matter beyond the control of mere mortals. These same people may also believe that the Brooklyn Bridge is for sale, that the stars in the sky are God's daisy chain, or that every time a wee bunny wiggles its nose, a child is born.

---

91. Properly sung to the George and Ira Gershwin collaboration "Let's Call the Whole Thing Off" written for the 1937 film "Shall We Dance" and sung in the film by Fred Astaire and Ginger Rogers.

92. Ecclesiastes 1:9.

There is little debate on the question among our thoroughly modern, up-to-date economic thinkers as to which of the two outcomes—inflation or deflation—is preferable. The consensus comes down strongly in favor of inflation; the only remaining issue is how much inflation is ideal and how much may be a problem.

Inflation is preferable, our deep thinkers tell us, not because it is all that good, but because deflation is much worse. Former Federal Reserve Bank official Ben Bernanke gave a speech back in 2002 concerning the deflationary situation in Japan entitled, "Deflation: Making Sure 'It' Doesn't Happen Here."[93] This was mainstream opinion, the idea that deflation had to be fought at all costs, and it was the sort of attitude that did not dim his prospects for later becoming chairman of the Federal Reserve Board of Governors.

Less influential economists join the chorus. Following the economic collapse of 2008, one Nobel Prize winner in the Dismal Science criticized the Fed, signaling out then chairman Ben Bernanke, calling him "feckless" for even talking about the possibility of deflation without preparing an all-out war against the possibility.[94]

Another interesting and related question, one that does date back to antiquity, is simply this: *cui bono*? Who benefits? And conversely, who loses? The idea that a public policy calling for inflation of the currency could be an unalloyed benefit to all citizens is simply ridiculous. Perhaps the losers are not numerous, or not particularly sympathetic characters, or largely invisible to the public—but there are losers. The interesting question is who are they? And should they (as well as the rest of us) be made aware of it?

The simple answer is that inflation favors debtors and deflation favors creditors. Debtors benefit because their interest payments

93. Speech before the national Economists Club by Ben S. Bernanke, November 21, 2002.
94. "The Feckless Fed" by P. Krugman, The New York Times, July 11, 2010.

become easier to pay when inflation is occurring. And creditors' capital becomes more valuable over time during deflation; however, this is only partially satisfactory. Most of us feel the weight of our mortgage and credit card balances, and as a result most of us feel that we are debtors rather than creditors, so part of the answer as to why inflation is preferable is that it is popular—a very relevant fact in a democracy. Inflation perhaps doesn't win elections, but deflation almost certainly loses them. Herbert Hoover, were he alive today, would testify to this. Those who identify themselves as creditors are institutions like banks and insurance companies and are not the sort of entities that evoke sympathy from voters.

Such a black-and-white view of the economics, however, reflect an absence of imagination. Creditors are, finally, human beings—not institutions. Banks and insurance companies forced to settle for poor returns eroded by inflation must, in turn, pay those poor inflation-eroded rates and benefits to depositors and policy holders.

The other reason the thoroughly modern economist prefers inflation has more to do with contract law than economics. One weekly news magazine gave a hint of this when it told us recently that deflation is not merely bad. "It's a disaster," the magazine opined. "Falling prices means lower revenue and profit margins for companies, which as we know leads to layoffs, less hiring, stagnant wages, and outright pay cuts."[95]

That last part is critical, but perhaps not in the way the author intended. The modern service-producing economy is staffed with people on a salary, a salary fixed and calcified in the near-term by elaborate, wide-ranging employment contracts. Employers, such as those who employ economics professors, therefore cannot adjust labor expenses quickly when faced with a serious deflationary spiral. These salaried employees

---

95. "Why Deflation is Worse than Inflation," U.S. New and World Report, July 16, 2010.

now often devote 30 percent and more of that after-tax salary to mortgage or rent payments, much more than they did a century ago, which of course are also fixed amounts. Governments also now devote a large percentage of their outlays to debt service, another fixed expense requiring growing revenues to keep up the interest payments. As a result of all this, deflation has become completely unwieldy and impractical because "outright pay cuts" across a large swath of the economy have become—in the near term—legally and practically impossible to implement.

It is perhaps useful to recall that the world only a single century ago, and many years after the Book of Ecclesiastes was put to paper, was quite different than today.

Deflation, Up Close and Personal

How 3M Conquered the Depression of 1921[96]

Most readers of economic and financial history have digested and interpreted the many big financial events of the twentieth century: the Great Depression, the war mobilizations, the oil shocks and inflations, etc. Such economic events demanded attention and interpretation not only because of their importance but also because of their duration. The Great Depression, for example, is often thought to have begun with the stock market crash of October 1929, but its effects lingered into the late 1930s.

The economic record of the tumultuous twentieth century contains other interesting but largely ignored or undigested events. This may be due to their brevity. The stock market crash of October 1987, for example, a much sharper decline than that of October 1929, is now largely ignored by all but historians of stock market technical detail,

---

96. "Deflation: Up Close and Personal" appeared in the Summer 2019 issue of *Financial History* magazine.

perhaps because prices quickly recovered, and the crash had little long-term effect on the nation's economic life.

One of the most startling of these undigested events, the details of which are simply mystifying to us today, is the quick and sharp depression and deflation of 1920-1921. Inflation, not deflation, has been the constant in monetary affairs over the last century, one during which increasing prices of goods and services became relentlessly commonplace.

The 1921 depression/deflation is hard to ignore from the economic data. A scan of some of the nation's most studied economic measurements reveals only two real bouts of deflation over the last 100 years. The most famous of these, the Great Depression and the dreadful economic year of 1932 that saw the consumer price index decline by 10.3 percent, has been studied to death. The drop in prices in 1932 did not set a calendar year record, however. The calendar-year deflation record is held by 1921, when consumer prices declined by 10.9 percent. Monetary historians Milton Friedman and Anna Jacobson Schwartz could not ignore the 1920-1921 slump: They called the deflation "unprecedented," the related drop-off in economic activity "one of the most rapid declines on record."[97]

1921? The beginning of The Roaring Twenties? What could have happened to cause such a drop? And what has allowed many of us to ignore those 1921 events?

The answer to that last question, hinted at earlier, is that the downturn in prices and economic activity in 1921 was sharp but brief—very brief by modern standards. Given that such downturns occur with frustrating regularity, a look back at the details surrounding the 1921 depression might be useful.

Let us then focus on the year 1921, and let us not confine ourselves

---

97. Milton Friedman and Anna Jacobson Schwartz, *A Monetary History of the United States 1867-1960* (Princeton, 1963), p. 231.

to platitudinous, macroeconomic generalities devoid of detail. Let us consider, instead, "all things both great and small."

The Minnesota Mining and Manufacturing Company, now known the world over as 3M, was a small, fledgling sandpaper maker in 1921. The company name was a little presumptuous. There were plenty of other, larger mining and manufacturing concerns in the state (although fewer did both), and sandpaper was not the most important of manufactured goods. The process for making sandpaper, however—straining rock granules of a required hardness by diameter, sprinkling them onto a soft base coating, then sizing, drying, and curing—was the sort of process that might be extended to the production of other products.

The 3M we know today as an American industrial behemoth, a mainstay of the Dow Jones Industrial Average, had been an even smaller, money losing outfit when World War I began in 1914. The onset of war didn't help at all. There was great economic as well as political uncertainty, and stock markets around the world closed for months for fear of panic selling. After the initial shots were fired, however, and the belligerents put their economies on a war footing, it became clear that demand for industrial goods of all kinds would increase, and that inflation of the currencies of the warring countries would result. The United States did not initially join the fray, but American prices drifted upward along with those of the warring countries.

Inflation is the industrialist's best friend, at least when it is just beginning or kept from spiraling out of control. Raw material inventory acquired at low prices is gradually transformed into final product that can be sold months later at higher prices due to the general increase in all prices that characterizes a currency inflation. Operating margins almost can't help but improve.

The struggling 3M Company would benefit mightily from this combination of war spending and inflation. Its sales totaled a mere

$263,000 in 1914, and its expenses easily exceeded that figure. By August 1916, however, the company president could tell the Board that, "Business has more than doubled in the last two years," adding "we'll have enough left over after expenses to pay a dividend."[98]

Sandpaper was perhaps a prosaic item, but because it was used in automobile production and repair, it was in high demand nonetheless. American-made military vehicles were being shipped to Europe even before America entered the war, and civilian automobile sales grew by leaps and bounds following the armistice in November 1918. Automobile production doubled in 1919 from 1918 levels. This growth in the automobile business combined with the war-induced inflation to cause company sales for 1919 to ring in at a stunning $1.4 million, a figure exceeding expenses by $440,000.[99] Profits in 1919 were greater than total sales only five years before.

It was as the 3M accounting department was tallying these surprising figures that economic conditions began to turn. The culprit behind the turn was interest rates. The Federal Reserve, looking to curb inflation-fueled borrowing, increased the lending rate it charged its member banks from 4.75 percent to 6 percent on January 21, 1920, and from there to an almost punitive 7 percent rate on June 1st.[100]

This set the stage for massive de-leveraging. Banks sought to cut back their lending in order to reduce their high interest borrowing, and the rout was on. Automobile sales, then as now dependent on financing, dropped like a rock. From levels of roughly 50,000 per month in early 1920, sales of General Motors vehicles declined to 13,000 by November, and to less than 6,200 in January 1921.[101] General Motors

---

98. Virginia Huck, *Brand of the Tartan: The 3M Story* (1955, 1995), p.105.

99. Ibid, p. 102

100. Friedman and Schwartz, p. 230-232

101. James Grant, *The Forgotten Depression* (New York, 2014), p. 73.

continued to ramp up production until the very end of the year, however, which left it with a mountain of inventory, finished and unfinished, when production was finally curtailed in late 1920.

1920 automobile: Slow-moving inventory

The effect on a small, automobile-oriented enterprise like Minnesota Mining and Manufacturing was huge. As auto sales dropped, demand for their product sagged. The beneficial effect that the general inflation of 1914-1919 had on company margins now began running in reverse. Inventory generated at boom prices had to be marked down significantly to move at all, and the downward effect on revenue and margins was thus compounded. Company leaders must have looked at the situation and wondered if the inflation-aided prosperity of 1919 would be the high-water mark of company fortunes.

The early months of 1921 saw things reach a critical juncture. With demand dwindling for a product that was declining in price, company management was faced with a stark choice: Reduce workers or reduce wages. Sandpaper production had increased markedly in the years leading up to the break, and it was clear that the skills their workforce had developed were responsible for this improved productivity. It didn't seem the brightest idea to lay off a work force that had developed such skills.

The choice was made easier by the simple realization that prices of other goods, the various necessities of life, were also falling through the floor. Crop prices had declined by more than half in the last six months of 1920, and grocery prices followed. One dramatic example, made worse by inflation-fueled lending to Cuban sugar planters, was the price of sugar: From a per pound high of 22 cents in early 1920, sugar prices declined by over 90 percent, to 2 cents in 1921.[102]

The rout was acknowledged by incoming President Warren Harding, whose inaugural speech on March 4, 1921 commiserated with the nation's workers and businessmen. "Our people must give and take," he said, acknowledging the slings and arrows they had suffered. "Perhaps we shall never know the old level of wages again," he speculated, concluding that, "We must face a condition of grim reality, charge off our losses and start afresh. It is the oldest lesson of civilization."

The decision made later that month by Minnesota Mining management was spelled out in Company Bulletins #71 and #72. "Owing to a change of business conditions," the bulletins announced, hourly pay would have to be cut across all pay grades. Such grades were arranged by gender and years of service, with the women who did much of the office work earning substantially less than the men who worked the production lines. From levels of 52-57c/hour (~$25-30/hour today), the

---

102. Philip L. Carret, *The Art of Speculation* (New York, 1931), p. 2-3.

men saw their pay sliced by 7.5 cents per hour across all pay grades—a stunning 14.3 percent cut for the lowest pay grade. From levels of 29-34c/hour, pay for women was cut by 3 cents—a slightly lower percentage—from these lower pay rates. The decline in company and worker outlook in just fifteen short months must have been sobering.

These financial difficulties were occurring just as the company was preparing to introduce its first new and improved product. Company leaders had been working with an inventor in Pennsylvania named Francis Okie, who had sent them an odd letter many months before expressing interest in buying samples of their granules. Subsequent conversations revealed that Mr. Okie had developed a water-proof coating to anchor the granules. Sandpaper manufacturers near Mr. Okie in Pennsylvania were willing to allow him to use their production lines to make small experimental runs but refused to sell him large quantities of their granules to expand his production. Mr. Okie wrote to the only other sandpaper maker he could identify, little Minnesota Mining way out west in St. Paul.[103]

3M employees knew well that use of the company's sandpaper sent dust airborne, dust that was hardly a salutary addition to the workplace. A water-proof sandpaper held out the possibility of sanding in water, which would allow users to wash away the dust rather than send it into the air. They immediately set out to work with Okie, and Okie sent 5-gallon pails of his chemical coating from Pennsylvania to St. Paul. Batch quality varied in a matter that frustrated all involved, and Okie eventually moved to St. Paul to be closer to the production process. May 1921 saw the first sales of this new product—called WETORDRY™—to Maxwell (now Fiat Chrysler) and Buick Motors.[104] Automobile makers and automobile body repairmen soon developed the technique

---

103. Huck, p. 112
104. Ibid, p. 116

of running water over the area being sanded—"wet sanding"—with WETORDRY sandpaper, which washed away the dust and prevented it from accumulating around the granules on the paper.

The deflationary depression that clouded the introduction of WETORDRY, with all its distress and slashed wages, was sharp and sudden—and short. Interest rates were lowered and business activity bottomed in mid-year 1921, although consumer prices continued downward. Prices declined a little further in 1922, but GNP jumped 6.6 percent from 1921 levels, and the rebound in business activity trumped the decline in prices. Leveraged measurements of economic activity jumped even higher: The earnings of the Dow Industrial companies increased by over 300 percent in 1922 from the depressed levels of the year before, and the number of businesses reporting 1922 profits in excess of $100,000 increased 66 percent from their numbers in 1921.

One of those companies was little Minnesota Mining and Manufacturing. Sales snapped back. The WETORDRY product helped bring the yearly sales total to over $2 million in 1923, with profits for the year greater than those inflation-fueled levels of 1919.

The 1920s would roar on. The 3M Company created a research laboratory in 1924, initially to monitor the quality of their new waterproof coating and sandpaper. The following year their researchers branched out to develop and introduce masking tape, the first version of what the company later called Scotch™ tape, an adhesive in place of the base coating applied to a paper backing that permitted auto workers to quickly mask off and control paint areas to create 'two-tone' automobiles. In 1930 they introduced a cellophane tape—popular now for gift wrapping (Magic™ tape)—by substituting a water-resistant film to support the adhesive, their first of thousands of consumer products. It was a tremendous decade of growth for the company: Little Minnesota Mining and Manufacturing increased sales over five-fold during the period 1921-1930, and by the end of the decade, the company name didn't seem quite so presumptuous.

These variations on the general method used to make the original sandpaper product were possible because the company weathered the financial storm that was 1920-1921. Faced with the financial difficulties of that wicked, seemingly bottomless depression and deflation, 3M had the flexibility to quickly adjust their labor expenses in line with demand and general prices.

The early months of the downturn that began eight years later, in 1929, were much less severe than the downturn of 1920-1921. Prominent Yale economist Irving Fisher announced in May 1930 that "thus far the difference between the present comparatively mild business recession and the severe depression of 1920-1921 is like that between a thunder-shower and a tornado."[105] This 'mild business recession' was met this time by the nation's leaders with a very different response. Businesses fought to keep wage levels up for fear of reducing what was beginning to be called "aggregate demand." The most prominent proponent of this effort was Henry Ford and his Ford Motor Company. Ford stubbornly raised workers' wages in 1930 to combat the decline. President Hoover announced in May 1930 that "for the first time in the history of great slumps, we have had no substantial reduction in wages." Of those firms reporting their activity to the Bureau of Labor Statistics, 92 percent had reduced wages in 1921, while just 7 percent did so in 1930.[106]

This stubborn approach to keep up wages and 'aggregate demand' did not work. Other factors—the Smoot-Hawley tariff bill, income tax hikes, the repeal of dollar-gold convertibility—contributed to cause the

---

105. Walter A. Friedman, *Fortune Tellers: The Story of America's First Economic Forecasters* (Princeton, 2014), p. 200.

106. William H. Barber, *From New Era to New Deal: Herbert Hoover, the Economists, and American Economic Policy, 1921-1933* (Cambridge, 1985), p. 84-85.

mild recession described in May 1930 to deepen. The year 1931 would be one of the most difficult of the twentieth century, and by mid-year 1932 things had completely collapsed. Unemployment soared. The economic rout that was the 1930s was on, and the difficult days of 1920-1921 and the lessons that those events might hold began being erased from the nation's collective memory.

★ ★ ★

Postscript: For those forced to live through it, there is no getting around the fact that deflation is much more painful than inflation. This is perhaps why our policy makers have chosen inflation and a currency that gradually declines in value over a stable currency that can under certain economic conditions cause prices to plummet. For as pleasant as it is to find food and gasoline available for purchase at lower prices, the havoc wrought by deflation on the nominal value of one's house and car and 401K is distinctly worse. Business owners who discover that the inventory they acquired at considerable expense is no longer saleable for remotely what they had planned are also not likely to regard deflation with broad-minded equanimity.

The fallout of the 1920-1921 depression was short-lived, and Americans at the time may have expected that the inflationary bout resulting from World War I would end with some sort of deflation to correct for the war spending splurge; they were used to it. The deflation that occurred a decade later was a different thing entirely. It lasted longer. It probably seemed endless to those living through it, and the vast American farm-belt economy had never seen crop prices collapse like they did in 1932-1933.

America's leaders formulated a different monetary solution, a solution whose effects are an integral part of our world today.

Chapter 10

FDR, MONETARY EXPERIMENTALIST

Nearly all financial historians have reached their own conclusions about the Great Depression of the 1930s. The convulsions of those difficult years offer fodder enough for all. Some have focused blame on the laissez-faire spirit of the 1920s that led to lax regulation; others blamed the excessive margin trading in stocks; still others blamed what they regard as inadequate monetary policy in response to the market crash. [107]

Such pat analyses of events, so easily 'understood' with the advantage of hindsight, can easily overlook the confusion that consumed policy makers at the time. That angst and confusion—searing for those who lived through it and easily glossed-over later on—should not be forgotten by historians.

The first year of the Franklin Roosevelt presidency provides an interesting example. Roosevelt met the economic problems of the early 1930s with his characteristic show of breezy self-confidence, but he occasionally confessed to, if not angst, at least some uncertainty. "It is common sense to take a method and try it," he explained concerning the dismal state of the economy in a commencement address delivered during the 1932 campaign. "If it fails, admit it frankly and try another. But above all, try something."

One such problem that Mr. Roosevelt met with this improvisational approach was the problem of low commodity prices, specifically low

---

107. "FDR, Monetary Experimentalist" appeared in the Fall 2021 issue of "Financial History" magazine.

farm prices. The collapse of farm prices, such as corn, wheat, hogs, in the early 1930s is a little-remembered but critical fact of those early Depression years. The declines in the stock averages are well known and easily displayed on one's computer, but the decline in farm prices, which had the pleasant upside of low grocery prices for the urban dwellers who write the history books, was in many ways more serious.

The years 1915–1920 had been boom years for U.S. farmers, a boom resulting from the drop in European farm output due to the Great War. From such peak levels, prices somewhat naturally declined in the 1920s: European farmers increased their output, and prices gradually fell by roughly half from those peak levels over the course of the decade. This became a slow-motion problem in parts of farm-belt America as the 1920s roared on in urban areas, and some farmers and their rural bankers found themselves sliding into financial difficulty.

Then the bottom fell out. The slow decline became a rout in the early 1930s. Prices collapsed by another 50+%: Corn had declined slowly from $2/bushel in 1920 to $1.20 in 1929, then fell precipitously to as low as 25c in 1933. Wholesale wheat went from $2.40/bushel in 1920 to $1 by the end of the decade, then dropped to 50c by 1932-1933.[108] Farmers in 1932-1933 faced prices so low, they simply could not cover their costs.

President Roosevelt knew that the economy could not recover without an increase in crop prices. It was unclear how to bring about an increase, but the new President approached the problem with a willing-ness to 'try something.'

Crop prices in the United States in 1933 were denominated in U.S. dollars that were in turn exchangeable for gold at a fixed rate of $20.67

---

108. "Prices" by G. Warren and F. Pearson (New York, 1933), p. 28-29.

per troy ounce. The economy and prices had their ups and downs under this 'gold-based system,' but long-term price inflation was almost unknown: One U.S. dollar bought roughly the same basket of goods in 1933 that it could purchase when the U.S. Treasury began operations in 1790. During all that time—with the exception of a period during and just after the Civil War—the dollar's value was officially pegged at roughly 1/20 of an ounce of gold.

This equivalency between the dollar and gold was seen by some as the problem at the root of those low farm prices. The thinking went that if the dollar continued to be defined by this fixed amount of gold and therefore remained highly valued, crop prices denominated in these highly valued, gold-backed dollars would remain stuck at low levels.

Most people of Roosevelt's age, however, did not question this equivalency: The $20.67 per troy ounce had been in place their entire lives, and for many it was almost a law of nature. Roosevelt's concern with farm prices was central for him, however: In an April 1933 press conference concerning monetary matters, he announced that, "The whole problem before us is to raise commodity prices."[109] Roosevelt was determined to 'try something,' and he was at least open to such ideas involving re-valuing gold.

The newly empaneled Congress had passed the Emergency Banking Act on March 9, 1933, giving Roosevelt broad monetary powers. He used this new power to declare it illegal for American citizens to hold gold coins or bullion or gold certificates or to export gold abroad. All such gold was to be returned to the government at the statutory rate of $20.67 per troy ounce.[110] The reasons behind the order were vague— the financially sophisticated probably guessed some form of inflation

---

109. "American Default" by S. Edwards (New York, 2018), p. xi.
110. "Money of the Mind" by J. Grant (New York, 1992), p. 227.

was in the works, and some even began investing in gold mining companies[111], but most Americans dutifully complied.

The world-wide economic slump was a central subject at the International Monetary and Economic Conference held in London in the early summer of 1933. The U.S. dollar had gyrated wildly on foreign exchange markets during the spring with the uncertainty concerning the new Roosevelt administration's monetary policy. The ban on gold exports had caused a sharp dollar decline, and many of the conferees sought a way to stabilize exchange rates. They had different and somewhat irreconcilable ideas, however. France, for example, was committed to a gold-backed currency, while Great Britain had recently abandoned the gold-standard.

President Roosevelt was kept apprised of events, but he did not help the search for consensus: Shortly after the conference began, he cabled from a military cruiser that exchange rate stabilization was "a purely artificial and temporary expedient ... [a] specious fallacy."[112] The President's negative cable killed any hope that a stabilization plan would emerge.

Exchange rate stabilization was perhaps simply an insufficiently pointed cure for what Roosevelt saw as America's real problem: low farm prices. The President was casting about for ideas as to how to increase crop prices and was perhaps impatient with efforts that were not aimed at doing just that.

---

111. Ibid, p. 229. Bernard Baruch, when asked by the Treasury Secretary years later to explain his investments in gold mining companies at about this time, said "I was commencing to have doubts about the currency."

112. "Once in Golconda" by J. Brooks (New York, 1969), p. 159.

The Saga of George Warren and His Book

Enter George F. Warren, agricultural economist at Cornell University and a co-author with statistician Frank Pearson of a new book with the right title at the right time. *Prices* appeared late in 1931, and in its pages Professor Warren released a flurry of somewhat disjointed charts and graphs attempting to explain farm and other commodity prices through the ages. Of interest to some in Mr. Roosevelt's inner circle was Warren's conclusion that, "Unless the price of gold is raised, the process of bankruptcy and deflation has been only temporarily arrested."

This was intriguing. Warren's views were unorthodox, but his data were compendious, and nobody doubted his sincerity. If one followed his argument, all that was required to get U.S. farm prices up was an increase in the U.S. dollar price of gold.

The President knew Warren from his days as New York governor when Warren advised him on agricultural matters. Roosevelt and his aides watched farm prices closely through the spring and summer and early fall of 1933 and noticed that they did seem to vary somewhat with the trading price of gold. Roosevelt conferenced with Warren, to the consternation of the few establishment bankers in the President's inner circle. By mid-October things had come to such a pass that Roosevelt decided to give Warren's ideas a try.

George Warren (center, standing): A man
whose time came...and went.

The public's fascination with the new Roosevelt administration and its new ideas was such that Mr. Warren attained minor-celebrity status. He was not an official member of the Roosevelt administration, and yet he appeared in full portrait on the cover of *Time* magazine, his calculating pens prominently displayed in the front breast pocket of his suitcoat.[113]

Professor Warren saw his calling as scientific in nature. He wrote in *Prices* that "the ability to forecast results of a given force is one of the important tests to determine whether or not it is science."[114] Warren drove home the point by adding that the depression of the early 1930s "is not an act of God for the purification of men's souls."[115]

Roosevelt met with Warren to discuss the writer's ideas. Little is known, however, of precisely what Warren advised. "Since he has been in Washington," *Time* magazine wrote of the mysterious Mr. Warren, "he has spoken no word to the Press, written no articles, refused to express his opinions even by letter." The best account we have is the

---

113. Time Magazine, Nov. 27, 1933. Mr. Warren was profiled along with the other, official members of President Roosevelt's cabinet.

114. "Prices" by G. Warren and F. Pearson, p. 117.

115. Ibid, p.125.

diary of Henry Morgenthau, Roosevelt's friend and neighbor and then governor of the Farm Credit Administration, but Morgenthau does not go into detail concerning the specific monetary advice offered the President. The flow of subsequent events have led some to conclude that Warren counseled that an increase in gold prices, no matter how it was brought about, would cause an increase in farm and commodity prices.[116]

A close reading of *Prices* finds only partial support for this. Dr. Warren's book does not suggest an increase in gold prices, in and of itself, would increase commodity prices. The passage mentioned earlier regarding raising the price of gold is lifted from the last section of the last chapter of *Prices* in a section entitled, "Short-term price outlook," and is mentioned only after other options are discussed, one of which was legal devaluation of the currency in terms of gold.

Dr. Warren's scientific analysis yielded one conclusion concerning which he was adamant: Inflation is to be preferred to deflation, which he called an "infinitely worse disease."[117] He wrote favorably in *Prices* of the inflationary policies adopted by France, Belgium, and Italy in the early 1920s that allowed those countries to avoid the deflationary depression of 1921 that caused havoc in the United States, and of the way those countries revalued their currencies in the mid-1920s in terms of gold to account for those earlier inflationary policies. Warren even found something to like in Weimar Germany's hyper-inflation of the early 1920s, writing that although the hyper-inflation that culminated in a trillion-to-one revaluation of the German mark in 1923 "was extremely serious for the country…the serious effects of deflation were avoided."[118]

---

116. Edwards, p.70.

117. Warren and Pearson, p. 180.

118. Ibid, p. 170-171.

Regardless of the specifics, Warren's attitude was perfectly attuned to President Roosevelt's goals, and Warren's influence over policy responded accordingly. "During the second half of 1933," financial historian Sebastian Edwards has concluded, "George F. Warren was the most influential economist in the world."[119]

The Roosevelt administration commenced experimentation with what they took to be Dr. Warren's scientific teachings. For six weeks during the late fall of 1933—with the official gold exchange rate of the United States dollar still fixed at $20.67/troy ounce but with the trading price north of $30—Roosevelt and a group of his inner circle of advisors met each morning to determine how much to increase the gold price in commodity trading that day, using U.S. government money to do so. Ten cents an ounce? Twenty cents? Henry Morgenthau records that the decision was made one day to increase the gold price by twenty-one cents per ounce. When asked why, the President replied airily that, "It's a lucky number, because it's three times seven."[120]

The experiment was destined to fail: The U.S. government could increase the gold price, but in doing so agricultural prices barely budged.

Chroniclers of those difficult and uncertain times have not been kind to Mr. Warren. One critic of Roosevelt's New Deal policies summarized Warren's views as suggesting that "a historical relationship existed between the price of gold and the price of farm commodities—they rose and fell together."[121] The *New Yorker* magazine's financial writer wrote in the 1960s that Warren was "a monetary nut" who postulated that, "The price of commodities...went up and down

---

119. Edwards, p. 103.

120. The Diary of Henry Morgenthau, from the section entitled "Farm Credit Diary, April 27 – November 16, 1933," page 96.

121. "New Deal or Raw Deal" by B. Folsom (New York, 2008), p. 105.

automatically with the price of gold in terms of paper currency, and... adduced a bewildering array of historical statistics and charts going back beyond the California and Australia gold rushes of the middle nineteenth century to the Spanish Conquest, and even further. Therefore ... all one had to do to control the price of commodities was to control the price of gold."[122]

The Roosevelt administration's experiment, perhaps laudable in spirit, did not reflect a truly accurate reading of *Prices*. The early pages present graphs showing that "gold" follows commodity prices very closely over hundreds of years of English history, but the "gold" in these graphs is not the gold *price* but rather the prices of these commodities expressed in gold *coin*. England was on the gold standard during most of these years, so these lines should be expected to follow one another, and the lines diverged only during the Napoleonic and Great-War periods, when England discontinued gold convertibility.

Gold and commodities can certainly be observed going up and down together because of shortages of both, but this is rare. More often, their concerted movement is because the currency in which they are priced is either declining or increasing in value. Prices expressed in that currency then naturally move together. Simply put, gold is just another commodity being influenced by a third variable, namely the market assessment of the value of the currency in which gold and other commodities are being priced.

A thorough reading of *Prices* tells a different story. The charts and graphs that show the paper currency price of gold moving up in tandem with wholesale prices do so in countries like France and Italy as they devalued their currencies in terms of gold in the 1920s.[123] In gold standard countries like Britain and the United States, Warren opined that wholesale

---

122. Brooks, p. 161.
123. "Prices," p. 171.

prices rose up and down not with the *price* of gold but inversely with the *value* of gold[124], a value he measured by the size of a basket of commodities that could be purchased with a certain amount of gold.[125]

Warren was perhaps too sanguine about the adverse effects of inflation, but he was quite accurate as to its causes. Inflation was caused by "large issues of paper money, reducing the weight of metal in the monetary unit, reduced demand for the monetary metal, or large additions in supplies of metal."[126] Nowhere does he suggest a rise in the price of the metal, a step consistent with increased, not reduced demand, would inflate other prices.

Warren's verbiage is a little strange to us now. The first two of these causes of inflation we can understand well enough, and the fourth refers to the inflation caused by big gold mine discoveries that add to the supply of gold and therefore the supply of money.

The third of these causes, the one having to do with reduced demand for a monetary metal such as gold, is one we might find confusing. Warren postulated that as demand for gold falls, the value of gold falls, and as it does, commodity prices increase. Such a drop in demand, Warren asserted, occurred in 1850-1856 and again in 1897-1906 as gold flowed into the country, first from the mines in California, later from Alaska and South Africa,[127] but these drops in demand we moderns might describe as increases in the supply of gold rather than a drop in demand. Warren found a similar drop in gold 'demand' in the United States in 1914–1920 as monetary gold flowed from Europe to the United States when war broke out. In each case, 'gold demand' declined, in Warren's parlance, with increased supply. To associate

124. Ibid, p. 37-38.

125. Ibid, p.70-71.

126. Ibid, p. 178.

127. Ibid, p. 96.

such events with "reduced demand for the monetary metal" is a clumsy way of expressing things. However, with each such drop in "demand for the monetary metal," prices in the United States did indeed surge.

These fine points were lost in the excitement surrounding Warren's possible connection between the price of gold and farm prices.

The gold buying program failed to raise farm prices during those six weeks in late 1933, but this did not cause Warren to be expelled from Roosevelt's inner circle, perhaps because he had warned that the experiment intervening in the gold market might not work. Such bidding up of the price of gold in daily trading did not increase farm prices, but an accurate reading of *Prices* did not suggest it would.

Warren was much more optimistic that "reducing the weight of metal in the monetary unit" would do the trick, and the Roosevelt administration did just that in early 1934. The exchange value of the dollar into gold was changed from $20.67 to $35 per troy ounce, a 59 percent reduction in value of the dollars in the pockets of Americans. This is what had been done in France and Belgium and Italy a few years earlier, steps that received the blessing of Dr. Warren in *Prices*. President Roosevelt took Warren's advice, in the process ignoring 140 years of U.S. monetary history, and simply changed the value of the dollar in terms of gold.

The Roosevelt dollar devaluation, a step fully consonant with George Warren's views expressed in *Prices*, did finally halt the deflationary slide. *Prices* stopped declining and began to increase: Corn nearly doubled in 1934, and wheat rose almost 50 percent. Consumer prices had declined by 5.2 percent in 1933, but following devaluation, they reversed course, increasing by 3.5 percent in 1934 and by another 2.6 percent in 1935. These price-level increases were not perhaps as rapid as Warren had predicted, but the President wanted to stem the deflationary tide, and the advice offered by George Warren in *Prices* had finally done just that.

★ ★ ★

Postscript: The much more common problem in the modern age is not deflation but inflation, or—less euphemistically—devaluation. This is largely because the political process has gradually hit upon a way to keep people employed more reliably through slowly lowering the value of the currency in which workers are paid. This is a pretty good trick and goes largely unnoticed.

One way to figure out who wins and who loses under this system is to analyze what happens when the inflation gets a little out of control (for whatever reason). This happens routinely now. The trick in examining financial history to isolate the winners and losers is to find an instance that has 1) experienced this rampant inflation, 2) had a modern, diversified economy at the time, and 3) kept scrupulous records ...

The German Hyperinflation of the Early 1920s[128]

A Financial Look

Hyperinflation—i.e., inflation running at or over 40-50 percent per month—is not an uncommon event in the modern world. It has occurred recently in places as remote from one another as Argentina, Zimbabwe, Turkey, and Venezuela. These countries slid into hyperinflation in their own unique ways, and yet they ended up in the same monetary and financial difficulty.

For purposes of extracting general principles and interesting historical parallels, however, one such event stands out. The hyperinflation that racked Germany, Austria and Hungary in the years leading up to the trillion-to-one devaluation of the German mark in November 1923 is instructive not only because those events are documented with

---

128. "The German Hyperinflation of the Early 1920s" appeared in the Summer 2022 issue of *Financial History* magazine.

Teutonic thoroughness, but also because their economies were diversified and similar in many ways to the United States today.

This is not a journal of lay opinion, so let us begin by skewering a few half-truths that haunt simplistic discussions concerning the German-Austrian hyperinflation of the early 1920s.

Many believe that the hyperinflation ushered the Nazis and Adolf Hitler to power. This is not completely wrong in that the hyperinflation set to low heat trends that would boil over years later, but it is not really accurate. The Nazis were a small, regional political force during the hyperinflation and remained so for years afterwards. It was the worldwide depression of the early 1930s that finally vaulted them to national political power, not the hyperinflation.

Others believe it was caused by the reparation payments required of Germany by the Versailles Treaty, and of Austria and Hungary by the parallel treaties of St. Germain and Trianon. Those payments certainly made things worse, but Germany and Austria-Hungary were on the road to financial trouble long before those payments began. Germany's World War I costs had run to 165 billion marks, but the war-profits and transport taxes instituted to 'pay' for the war raised only about 1/10 of those costs.[129] Fiscal deficits financed the German war effort, deficits papered over with patriotic war bond appeals—"I gave gold for iron"—bonds whose values were destined to plummet. The obligation to redeem notes in gold had been suspended in 1914, and foreign exchange quotations went un-published during the war, so the value of the German mark was a bit of a mystery when the war ended. During the chaotic post-war year of 1919, as quotations resumed and as German deficits became known but before the Versailles Treaty terms kicked in, the mark declined in value from 10 to 40 to the U.S. dollar.

---

129. *When Money Dies* by A. Ferguson (London, 1975), p. 10

In Austria, a similar war-funding deficit caused monetary events to spin out of control even faster than in Germany. The empire centered in Vienna was reduced in size by roughly two thirds, and with that went any hope for the Austrian currency.

The disastrous effects of these post-war events upon the Austrian citizenry is captured in grisly detail in the diary of a middle-class Viennese widow, Anna Eisenmenger, published in the early 1930s. The war's end left Frau Eisenmenger with a war-blinded son, a daughter with tuberculosis, and a son-in-law with amputated legs. She struggled to keep the family together, relying on a trusted banker to help her navigate the chaos, but it occasionally overwhelmed her. The banker advised converting her Austrian currency into Swiss francs, but she nervously declined, only to later watch her savings and her son's pension that he had converted to Austrian government bonds decline in value by three fourths almost overnight. The scant food shipments into the city were priced at 4-5 times what she had paid a few months before; fruit was nowhere to be found, and she watched in anguish as her grandson developed scurvy.[130]

The treaty terms caused things to go from bad to worse. British economist J. Maynard Keynes warned the Allies that the terms imposed were too harsh. He wrote a book, *The Economic Consequences of the Peace*, in which he detailed the problems. He did so, however, in compendious numerical detail, a prose style that probably did little to increase the book's appeal for the politicians who were the intended audience.

Keynes enumerated the claims made by the Allies and the extent to which they probably exceeded actual war damages, claims that included pensions for the widows and orphans of Allied soldiers. He

---

130. *Blockade, the diary of an Austrian middle-class woman, 1914-1924* by A. Eisenmenger (London, 1932)

analyzed Germany's ability to make the required payments, concluding "It is, in my judgment, as certain as anything can be…that Germany cannot pay anything approaching this sum."[131]

The new German 'Weimar' Republican government responded to this inability the same way most governments have: They printed more money. As reparation payments came due, the German mark would take a fresh drop in value: By the close of 1921, over 200 marks were required to buy a dollar, a decline that was only gaining steam. British Embassy staff in Berlin reported to London that, "The daily creation of fresh paper money which the government requires in order to meet its obligations both at home and abroad inevitably decreases the purchasing value of the mark, and in turn [brings] about a further decline, and so on *ad infinitum*," concluding that "I hardly know a single German of either sex who is not speculating in foreign currencies."[132]

The skids were thus greased.

All of this is intriguing in the way a car crash is intriguing, but we're interested in whether history provides a few 'financial survival' suggestions for such unsettled times.

The losers under such an inflationary policy are numerous and easy to spot: Working men and women struggled when their wages failed to keep pace with inflation. The same was true of salaried people who were without equity interest in the profits of their companies. The rentier middle class living off the fixed interest on bonds and mortgages paid in paper currency watched their capital slowly devalued and destroyed: Interest and dividends fell from 15 percent of national income before the war to a mere 3 percent ten years later.[133] Worse off of all were pensioners and the disabled living on some fixed amount of

---

131. *The Economic Consequences of the Peace* by J.M. Keynes (London, 1920), Chapter V

132. Ferguson, from British Foreign Office Files, 1921

133. *The Downfall of Money* by F. Taylor (New York, 2013), p. 214.

government largess. They were often reduced to destitution. "Former civil servants and officers are undoubtedly the poorest of the poor in Austria today," Frau Eisenmenger observed. "Thus it happens every day…that elderly, retired officials of high rank collapse on the streets of Vienna from hunger."[134]

Farmers could remain indifferent to the chaos and could even benefit from the currency decline. They had food to eat and barter, and what produce they didn't need for themselves, they watched increase in price almost daily. The instability of the currency often led farmers to refuse to even send produce to the cities. Those who had mortgages on their farms watched the principal balance wither into insignificance. A young German woman who lived in the city but who worked for a summer on a farm in the early 1920s was simply shocked by the difference. "The contrast between country and city was so enormous," she recalled, "that it cannot be understood by people who have not lived through it."[135]

Business owners and stock investors shielded themselves somewhat. Inflation permits industrialists to buy low and sell high almost without fail as they transform input materials into final product. Frau Eisenmenger in Vienna observed this in the increased nominal value of her industrial shares and found it vaguely unsettling, although she later realized the prices of her stocks did not keep pace with the cost of living. Investing in common stocks wasn't error-proof, either: When the German mark rebounded temporarily in late-1921, stock prices tumbled.

Savers were big losers. Savings declined precipitously—and to many simple Germans inexplicably—in purchasing power. Those

---

134. Eisenmenger, diary entry from January 22, 1920.

135. *How It Happens: Talk About the German People 1914-1933* by P.S. Buck (New York, 1947), p. 157.

who had 'prudently' placed their savings in banks and in war bonds were punished in the same way as their interest payments shrunk in real value to a pittance. They couldn't help pondering on the chaos that was created. "Saving is the very source of wealth and health of a sound nation," reminisced one German who had grown to adulthood during the inflation and could see years later the moral damage done by those days, "but we were no longer a sound nation. We were on our way to become a crazy, a neurotic, a mad nation."[136]

Rampant inflation encourages what appears to be odd, irrational behavior because it turns money into a wasting asset. Stories were told during those years of bachelors resorting to buying swaddling clothes when little else was left in the stores; and fine grand pianos were found in the houses of unmusical families, etc. A stable currency is in this way not merely a convenience; it may be a pre-condition for any attempt at rational resource allocation in a diversified economy.

Workers' wages trailed inflation, so German industrialists were able to take advantage of the declining real costs of their employee wages by pricing below their foreign competitors. The revenues generated in foreign markets were then often kept in foreign currency in foreign banks, bank deposits that acted as bets against the German mark and a way to avoid German taxes. Bankruptcies actually declined during those months in which the mark lost value, and perversely increased when it rebounded. "It gives some inkling," wrote the *Frankfurter Zeitung* in 1921, "of the awful debacle which may be expected if a rapid and permanent improvement of the mark actually takes place."[137]

The *Frankfurter Zeitung* needn't have worried. French political opinion stiffened against the Germans in late 1921, and as reparation payments resumed in 1922, the mark experienced a fresh wave of

---

136. Buck, p. 180.

137. Ferguson, p. 66.

selling. The payments became a growing source of resentment as they became associated with the decline of the currency.

Germany's Foreign Minister Walter Rathenau believed the Treaty payments should be made until Germany could get the Allies to modify them, a position that angered the militant wing in the Reichstag—the German Parliament—who wanted to refuse to pay. In late June of 1922, Walter Rathenau—erudite, cosmopolitan, Jewish—was assassinated during his morning commute to the Foreign Office by two fanatical, young, former German military officers (part of a large anti-Weimar group).

The financial world was shocked by the event, and the mark resumed its slide. Food prices jumped over 50 percent in July 1922. The cost of living became impossibly high for pensioners and salarymen, widening the schism between city and country, and in the cities between civil servants and those few who speculated in currency and stocks.

Pearl S. Buck, the widely traveled Nobel Prize-winning American writer, chronicled those times using the reminiscences of Erna von Pustau, a well-educated and perceptive German woman of aristocratic bearing who came of age during those years and who had emigrated to New York in the early 1940s. Frau von Pustau told Buck of her childhood in Hamburg as the youngest of three daughters in a respected merchant family, and how she observed anti-Semitism creep into her circle. It became more acceptable, she said, with "the lie that the Jews were the 'guilty ones' for inflation...' Stock exchange' and 'Jews' were very much connected in the minds of the people...Looking around for the guilty ones, in a situation which nobody really understood, made those who lost their fortune, especially the middle class, ready prey for anti-Semitic propaganda."[138] She was taken aback by the changes in

---

138. Buck, p. 188

her own father's attitudes, recalling sadly his new view in the 1920s that "creative capital is the capital we Germans have: parasitic capital is the capital of the Jews," and she recalled lamenting to a friend that, "You should have known my father as he used to be."[139]

British economist Maynard Keynes had underestimated the rate of depreciation of the German mark in his 1920 book, but he watched events closely and updated his views in a September 1922 editorial. He reiterated his main point that to expect Germany to pay more than about 2 billion in "gold marks" per year was "in the realm of phantasy" that derived, he wrote, from the belief that "the extremity of France's need enlarges Germany's capacity [to pay]."[140]

Complicating the problem was the German central bank president Rudolf Havenstein's inability to understand the situation. Havenstein was a civil servant, a lawyer, not a banker or economist. His successor, Hjalmar Schacht, later wrote that Havenstein "would hardly have claimed... [to be] a specialist on monetary theory" and that Havenstein was also "limited by a certain obstinacy of outlook."[141] President Havenstein saw the decline in the exchange value of the mark as the core problem, one he stubbornly addressed by printing more currency to ensure that Germans would have the needed purchasing power.[142]

The core problem, of course, was the money printing itself. Thirty paper mills and nearly 150 printing firms and 2,000 printing presses worked round-the-clock to create the blizzard of bank notes that Havenstein thought were needed to compensate for the drop in the exchange value of the mark.

---

139. Ibid, p. 190

140. Ferguson, p. 112.

141. *The Stabilization of the Mark* by H. Schacht (New York, 1927), p.122.

142. Ferguson, p. 252: "The Reichsbank's display of naivete in its credit policies of 1922 and 1923 should finally dispel any suspicions of financial Machiavellianism on the part of Havenstein and his associates."

In the end, investors in common stocks could not escape the crazy, neurotic mess. Share prices increased during the period 1914–July 1922 by over 13 times in terms of paper marks, but this increase fell far short of the 140-fold decline in the paper mark versus the non-inflated, gold-backed mark. This decline was crystallized in the price of shares of Daimler Motor Company, whose high-quality cars commanded a premium price as the shares languished: By October 1922, stock market wags were amused to observe that all the Daimler shares outstanding could be purchased for the same price as 327 of its cars.[143]

The conventional way to discourage speculating on a continued decline in the currency is by increasing interest rates. The German central bank did nothing of the sort. "The discount rate for commercial bills remained at 6 per cent throughout August [of 1922]," summarized historian Adam Ferguson, "while during the same month the mark fell by 250 per cent against the [British] pound." Under such a monetary policy, speculation against the mark by commercial borrowers with access to this discount rate was a 'no brainer.' Those who could not borrow from the central bank paid much higher rates.

The mark's downward slide accelerated. At roughly 9,000 marks to the dollar on New Year's Day 1923, it was 26,000 in April; 55,000 in May; 4 million in August; 65 million in September; 300 million by early October; and 17 billion by the end of the month. There seemed to be no bottom.

---

143. Ferguson, p. 118.

Germany, 1923

At this point a banker, Hjalmar Schacht, was appointed to a new position, Commissioner for National Currency. Eight days later Havenstein suddenly died of a heart attack, and Schacht was given control of monetary policy. Schacht reversed course: He refused to continue to monetize government debts and defined a new 'Rentenmark' equal in value to one trillion paper marks. He refused to honor the private notes—'Notgeld'—that had been used by industry and by municipal governments instead of paper marks. There were howls of protest, but Schacht held firm. He got agreement from London financiers to back the nation's gold (not the paper) marks.[144] His secretary recalled that during these hectic days Herr Schacht often sat in a small makeshift office in the Finance Ministry, chain-smoking. He tirelessly

---

144. Schacht, p. 130.

lobbied foreign exchange market-makers via telephone on behalf of the Rentenmark, attempting to peg it to the U.S. dollar and gold.[145]

It worked: The Rentenmark initially declined against the dollar, but by early-December 1923, it began to stabilize. It would later be replaced by a new Reichsmark. Distrust of the currency lingered—increasing interest rates to dampen speculative borrowing was thought futile—so credit was frozen and then rationed instead.[146] Unemployment loomed for many industrial workers, but faith in the new direction taken by Schacht was tangible: By mid-December 1923 farmers began increasing shipments of produce to the cities. "Not even the most fanatical advocate of stabilization," wrote the British ambassador on Christmas Day 1923, "could have anticipated more remarkable results."[147]

The damage to the larger society, however, had been done. The many patriotic citizens who had put their savings in government bonds watched those savings wiped out. The deprivation of most and the profligate spending and speculating of some produced cynicism. Inflation picked a few winners, and millions of losers, fomenting suspicion and contempt—a dangerous result in a place like Weimar Germany, a fledgling democracy with considerable technological and military resources.

How dangerous? "I once studied the curriculum booklet which the Reichstag published of its members," Frau von Pustau recalled. "A high percentage of National Socialist [i.e., Nazi] members gave the same story: War, then demobilization, then college, then the necessity to leave college because of inflation."[148]

---

145. Ferguson, p. 211.

146. Schacht, p. 158-159.

147. Ferguson, p. 216, quoting Britain's Ambassador to Germany D'Abernon, from his diary published in 1929.

148. Buck, p.133.

In the same way that the fluttering of a butterfly's wings can influence physical events far away, financial policy decisions can reverberate in unexpected ways.[149] An expedient, inflationary monetary policy can result in bizarre, unexpected aftershocks—shocks far removed in time and/or place from the direct financial effects. Citizens left in difficult financial circumstances may not respond in ways that policymakers expect or desire, and the response may set in motion bizarre societal changes. A thorough study of the aftershocks wrought upon those German-speaking peoples roughly a century ago should give policymakers pause.

---

149. George Warren can perhaps be forgiven for his attitude towards the German hyperinflation. Warren wrote *Prices* in 1931, before the disaster that was Nazism could be fully known.

Chapter 11

'AUSTRIAN' ECONOMICS VS. DEMOCRACY

The Austrian School of Economics is popular among 'small government' libertarian thinkers living throughout the world. 'The Austrians' believe that interest rates and the money supply are integral parts of the economic world and of individual economic calculations. They theorize that when government dictates the rates or adjusts the money supply, the inevitable result is either 1) rates higher than the 'correct' rate, which would tend to retard investment and economic growth or, 2) more commonly, rates lower than this correct rate, thereby causing some immediate economic growth as well as some of what the Austrians called 'mal investment.' Both outcomes, the 'Austrians' assert, distort the workings of the economy and will eventually cause harm. The leading light of the Austrian school was one Ludwig Von Mises, who had the twin-edged fortune of being able to observe at painfully close range the mal-investments and hyper-inflation of early twentieth century Austria.

Von Mises was interested in the motivations of central bankers and the politicians who appoint them because he believed the mischief that resulted in these distortions had its origins there. Central banks are often created with the best of stated intentions, but they are always staffed by human beings of the flawed variety. The legislation establishing such central banks often mention the advantages of such a bank in glowing terms; and indeed, an expandable currency is very convenient when a country is faced with war or some other dire economic emergency like hurricanes or earthquakes or crop failures. Von Mises pointed out that the political process is filled with lesser 'emergencies' that invariably call for the politicians' attention, as well as freshly printed money from the central bank.

One of Von Mises' central insights was that the process of spending government money that the government does not currently have—a depressingly common problem—encourages non-democratic impulses. When confronted with such a situation, "a government always finds itself obliged to resort to inflationary measures," he wrote, "when it cannot negotiate loans and dare not levy taxes, because it has reason to fear that it will forfeit approval of the policy it is following if it reveals too soon the financial and general economic consequences of that policy."[150]

The need for public approval is the real engine of democracy, of course, and majority approval of the citizenry is a somewhat predictable thing. The average citizen, when confronted with a stiff bill to pay, can be sure to prefer putting it off. Those seeking evidence of this need only ask the credit card companies. "I'd gladly pay you Tuesday for a hamburger today," was the time-honored economic wisdom of J. Wellington Wimpy in the *Popeye the Sailor* comic strip back in the 1930s and 1940s, and average sentiment in a democracy invariably agrees with Wimpy.

This situation creates a problem for Von Mises and the Austrians, what he sees as a flaw in democracy. "Inflation becomes the most important psychological resource of any economic policy whose consequences have to be concealed; and so in this sense it can be called an instrument of unpopular, that is, of antidemocratic, policy, since by misleading public opinion it makes possible the continued existence of a system of government that would have no hope of the consent of the

150. "The Theory of Money and Credit" by L. von Mises (1912, 1953)

people if the circumstances were clearly laid before them."[151]

Well, maybe. On the other hand, perhaps voters are a little smarter than we give them credit for, and perhaps they are a little vain. They may know that the policies they prefer are inflationary, and that inflation favors debtors like themselves, but they also may like to be flattered, or at least not told to their face by politicians that they are welshers or deadbeats like J. Wellington Wimpy.

American political and economic history, for example, while it may not reach back as far as that of Austria, is nevertheless filled with interesting characters and dramatic ups and downs. American voters have been pointedly asked at different times to vote for policies they understood to be inflationary, with results that tell a slightly different story.

The Pan, the Sluice Box, and American Monetary History[152]

Those students of economic history with a fondness for the precision of the gold standard of money, where currency is exchangeable for a governmentally mandated amount of gold, tend to gloss over its shortcomings. A gold standard system has some features that can appeal to us today—fixed exchange rates, zero inflation, no cryptic, market-gyrating pronouncements by central bankers, but it is not without its limitations.

The nineteenth and early twentieth centuries saw the popularity of the gold standard reach high tide, when it was used in western Europe, the British Commonwealth, and the United States–Britain's opinionated and independent son. This was also perhaps the most economically

---

151. ibid

152. "The Pan, the Sluice Box, and American Monetary History" appeared in the Winter 2020 issue of *Financial History* magazine.

vibrant and technologically innovative period in human history, so the reliance on gold exposed its central shortcoming: namely, the inability of gold stores to expand as rapidly as the economy itself.

This inability of gold stores to track economic growth and prevent occasional bouts of deflation laid the groundwork for gold's eventual loss of governmentally sanctioned monetary status. In the United States, it didn't happen suddenly; it was more a matter of decades of trial and error driven by political expedience.

The founders and framers of the U.S. government rebelled against the British crown and its parliamentary system, but in monetary matters they followed Britain's lead. Gold coins were minted, and the U.S. dollar was exchangeable for gold at roughly $20/troy ounce. The federal government's first fifty years were filled with controversies, but few involved this dollar-gold connection.

Reliance on gold got its first big shake-up when gold was found in large amounts in the streams flowing west out of the Sierra Nevada mountains in California in 1848, gold that then coursed through the nation's banking system like a bocce ball through a snake. Capital projects—many of them railroad projects—arose to meet this new supply of money. The economy soared. A big economic slump resulted in 1857 when some of those loans went bad just as gold mining output began to decline and as gold drained from U.S. to European banks to pay for imported goods.

Monetary affairs then experienced a still bigger jolt with the coming of the Civil War and the printing of unsecured 'greenback' paper currency necessary to finance the war. The nation's citizens, especially the farmers, noticed an odd—and for the farmers, fortuitous—fact: Crop prices consistently rose during the conflict, fueled by the gradual decline in value of the greenback as the war dragged on. Illinois farmer John Griffiths watched his son go off to fight and began working the farm by himself. "It has been a good time for making money in the north since the war began," he wrote later. "Everything was so high[153]," he recalled, referring to crop prices denominated in greenbacks.

Farmers didn't forget this little bout of prosperity. The nation returned to the gold standard in the early 1870s, and as it did farm profits declined. The agricultural interest could have chalked up those Civil War-era profits to fewer workers and, therefore, lower supply or to a war-induced bump in demand, but many chose to attribute them to the use of the greenback. The Greenback Party coalesced in the 1870s around the idea of returning to an unsecured paper currency. Most voters still regarded paper money with suspicion, however, and the Party never achieved any nation-wide success.

The Greenback Party disappeared in the late-1880s, but their monetary motives survived. The Populist Party of 1892 advocated minting silver-based dollars—something they called 'bimetallism'—with the same goal in mind: to increase prices through expansion of the money supply. Their platform was explicit: Silver-based money should be minted and valued at 1/16 that of gold, and the aggregate money supply should be increased to the point where it was equal to $50 per capita. The Populists won four states and 8.5 percent of the vote in the 1892 election, but this would be the Party's best showing. Their monetary ideas, however, were yet to crest.

The 16:1 valuation ratio of gold to silver was an integral part of 'bimetallism' because it deliberately over-valued silver. Silver was being mined in large quantities in the 1870s and 1880s in Nevada and Colorado, but even under normal conditions, the ratio is much greater than 16 to 1. Today's ratio is over 80 to 1. By over-valuing silver, politicians sought to encourage its monetary use in the same

---

153. "A People's Contest" by Philip Shaw Paludan (Kansas, 1988), p. 169

way that greenbacks displaced gold from use in the 1860s. For farmers struggling to pay back loans denominated in gold, silver was a metallic version of the greenback.

The gold standard problem mentioned earlier—its inability to keep prices from falling occasionally—grew intractable in the early 1890s. Gold mine output had peaked in 1853 with the California gold rush, and by the early 1890s it had declined to only half the levels of the early 1850s. The decline caused gold to increase in value, lowering prices and making debt-service difficult. By 1893 the United States was in recession, and as it deepened with each passing month, the nation's leaders struggled to find a solution.

The Populist Party's bimetallism ideas were given another look. Initially it was an eclectic group comprised of Democratic farmers and Republicans from silver mining areas, but as the movement gained adherents, it coalesced under the Democratic tent. Democrats controlled the South and parts of the Midwest–agricultural areas where some currency inflation would be a welcome relief—and although their eastern banking wing was influential (its leading figure was President Grover Cleveland), their agrarian wing was numerically larger.

In the wake of a run on U.S. Treasury gold reserves during the winter of 1894-1895[154] these 'silver men' convened small state conventions and sent members to a national conclave in Washington, DC that August. They called the event the "Bimetallic DNC," and it was dedicated to these monetary principles and not to any one leader. With a Democrat in the White House committed to gold-backed money, it was clearly an attempt to wrest control from the Cleveland wing of the party.

When the Democrats convened in Chicago in July 1896, and it

---

154. "Morgan: American Financier" by Jean Strouse (New York, 1999), p. 340-354.

became clear that the silver men would control the party platform (right down to the 16 to 1 ratio that had been used by the Populist Party four years before), they needed a presidential candidate to champion their cause. Speeches were delivered making the case for bimetallism, but they were uninspiring. Opponent William Russell, the governor of Massachusetts, warned the convention that such a "new and radical policy" would lead the party to the "darkness of defeat and disaster" in the fall.[155]

William Jennings Bryan—a two-term congressman from Nebraska and little known outside the Midwest—responded with the speech of a lifetime. He summarized the economic approach of his opponents as follows: "If you just legislate to make the well-to-do prosperous, their prosperity will leak through on those below." He warned his allies that, "If they [their opponents] dare to come out and in the open defend the gold standard as a good thing, we shall fight to the uttermost." He concluded with powerful words still remembered today: 'You shall not crucify mankind on a cross of gold.'[156]

The crowd went wild. 'I had never dreamed that a mortal man could so grip and fill thousands of men with enthusiasm,' one delegate later wrote.

★ ★ ★

Some 2500 miles northwest of the madding crowd in the Chicago Coliseum, Joe Ladue ran a trading post in the Yukon Territory where the Sixty Mile River empties into the Yukon River. He and his neighbors lived solitary, hardscrabble lives largely deaf to American political oratory. The Yukon River flows east and north out of the mountains

---

155. "The Triumph of William McKinley" by Karl Rove (New York, 2015), p. 272
156. Ibid, p. 275-276.

that push up against the Pacific Ocean and drains a vast taiga landscape sandwiched between mountain ranges. The area was rumored to contain gold in the mountains and in the placer deposits below, but the pickings as of July 1896 had been sparse. Ladue made it his business to gather details of any gold finds in the area, however, and pass such information on to his customers to encourage trade in the goods he had for sale.[157]

William Jennings Bryan was likely still basking in his nomination and in that thunderous applause when a visitor entered Ladue's trading post. Robert Henderson, an inveterate gold prospector, had stopped by Ladue's place two summers before, when Ladue had recommended Henderson try panning the Indian River, which flows into the Yukon some ten miles upstream of Ladue's place. Henderson had done so, with little success. When Henderson went to the headwaters of the Indian River and crossed over the divide to a small creek that drains into the Klondike River he had better luck. Encouraged, Henderson followed the Klondike downstream to the Yukon River that summer of 1896 and back to Ladue's place to buy more provisions. He settled his account with Ladue using some of the gold he had found.

Ladue was impressed by Henderson's persistence as well as his gold. Ladue advised Henderson to retrace his steps to the Klondike River rather than via the Indian River, and Henderson took his advice. At the mouth of the Klondike, Henderson met George Carmack, an American fishing and living with the native Tagish Indians. He told George of his find, and suggested George try panning some of the other small creeks that flow into the Klondike, but shortly afterwards Henderson hurt his leg badly and had to leave the area. George and his fishing partners, a strapping Tagish man and George's brother-in-law

---

157."The Alaaska Gold Rush" By David B. Wharton (Indiana, 1973), p. 78-82..

"Skookum" Jim Mason[158]—Skookum is the native word for strong—and Mason's nephew Charlie, tried panning in nearby Rabbit Creek, and there they discovered copious gold flakes in the placer deposits in the stream.

Rabbit Creek[159] was a remote place, but of the few human beings living within fifty miles, many were potential prospectors. Word traveled fast. One member of the Royal Canadian Mounted Police heard about the gold strike and left his post in late August to try his luck, but on reaching Rabbit Creek on September 1, he discovered that both sides of the creek were staked out. The Alaska Gold Rush was on.

The rest of the world would remain in the dark for quite a while about the magnitude of the gold strike along the Klondike. George Carmack wrote his sister in California of his good fortune late in 1896, but she did little with the information. Three grizzled prospectors found their way to Seattle in November 1896 and reported that gold had been found, but such reports were common, and Alaska was already known to contain gold. Winter settled over the Yukon, and the freezing of the rivers would isolate the frenzied activity of those Klondike prospectors from the rest of the world.

Bryan lost the election to William McKinley that November. Critical agricultural states in the Midwest were strongly Republican and remained suspicious of Bryan's 'new and radical policy.'[160] Bryan did well enough though. His newly cast Democratic party could legitimately hope to grow its base of voters. After all, there were many persuadable 'silver men' among Republican voters.

The spring thaw of 1897 would change that political landscape. It set in motion the fruits of nearly a year's worth of gold sluicing and

---

158. Jim Mason's native Tagish name was Keish.

159. Prospectors quickly renamed Rabbit Creek "Bonanza Creek," the name it has today.

160. Rove, p. 368

panning moving down the Klondike and Yukon Rivers, into the Bering Sea, and south to the nation's banks. On July 16, $400,000 of Klondike gold (worth $40 million today) arrived in San Francisco. Two days later, over a ton of the mesmerizing metal worth $700,000 reached Seattle along with its newly rich owners. Papers throughout the country shouted the news.[161] A stampede to the Klondike began.

William Jennings Bryan in the fateful year of 1896.

Over $400 million of gold flowed into the nation's banking system from 1897 to 1900 (some of it from South Africa and Australia).[162] The economy boomed, and grain prices increased. This gold-fueled economic growth dimmed William Jennings Bryan's once incandescent

---

161. Wharton, p. 86

162. "A Godly Hero: The Life of William Jennings Bryan" by M. Kazin (New York, 2006), p.84.

political future. Bryan was nominated again in 1900, but he lost even more soundly to McKinley. He was put forward yet again by the Democrats in 1908 with the economy mired in a slump, just as in 1896. The 1908 slump was blamed on a New York banking crisis rather than the gold standard, and Bryan lost to William Howard Taft.

The prosperity that rained down on George Carmack, "Skookum" Jim Mason and "Dawson" Charlie was hard for them to control. Carmack abandoned his Yukon-born wife and moved to California and then Seattle. Rich but restless, he spent his last years working claims in the Sierra Nevada range and the Cascades, hoping to re-live the excitement of Rabbit Creek. Jim and Charlie moved to Seattle; ensconced in nice quarters they went through money like water, at one point reportedly causing a commotion in the street below by throwing bills out a hotel window. They grew bored with city life after a few years and moved back to the Yukon, where Charlie died falling from a railroad bridge in 1908. A series of bad investments revived a prudent streak in "Skookum" Jim, and he set up a trust with the money he had left. He lived out his remaining years in the peace and quiet of the Yukon.[163]

George, Jim, and Charlie's gold strike may have dimmed Bryan's political light, but Bryan's ideas, when marketed differently, would later carry the day.

Gold production remained healthy for twenty years following the Alaska gold strike, but then declined throughout the 1920s. Farm prices softened, and when the economy and prices collapsed in the early 1930s, the nation's politicians were again confronted with a crisis.

Democrats had learned their lesson. It was clearly unwise to advocate devaluing the currency to increase prices, but was it necessarily unwise to simply devalue? The Franklin D. Roosevelt campaign of

---

163. "Skookum Jim Biography" by G. Bennett (1980)

1932 was staunchly anti-inflationary. Their platform advocated "a sound currency to be preserved at all hazards," but upon assuming office, Roosevelt devalued the dollar to $35/troy ounce from $20.67 and prevented creditors from demanding re-payment in gold. Prices increased, and Roosevelt's popularity did not decline. Roosevelt legalized Federal Reserve "open market operations,"[164] paving the way for today's gold-free, "inflation targeting" (i.e., gradual devaluation) system.

The Democrat's very successful 1936 platform asserted "We approve of a permanently sound currency" while also taking credit for increased prices: "The farmer is no longer suffering from 15-cent corn, 3-cent hogs, 2 1/2-cent beef, 5-cent wool, 30-cent wheat, 5-cent cotton, and 8-cent sugar." In 1940, the Democrat's platform claimed that "We have steered a steady course between a bankruptcy-producing deflation and a thrift-destroying inflation, so that today the dollar is the most stable and sought-after currency in the world."

The political box score: No wins and three losses when campaigning for dollar devaluation (i.e., the Bryan record), four wins and no losses when campaigning for a sound currency and putting in place devaluation measures (the FDR record). Roosevelt learned from Bryan's defeats, and the lessons he taught the nation's politicians–Democrats and Republicans–guide them to this day.

---

164. See the Thomas Amendment to the Agricultural Adjustment Act of 1933.

Chapter 12

SEIGNIORAGE FOR FUN AND PROFIT

"Inflation," as a financial-monetary term, is not fully satisfactory. To inflate means to expand or make larger, and certainly during times of inflation, the prices of things tend to get larger. The root cause of the general increase in prices across a whole range of goods—the definition of "inflation"—is not at bottom an expansion, however. It is more accurately described as a contraction. The reason a large basket of different sorts of goods increases in price simultaneously is that the currency used to purchase those goods is contracting in value. It is deflating in value, not inflating. It is only after this process of "deflating," or "devaluation" of the value of the currency has begun that the prices of most things begin to increase.

This decline in the value of paper currency is a recurring theme in financial history. At almost any time, somewhere in the world, there is occurring a rapid deflation, or contraction, in the value of the nearby government's paper money, thereby causing a notable rise in the prices of things priced in that currency. This widespread tendency is, at bottom, because humans in general are one with Oscar Wilde in that they can "resist anything except temptation." The leaders of most governments are, alas, some of the most human and Wilde-like of us all.

Put yourself in the position of a political leader. You are surrounded day and night by courtiers of one sort or another—military experts, political experts, engineering experts—lobbing ideas at you for the betterment of the country you love so dearly. They just need to be given the word, and all the plans they've sketched out for you that fulfill so perfectly your hopes for the future. They are your courtiers, after all, because their ideas fit your hopes so perfectly. You want nothing more than to give them the go-ahead. All that stands in the way is money.

You could tax your citizens to raise the money, but you don't need to take a survey or a poll to know that this will reduce your popularity. You could reduce expenses elsewhere, but the people whose projects you are currently supporting are your friends, too. You therefore do what political leaders since time immemorial have done: You print the money.

Well, no. Not quite. Technically what you do nowadays is mandate the creation of a central bank, a bank that will be given the power to mint coins or print currency—and pocket the difference between the value of the currency and the cost to produce it (i.e., seigniorage) and turn it over to the government. You assure the public this central bank will be independent of political influence, but the leaders of this bank will be people you choose. You then issue bonds to finance the projects you have in mind, and you make sure that the leaders of the central bank understand that their job is to buy any of the bonds that you issue that don't find a willing buyer, and at prices that you approve of using money that they may have to print if necessary. It is a distinction without a real difference, of course, but it does fool enough of your citizenry enough of the time to be politically practical.

The end is always the same. The political leader finds more projects, the central bank makes sure all the bonds issued to finance them are snapped up. The printing of money nearly always proves necessary to buy up these later bonds at good prices. Meanwhile, the costs of the projects escalate as all the money put into circulation by the central bank causes the sellers of actual stuff—concrete, fresh vegetables, human labor—to realize that their costs of providing these goods are going up and to demand more of the currency in exchange. This then requires that more bonds be issued, more money be printed to buy up the bonds, more price increases for the goods purchased with the money thus printed. Etcetera, etcetera.

There have been rare instances when paper money has held its value over time. These rare paper currencies have been issued in times and places where government leaders have been prevented from exercising their full genius by certain constraints. These constraints have been very popular with the ordinary citizen because a currency that holds its value allows such citizens to save money during their working lives and retire with a certain degree of financial and spiritual ease. These constraints are, however, a constant source of irritation for the sovereign and his courtiers.

Did I mention that such instances are rare?

The Gold Standard Days in Word and Song

First published in 2009.[165]

The Presidential candidacies of Ron Paul of Texas in 2008 and 2012 were very odd on any number of levels: his thin, dyspeptic, non-political countenance, his resignation to defeat from the start, his confrontational manner in dealing with the leaders of his own party. Oddest of all perhaps was his policy prescription abolishing the Federal Reserve Bank system and returning the United States to the gold standard, under which a unit of currency would be convertible into a fixed amount of gold. "History has shown that fiat currencies eternally self-destruct," Presidential candidate Paul explained, "and they always go back to gold."

Many Republicans secretly agreed with some of his many criticisms

---

165. "The Gold Standard Days in Word and Song" appeared on the Kitco.com web site on October 21, 2009 and the *W. S. Gilbert Society Journal*, Volume 4, Issue 30, p. 50.

of government intrusions and mounting government debts. His views on returning the country to the gold standard, however, struck much of the party as nothing short of insanity.

In 2016, Donald Trump successfully sought the Republican nomination for President while saying that a return to the gold standard, "would be very hard to do, but boy would it be wonderful." Trump did not make such a return a real part of his candidacy, and as President, he said and did nothing more about it. Most assume that his affinity for the gold standard was fleeting and irrelevant and a subject best left alone, perhaps out of concern for needlessly scaring the financial markets.

It was not always thus. The gold standard was the way in which the advanced countries of the world organized their monetary affairs and settled their accounts throughout most of the nineteenth century and until 1914, and then again following the war sporadically and up until the early 1930s. It was a period of great economic and technical progress.

It was a world of precise weights and measures, and of non-wavering exchange rates. In 1816, following the Napoleonic Wars, the British Parliament passed The Great Recoinage Act, which mandated that 12 troy ounces (one troy pound) of 'standard' 22-karat gold would be convertible into precisely 44-1/2 guineas, or 46 pounds 14 shillings and 6 pence. Both before and after passage of the Act, U.S dollars were exchangeable for British pounds at a rate of around $4.86 to the pound. This meant that following passage of the Act, U.S. dollars would be exchangeable for pure (i.e., 24 karat) gold at a rate of $20.65 per troy ounce. If this were a legitimate science text, proving these equivalencies would be an interesting exercise at this point. This precise system of exchange between these two important currencies and gold held for roughly a century. Amazing.

It was boring, though. The American historian and journalist Henry

Adams summarized the feelings of many in writing to his brother Brooks in 1895. "I support Pierpont Morgan for President on a distinct gold monometallic [i.e., no silver dollars] platform. As a man of sense, I am a gold-bug and support a gold-bug government and a gold-bug society. As a man of the world," he concluded wistfully, candidly, "I like confusion, anarchy, and war."

Conservative and libertarian thinkers, perhaps because they were more comfortable with boredom, have had a long love affair with the gold standard era. Such people are rare, however, and in a democracy, they're largely irrelevant. The gold standard limited a government's ability to create credit and currency and therefore prevented debtors from devaluing their debts—and debtors are far more numerous than libertarian intellectuals. Contemporary financial historians such as James Grant regales his niche readership with tales of the glory that was the gold standard and of J.P Morgan's central banking. The Austrian School economists and the few followers of Milton Friedman approve of the tightly controlled growth in the money supply that was the essence of the gold standard. The willingness of high government officials during the gold standard era to refrain from meddling with the operation of banking and free markets, and from the temptation to devalue the government's debts, is therefore an historical curiosity. British Prime Minister Robert Peel, U.S. Presidents Grover Cleveland and Calvin Coolidge, French central bank president Emile Moreau were among the lions of the gold standard age—and nearly all forgotten by most others.

The old photos leave the impression of a bygone and almost fairytale era: the celluloid collars, the outlandish mustaches. It is almost useless to read the pronouncements of these gold standard bearers for insight into what held the system together; they were nearly all of them taciturn on economic matters, and to many of them the gold

185

standard was a law of nature that didn't need explaining. We must look elsewhere to find the stuff, the temperamental glue, that held the gold standard system together.

I assert that the amber-preserved essence of this gold standard world is found not in life but in art, specifically in the light operas of Gilbert and Sullivan that were so popular at the time. William Schwenck Gilbert, the odd librettist who got top billing over the composer of the musical score, was the genius behind these artful Victorian comedies that so often poked fun at the powerful.

For those not up on their opera history, it is perhaps time to point out how popular these Gilbert and Sullivan entertainments were those many years ago. From the 1870s through the mid-1890s, their Savoy Theatre in London was The Place To Be, and opening night productions were the hottest tickets of the year. Their copyrights were valuable enough that the first productions were sometimes performed simultaneously in both Britain and the United States in order to secure the copyright in both jurisdictions. Their enthusiastic, upper middle-class audiences in London and New York, the financial nerve-centers of the gold standard world, were the staunch supporters of the gold standard system.

Modern sensibilities are easily put off by Gilbert's corny, sentimental young tenors and the eye-batting young objects of their affection. The supporting characters, however, are often skillfully drawn caricatures of public figures. The sophisticated yet good-natured irreverence of these send-ups is a lost art.

Some of Gilbert and Sullivan's fanciful characters

The main reason for adopting the gold standard is to control the government's issuance of paper money and credit, a control grounded in skepticism concerning governmental omniscience. Gilbert's high government officials usually lacked anything even close to such. Lord Mountararat in the opera *Iolanthe* (in a tune entitled "When Britain Really Ruled the Waves"[166] reflects on the record of the august legislative body of which he is a member:

> *The House of Peers made no pretense*
>
> *To intellectual eminence*
>
> *Or scholarship sublime...*

---

166. For those poor benighted souls unfamiliar with Gilbert and Sullivan operettas, the song titles enclosed in parentheses can be searched and You Tube videos accessed that will allow the reader to listen to and view productions done around the world involving the particular tune. They can then enjoy Arthur Sullivan's wonderful music as well as William Gilbert's lyrics.

When Wellington thrashed Bonaparte,

As every child can tell,

The House of Peers, throughout the war,

Did nothing in particular,

   And did it very well...

And while the House of Peers withholds

Its legislative hand

And noble statesmen do not itch

To interfere with matters which

   They do not understand,

Gilbert's audience knew as well that government officials more often owed their posts to palm-greasing and back-scratching than competence. The lawyer who becomes First Lord of the Admiralty in *H.M.S. Pinafore* ("When I Was a Lad") confesses:

Of legal knowledge I acquired such a grip

That they took me into the partnership.

And that junior partnership, I ween,

Was the only ship that I ever had seen...

I grew so rich that I was sent

By a pocket borough into Parliament.

I always voted at my party's call,

And I never thought of thinking for myself at all.

   I thought so little they rewarded me

   By making me the Ruler of the Queen's Navee!

Gilbert's audience found the idea of limiting the power of a government so constituted to be wholly desirable. He and his audience held out no such hope for the poor souls throughout the rest of the world living under autocratic, non-British, non-Western rule. The most imperial, and non-British, of Gilbert's titled characters was the Mikado, the all-powerful leader of Japan, who sought to encourage young Japanese men ("Our Great Mikado, Virtuous Man") to steady themselves and focus their energies,

So he decreed, in words succinct,

That all who flirted, leered or winked

(Unless connubially linked),

Should forthwith be beheaded.

Gilbert's audience knew that an all-powerful Mikado, no matter how ridiculous, would never lack for sycophantic, well-bred ministers, and Pooh Bah among them describes himself as "a particularly haughty and exclusive person" who "can trace [his] ancestry back to a protoplasmic primordial atomic globule." His exalted social position compels Pooh Bah to instruct young schoolgirls ("So please you, Sir") as follows:

I think you ought to recollect

You cannot show too much respect

Towards the highly titled few;

But nobody does, and why should you?

That youth at us should have its fling,

Is hard on us,

Is hard on us;

To our prerogative we cling –

Gilbert trusted his audience to recognize the public spirited man, the officious do-gooder, for the public menace that he was. In *Princess Ida* ("If You Give Me Your Attention") gossipy old King Gama introduces himself:

> *If you give me your attention, I will tell you what I am:*
>
> *I'm a genuine philanthropist – all other kinds are sham.*
>
> *Each little fault of temper and each social defect*
>
> *In my erring fellow creatures I endeavor to correct...*
>
> *A charitable action I can skillfully dissect;*
>
> *And interested motives I'm delighted to detect;*
>
> *I know everybody's income and what everybody earns;*
>
> *And I carefully compare it with the income-tax returns;*
>
> *But to benefit humanity however much I plan,*
>
> *Yet everybody says I'm such a disagreeable man!*
>
> *And I can't think why!*

What has happened to that Gilbert and Sullivan audience, that perceptive and "happy breed of men" that, on being confronted with such a philanthropist, would have gladly ignored him or quickly turned him out of any government post that he might have wrangled for himself?

The skepticism Gilbert assumed in his audience certainly extended to financial matters. He enjoyed creating characters who could use their social position and prominence to dupe the investing public.

The Gondoliers featured those delightful rogues, the Duke and Duchess of Plaza-Toro, Spanish nobility of the highest rank, whose beautiful daughter Casilda is somewhat appalled to learn of the various sordid methods used by her parents to trade upon and translate their noble rank into hard cash. The Duke explains ("To Help Unhappy Commoners"):

I sit, by selection,

Upon the direction,

> *Of several Companies bubble –*

As soon as they're floated

I'm freely Bank-noted –

> *I'm pretty well paid form my trouble...*

In short, if you'd kindle

The spark of a swindle,

> *Lure simpletons into your clutches –*

Or hoodwink a debtor,

You cannot do better

> *Than trot out a Duke or a Duchess!*

It is painful, perhaps, for the 'sophisticated' twenty-first century "Celebrity SPAC"[167] investor with his prospectuses and disclosure statements produced by big-name investment houses with offices in toney places like London and Zurich to learn that he would be regarded by this nineteenth century librettist and his chuckling audience as a credulous simpleton.

In Utopia Limited, a Mr. Goldbury, investment banker, explains ("Some Seven Men Form an Association") to a remote island people interested in freeing themselves of authoritarian shackles, that they might organize their finances along limited liability lines ...

---

167. The Celebrity SPAC, or Special Purpose Acquisition Company, often used celebrities to accomplish what the Duke and Duchess did for the investment bankers. Talk about life imitating art!

They start out with a public declaration
  To what extent they mean to pay their debts.
That's called their Capital: if they are wary
  They will not quote it at a sum immense.
The figure's immaterial – it may vary
  From eighteen million down to eighteen pence...
They then proceed to trade with all who'll trust `em
  Quite irrespective of their capital...
If you succeed, your profits are stupendous –
  And if you fail, pop goes your eighteen pence...
If you come to grief, and creditors are craving
  (For nothing that is planned by mortal head
Is certain in the Vale of Sorrow – saving
  That one's Liability is Limited), —
Do you suppose that signifies perdition?
  If so you're but a monetary dunce –
You merely file a Winding-Up Petition,
  And start another company at once!

Our contemporaries who were recently so horrified at the thin thread of capital that was used to balance the huge financial risks that came to such grief in 2008 would have been branded hopelessly naïve by the audience at the Savoy Theatre of the 1890s. Gilbert's great warning (from H.M.S. Pinafore) to those seeking clarity and transparency in human affairs, financial and otherwise, is that …

Things are seldom what they seem,
Skim milk masquerades as cream...

Later, driving home the monetary point a little less obliquely:

Black sheep dwell in every fold,

All that glitters is not gold...

Gild the farthing if you will,

Yet it is a farthing still...

Gilbert's contempt for the idea of governmental and financial omniscience spilled over easily into ridicule of intellectual pretension. In Patience ("If You're Anxious for to Shine"), we hear Bunthorne (a parody of the then popular young Oscar Wilde) instruct on the proper posture to use when developing Arcadian thoughts ...

If you're anxious for to shine in the high aesthetic line as a man of culture rare,

You must get up all the germs of the transcendental terms and plant them everywhere,

You must lie upon the daisies and discourse in novel phrases of your complicated state of mind,

The meaning doesn't matter if it's only idle chatter of a transcendental kind,

  And everyone will say,

  As you walk your mystic way,

"If this young man expresses himself in terms too deep for me,

Why, what a very singularly deep young man this deep young man must be!"

If only the 1880s audience that laughed out loud at this could somehow have been present in the Congressional committee room to listen to the illustrious and Delphic chairman of the Federal Reserve favor the nation with his 'complicated' testimony!

A democracy anxious to elect 'transformative' chief executives or imbue its politicians with meaning and power that would have caused Louis XV to blush, is not the sort that would question the limits of the wisdom of such an official. Those hordes of investors who made savants of CEOs showing growing profits on the strength of investing ever larger sums of borrowed money also lacked the skeptical spirit.

The requirement to back a government's currency with gold, or any other substance of fixed value, was one not of economic barbarism but of doubt regarding the value of paper money and of the wisdom of the people empowered to create and manage it.

★ ★ ★

One of the few bits of history that most economic historians agree about is the importance of the dreadful banking panic of 1907. It was bad, they all agree, and it led to the creation of the Federal Reserve banking system, a government-sanctioned bank whose functions included acting as a lender of last resort in times of trouble and panic of the sort that occurred in the early fall of 1907.

There were such lenders of last resort in 1907, of course. Men like J.P. Morgan, founder of the firm that still bears his name, and George F. Baker of the First National Bank, and James Stillman of National City Bank. They had performed well—all things considered—in 1907, but with the advantage of the hindsight often employed by politicians, not quite well enough. They were in the business of acting as central banks of sorts, protecting large stores of stable assets. They maintained a network of 'correspondent banks' out in the savage, untamed world west of the Hudson River. These smaller banks often borrowed money from the larger New York banks, and if they experienced some sort of calamity—a run perhaps, or a spate of bad loans connected to some local event—the New York bankers like Morgan and Baker and Stillman would rifle through their books to determine if these smaller banks were solvent enough to warrant a loan to tide them over.

The Panic of 1907 was exactly this sort of calamity. A series of loans made to a copper mining financier—copper was a hot commodity in 1907 with the growth in electrical service—went bad when they attempted to corner the market in the shares of one of their copper mines. General business conditions were not favorable: Commodity prices had begun to sag in mid-year 1907. When the corner failed, the shares collapsed, and the loans that had been made to try to achieve the corner were suddenly worthless.

A number of these loans were held by a few New York banks. Word began to get around, but nobody knew precisely which banks had made such loans and in what amounts. There was no deposit insurance in 1907, and by mid-October lines began to form, most visibly, outside the Knickerbocker Trust on 34th Street and 5th Avenue. There was a run on a number of other banks as well, and the panic landed in the library of Mr. Morgan. J.P. and his banking colleagues and his assistants and accountants were charged with sifting through the books of a number of banks, deciding which to save and which to let die. Viewed from the street outside the Morgan residence on 36th Street and Madison Avenue, it was all decidedly un-democratic.

The political groundswell against the idea of this cabal of influential private citizens running the nation's economy gave us, in 1913, the Federal Reserve Act. The Federal Reserve was going to make central banking a matter of public policy, not private gain. That was the idea. Public spirited types would meet and discuss matters prevailing at the nation's banks, and public policy would be made out in the clean, fresh, bracing air of democracy and not the smoke-filled air of Mr. Morgan's library.

The Federal Reserve would be granted one other teeny, tiny bit of power that J.P. Morgan and his cronies never had in racing to the rescue of banks in distress: They were given the power to print money. They would set national economic policy by, in part, regulating interest rates, and what would such a power be worth if the Federal Reserve could not decide to quickly adjust certain interest rates by buying up the distressed debt that was causing such rates to be sub-optimal? And what better way to ensure that the Federal Reserve maintains this ability than to allow it to create the currency with which to do it?

Things did not go particularly smoothly in the early years of the Federal Reserve. The depressions of 1920-1921 and 1929–1933 saw the Federal Reserve somewhat too passive in exercising these new powers. The 'Fed' really came into its own during and after World War II, when the United States economy became the center of the world economy, and the people and institutions willing to lend the U.S. government money began to seem limitless.

This insatiable appetite allowed the U.S. Fed to pursue abstract economic planning. If there was a downturn in the economy, even a break in the stock market, the Fed could race into the Treasury market, buy up the latest U.S. government bonds on offer and thereby lower interest rates, and in doing so be seen to be taking action to stem the downturn. They could also thus assure themselves of continued political support.

Such a habit is hard to break, and the U.S. currency began a slow, peaceful descent in value. The pair of boots that had not changed in price much between 1790 and 1913 began to shoot up dramatically. The price of crude oil–a critical commodity that was required to produce many other products—gyrated wildly with political events, but eventually increased over twenty-fold. Houses did the same.

This gradual devaluation created perverse incentives. Economists know that when everything is slowly increasing in price, spending today is preferable to saving for tomorrow. When the hoi polloi gradually figured this out, and the nation's savings rate declined, the government developed special tax-favored programs like IRA and 401K accounts to try to get people to save for their dotage, with only moderate success.

Almost exactly a century after the panic of 1907, the big panic of 2008 suddenly threw many of these very gradual changes into sharp relief. Just as in 1907, the problem was bad loans, mortgage loans, in unknown amounts coursing mysteriously through the banking system.

Financial commentators were somewhat stunned in 2008 by the complete absence of any financial institution that didn't lose huge amounts of money on what many shrewd types had pointed out in print years before were very risky investments. Certain banks were a little less profligate, but as a group, their behavior seemed nothing short of heedless. Erstwhile institutions with names like "New Century" and "Countrywide" were almost laughably mismanaged, as were the mortgage buying arms of the federal government, Fannie Mae and Freddie Mac. There were simply no big, financial institutions that behaved very prudently in the years leading up to the panic of 2008. In 1907 there had been at least a few such institutions headed by people like Morgan and Baker that behaved prudently.

What had happened to the conservative, prudent financial business leader between the years 1907 and 2008? The same thing that happened to the saver.

A Tale of Two Panics

Comparing 1907 and 2008[168]

Much has been written about the changes to the American financial

---

168. "A Tale of Two Panics" appeared in the Spring 2019 issue of *Financial History* magazine.

system and the American economy resulting from the establishment of the Federal Reserve Bank in 1913. These writings are interesting, but they often devolve into attempts at second-guessing the actions of the Federal Reserve in response to various economic conditions—depressions, speculative bubbles, etc.—with the convenient perspective of hindsight.

Another way to think about the effects of the Federal Reserve system is to ask what changes it has wrought on the behavior of the nation's citizens. Do our business people behave differently because there is a central bank? This question can be approached any number of ways, but one way is to look at similar sets of economic circumstances occurring with and without the presence of the Federal Reserve and observe the different reactions of the market participants.

Market panics can throw these differences into stark relief. In the same way that bad weather can expose the skill (or lack of skill) of ship captains and airplane pilots, bank failures and liquidity crises can throw bright light on the actions of a nation's financiers.

The panics of the late summer and early fall of 1907 and 2008 can serve. They were separated not merely by a clean century of time, but by the absence (1907) and the presence (2008) of a powerful central bank. A look back at the chaos and the action during those two panics can perhaps allow us to understand better the effects of central banking.

The facts surrounding the panics of 1907 and 2008 were different, but in precipitating features they were the same.[169] Credit conditions were strained in October 1907 and suddenly came completely unglued when the Knickerbocker Trust, a prominent New York bank, was rumored to have a big book of business with an over-extended

---

169. Nobel laureate Paul Krugman, writing of the 2008 crisis, concluded that "The parallel to the panic of 1907 should be obvious." *The Return of Depression Economics and the Crisis of 2008* (New York, 2009), pp. 155, 160.

copper mining financier who went bust attempting to force a 'short squeeze' in the shares of a company he controlled.[170] Troubles in 2008 culminated when Lehman Brothers was sunk by a large pile of lousy mortgages and real estate investments. In 1907, J. Pierpont Morgan sent his people to rifle through the books of the Knickerbocker Trust to assess if it was salvageable with an emergency loan and, similarly, in 2008 Lehman Brothers was examined by a number of potential buyers (including J.P Morgan Chase) in the days before its collapse.

The suspension of operations at the Knickerbocker Trust and the bankruptcy of Lehman Brothers had similar cascading effects: There was uncertainty concerning exactly which financial institutions held the bad loans and in what amounts, and this uncertainty led to reduced levels of lending. Asset prices declined sharply as the credit necessary to finance asset purchases dried up, and banks tried to call in loans and refused to make new loans until they could assess the damage.

The difference for investors is that in 2008, the benefit to being liquid was small. Interbank overnight rates increased a few percentage points in the weeks following the collapse of Lehman Brothers, then dropped precipitously to near zero. Margin lending rates, strictly limited in scope, barely budged. Long-dated Treasury securities, which while liquid do involve putting principal at risk, increased in value some 15-20 percent in the ensuing months as long-term rates declined. But, in general, those in cash and money market funds simply sat by

---

170. *The Panic of 1907* by R.F. Bruner and S.D. Carr (2007), p. 43-55. The short squeeze was to have been accomplished by acquiring a sufficiently large percentage of the shares outstanding and then demanding, or "calling," for the rest of the outstanding stock. The squeeze works only if those who are "short" the stock cannot deliver the shares they owe because there are few shares left to buy, and in the process of attempting to buy back these few shares the short sellers bid the share price up to very high levels. In this particular case, the squeeze failed because the financier discovered that there were not nearly as many short positions in the stock as he had calculated, so that when he called for the rest of the outstanding stock the shares were promptly delivered to him. The debts he had incurred to achieve the corner could not be repaid because the price of the shares collapsed when the squeeze failed.

and contented themselves with the thought that they hadn't lost any money.[171]

In 1907, however, a liquid investor unwilling to tie up money for years in buying depressed common stocks could still have made some real dough. In the wake of the closure of the Knickerbocker Trust, the market that lent short-term against stock market collateral–the 'call loan,' now the 'margin loan' market—needed lenders: The prevailing rate of roughly 6 percent was not high enough to induce sufficient supply.[172] Trust companies like the Knickerbocker routinely made unsecured loans to Wall Street brokers, but when the panic began and Trust depositors began queueing up to withdraw money, credit on Wall Street became very tight.[173]

J.P. Morgan's syndicate of banks sent funds, but the demand from the illiquid was insatiable. The nation's newspapers reported the dramatic events: on October 22—the day the Knickerbocker Trust suspended operations—the morning call loan rate of 10 percent produced insufficient supply, and by mid-afternoon, rates had skyrocketed to 60 percent and later 70 percent. On October 24, call money rates peaked at 90 percent.[174] The following day, call money temporarily reached 100 percent. Brokers in Philadelphia threw up their hands and simply discontinued all trading on margin.[175]

One person's high borrowing rate is another's payday, of course,

---

171. One money market fund, the Primary Fund, was actually forced to take a small loss in late 2008 (due to writing down the value of some Lehman Brothers securities) and was thereby said to have "broken the buck." The damage to investors in the Fund, however, was small.

172. Recall that this 6% rate was based on a gold-backed dollar, so it was a real 6% rate. It still proved woefully inadequate in late October 1907.

173. *The Panic of 1907* by Jon R. Moen and Ellis W. Taubman, federalreservehistory.org, Dec. 4, 2015.

174. *The New York Times*, October 24, 1907.

175. Ibid, October 25, 1907. "Stop Trading on Margin: Philadelphia Brokers Decline to Execute Orders Save for Cash."

and the market participant holding unencumbered cash in late 1907 might have felt that they were indeed living in "the best of all possible worlds." Those who could lend funds to the call loan market did so, earning 1 percent on their money in only a few days. These profitable rates persisted: Call loan rates remained well above 20 percent into early November, and averaged around 20 percent for months afterwards. Money was made by these same liquid folks in cashing checks and clearing house certificates, perhaps discounting them significantly from face value.[176]

My contemporaries may wish to avert their eyes. The business of charging 'usurious' rates to the financially distressed, the illiquid, is not a pretty sight. Those solvent souls in 1907 who saw themselves as fulfilling a useful function—providing cash at a time when it was needed—had to know that the country at-large probably thought of them as vultures.

The financial trauma of October 1907 did not pass quickly from public consciousness. It became known that the leaders of the major Wall Street banks, J.P. Morgan and his colleagues, had decided behind closed doors which banks and trust companies could be saved and which ones had to be shuttered. In the days before deposit insurance, this appeared to be incredible power wielded by private citizens accountable only to their partners or shareholders.

Members of the U.S. Congress decided to investigate this unaccountability. They held what became known as the Pujo Hearings, named after congressman Arsene Pujo of Louisiana, a House Banking and Currency subcommittee inquiry into whether there was a 'money trust' in Wall Street. "Trust" was both a legal and a colloquial term used to connote a

---

176. *Clearing House Loan Certificates and Substitutes for Money Used During the Panic of 1907* by J.G. Cannon (1910). Mr. Cannon records that such certificates were issued by bank check clearing houses throughout the country in lieu of cash. Holders of such certificates often preferred cash, and were willing to trade their certificates at a discount to face value.

concentration of power in any industry that might need to be broken up. A financial trust company like the Knickerbocker Trust was a lightly-regulated bank that paid slightly higher deposit rates but that generally took somewhat more risk with the depositors' money. The work of this subcommittee resulted in the passage of the Sixteenth Amendment authorizing a federal income tax, the Clayton Anti-Trust Act, and the Federal Reserve Act establishing a central bank, a bank designed to check the power of J.P. Morgan and his cronies that would—most significantly—be empowered to function as a "lender of last resort."

The establishment of the Federal Reserve sought to banish for eternity those all too conspicuous vultures. By empowering an institution to combat bank panics, the government made sure such vultures could never again profit from having 'ready money' in times of panic. Early on, its leaders were hesitant. But as the dollar's link to gold loosened until being cut entirely in 1971, the Federal Reserve became increasingly willing to provide cheap liquidity at any hint of trouble.

Federal Reserve officials like to quote the classic principles of central banking promulgated by nineteenth century British economist Walter Bagehot[177], who counseled that central bankers should—in times of panic—lend freely against good collateral, but at a high interest rate.[178] Modern central bankers have certainly mastered the first two of these precepts—lending freely against good collateral (if mortgages are considered 'good')—but the third concerning interest rates they seem to ignore entirely.

---

177. e.g., "Bagehot's Dictum in Practice: Formulating and Implementing Policies to Combat the Financial Crisis" by B.F. Madigan, Director, Federal Reserve Bank Division of Monetary Affairs, federalreserve.org (Aug. 21, 2009)

178. These general rules, "Bagehot's dictum," apply to those institutions acting as "lender of last resort" during a "credit crisis." Bagehot first described these general rules in his book *Lombard Street: A Description of the Money Market* (New York, 1873). The dictum was formalized by British economist Charles Goodhart in 1999 in an article entitled "Myths About the Lender of Last Resort" that appeared in *International Finance* 2/3, pp. 339-360.

Wall Street watched this and gradually concluded that liquidity doesn't pay. In the wake of the Lehman bankruptcy in 2008, when liquid funds were needed, short-term rates didn't spike upward. They declined! Federal Reserve infusions saw to it.

The lesson was obvious. What was the point of holding cash for such scarce times if the Fed could print all any bank needed? What large financial institution could afford to tilt against such a policy wind and do other than "borrow short, lend long, and hope for the best"? A century of financial gerrymandering has produced a system that simply doesn't reward risk-aversion in any positive way.

The implications of this policy change extend beyond 'solving' the liquidity problem of the moment. One is the decline of the currency: The Federal Reserve now manages interest rates to maximize economic growth and employment, meaning that interest rates are generally kept lower than they would be otherwise, which in turn requires the Federal Reserve to create money to bid up the price of government securities and suppress these rates. The call money rate, for example, has never returned to remotely the levels of October 1907. All the money and credit creation required has left U.S. dollar—now a "Federal Reserve Note"—a tiny 2 percent speck of the gold-backed dollar of 1907, and gradual devaluation (i.e., "inflation targeting") is now a governmental goal.[179]

The subtle, less visible effect is on the value of, and the potential returns accruing to, financial prudence. To illustrate, it helps to recall the actions of a few prominent financial figures from those bygone days of 1907:

Bernard Baruch was young and newly rich in 1907. He had made

---

179. Federal Reserve officials don't call it devaluation, preferring instead the lighter, more ambiguous term "inflation," which is simply the arithmetical inversion of the same quantity. Inflation-targeting is a goal of modern Federal Reserve policy. The current target is about 2% per year.

a fortune speculating on sugar prices, the end of the Spanish-American War in 1898, and the Northern Pacific ownership tussle and short squeeze of 1901. He was, nevertheless, a public-spirited man who would later volunteer his services to the government during the World Wars. The fall of 1907 found him worried about the markets and holding roughly $2 million in cash in safe-deposit boxes.[180] When the panic took hold, he saw his duty to be in shoring up the nation's financial condition. He thought of approaching J.P. Morgan directly with offers of help, but he knew Morgan regarded him as little more than a gambler. Baruch instead quietly deposited $1 million into a few strapped but solvent Manhattan banks, and shipped cash to a distressed copper mining concern in Utah while buying up its common stock.[181]

Jesse Livermore was also a newly rich speculator in 1907, but he was somewhat more flamboyant than his contemporary, Mr. Baruch. Known around Wall Street as the "Boy Plunger"[182] for his perennially youthful appearance and his investing style, Livermore was alternately barbarically liquid and then bankrupt as his speculative positions waxed and waned. October 1907 found him solidly short the market, and he was making hundreds of thousands per day in late October when the great man, J.P. Morgan himself, placed a discrete phone call to Livermore asking him to discontinue his shorting of the stock market. Livermore complied, later recalling the significance of Morgan's request as part of "a day of days for me," one in which his winnings were tallied in both money and in "intangibles."[183]

---

180. *Baruch: Portrait of a Citizen* by W.E. White (New York, 1951), p. 32.

181. *Bernard Baruch: The Adventures of a Wall Street Legend* by James Grant (New York, 1983), p.82.

182. A "plunger" was a market participant known for concentrating most of his/her assets into large bets on the price movement of specific stocks, bonds, or commodities.

183. *Reminiscences of a Stock Operator* by Edwin Lefevre (New York, 1923). A fascinating little book published in the middle of Livermore's career, it is written in the first person by a ghost writer, Mr. Lefevre.

Henrietta "Hetty" Green was a monstrously rich private investor in 1907. The sole surviving heiress to a New Bedford, Massachusetts whaling fortune accumulated in the 1830s-1850s, Green meticulously compounded her capital during the gilded age of the late nineteenth century. She was notoriously frugal, perhaps miserly, a trait that when combined with her willingness to sue—her spending on lawyers was positively profligate—earned her the name "The Witch of Wall Street." Green was nevertheless willing to speculate in greenbacks following the Civil War and in railroad stocks, but also made sure she kept considerable cash reserves to back up these somewhat speculative positions.

"I like to buy railroad stock and mortgage bonds," she told a reporter in 1905. "Government bonds are good, though they do not pay very high interest," she added. She went on to define her modus operandi as follows: "When I see a good thing going cheap because nobody wants it, I buy a lot of it and tuck it away."[184]

Two years later, when the panic of 1907 struck and the New York City government was starved for cash, Hetty Green wrote them a check for $1.1 million in exchange for some freshly-minted New York City revenue bonds. Her son supervised her holdings in Texas, and he later estimated her total emergency lending at that time to be at least $6 million (approximately $200 million today) in Texas alone.[185]

George Baker became president of the First National Bank of New York in 1877 at the age of 37, and he proceeded to run the bank for over 50 years. The First National, 'Baker's Bank,' operated in a way that is almost unthinkable today. There were only 20 holders of First National stock in Baker's early years, and the Bank's directors owned 92 percent

---

184. "Hetty Green: A Character Study," *National Magazine*, 1905, p. 633.

185. *The New York Times*, July 4, 1916, "Hetty Green Dies, Worth $100,000,000." Her son, Edward H. R. Green, was in charge of his mother's interests in Texas, and he was quoted in the article claiming her fresh lending in Texas alone totaled $6 million.

of the shares.[186] They did a big business in U.S. treasuries, turning over an astonishing $250 million of them in 1877.[187]

Baker's Bank was focused on liquidity, on trading in securities, not commercial loans. Deposits were taken only in six-figure or greater amounts, upon which a placid (but 'real') interest rate of 2 percent was paid. In those days before deposit insurance, Baker's reputation for prudence and discretion was such that conservative businesses kept large amounts with him: The privately-held Ford Motor Company often kept some $50 million with the First National, and Henry Ford himself often $5 million.[188] In October 1907, when J.P. Morgan convened a conference of his fellow New York bankers to organize a loan to support the call loan market, Baker's First National Bank was ready and willing to lend.[189]

Of these eccentric characters of yesteryear, the only one whose behavior in the days leading up to the panic of 1907 echoes down to us at all is that of the Boy Plunger, Jesse Livermore. His large positions 'shorting' the market were similar in spirit to those of the hedge fund managers of 2007-2008, like John Paulsen and Steve Eisman, who aggressively shorted the market for home mortgages. Livermore's plunging later caused him severe losses, just as it would later for those modern-day hedge fund managers.[190]

The conservative ways of Baruch, Green, Baker—their skeptical, liquid 1907 investing styles—have now been banished into irrelevance.

---

186. *Money of the Mind* by James Grant (New York, 1992), p. 50.

187. Ibid, p. 58.

188. Ibid, p. 41.

189. *The Panic of 1907* by Bruner and Carr, p. 74.

190. "One of John Paulson's Hedge Funds Crashed 70% Over the Last Four Years", *Bloomberg News*, January 9, 2018. Steve Eisman later closed the hedge fund—"Front Point Partners" — that so effectively shorted mortgages in 2008 and had to close the new one he started shortly thereafter —"Emrys Partners" — due to poor investing performance.

Their descendants on Wall Street today are a less skeptical group, one that trusts their central bank to provide when things get tough. When the call went out for liquid funds in September 2008, Wall Street turned to the Fed. Wall Street's residents would have explained that there was no point in holding cash, that short-term interest rates yielded next to nothing and even less after inflation, and that there was big money to be made in issuing and securitizing mortgages and thereby helping with the government's goal of creating an 'ownership society.'[191]

In the wake of the panic of 2008, that government, as mentioned, did provide. Many of the government's elected leaders, however, were critical of Wall Street's titans. In committee hearings similar to the Pujo Hearings, they announced that the denizens of Wall Street brought before them had been reckless and overpaid in the years leading up to the panic.[192] Lawmakers pointed to the 'leverage' employed by some of these financial firms–borrowing done to increase the size and potential profits of their investments—and made it look foolish and self-serving. Laws were passed (e.g., The Dodd-Frank Wall Street Reform and Consumer Protection Act) mandating risk reduction and aggregating to the government increased oversight of the surviving firms.

In passing laws and in more closely monitoring these firms, the law-making class acted on the assumption that the world could be controlled by a series of prohibitions and penalties. Wall Street, however, is governed by the profit motive, so these prohibitions represent barriers to be hurdled in a never-ending steeplechase race, not guidelines, not lodestars.

---

191. "The Ownership Society" *Forbes Magazine*, Sept. 3, 2004. President George W. Bush is quoted as follows: "Thanks to our policies, home ownership in America is at an all-time high. Tonight we set a new goal: seven million more affordable homes in the next ten years so more American families will be able to open the door and say, 'Welcome to my home.'"

192. e.g., The House Government and Government Reform Committee hearings convened in late 2008-2009 by Chairman Henry Waxman of California.

Mandating fiscal prudence on Wall Street may be difficult without some tangible payoff for such behavior. A Federal Reserve that manages short-term rates to encourage growth and employment and therefore often keeps such rates below the rate of inflation does not reward prudence. The shrewd, liquid, conservative management of funds practiced profitably by those wealthy characters of 1907 was grounded in the belief that prudence may someday be rewarded. That belief is perhaps as archaic as their buggy whips.

Postscript: The panic of 2008 caused central banks around the world to lower interest rates to zero. This was done to try to get the industrial economy going again, but it was difficult. Commercial and residential real estate was in oversupply, so low borrowing rates were not enough to tempt developers. The great, unwashed consuming public was largely left out of this binge as well: Their credit card lenders saw no reason to lower their rates, and home equity loans vaporized along with their home equity. The net effect was therefore simply to encourage re-financing of existing corporate debt and the issuing of new debt to buy back company stock. The upshot was that corporations became even more leveraged, meaning that the system became much more dependent on corporations making regularly scheduled interest payments.

The coronavirus pandemic and the related shutdowns of 2020 threw this new system the precise sort of pitch the new system could not handle. Businesses that are shut down cannot generate cash to make interest payments. The Federal Reserve and the Treasury were keenly aware of the dependence of this new structure on timely interest payments—their leaders had in some cases created the leveraged loans that were in such jeopardy—and they knew that the system was in danger of collapse. Within the span of a couple of weeks in the spring of 2020, the Fed authorized the printing of roughly $3 trillion of new dollars to *buy up some of the exotic loans created during those zero interest rate years by private equity companies to 'lever up' the mundane businesses they were cash flowing to generate huge fees for themselves.*

The Fed's actions at this juncture were not at all transparent, for the simple reason that if the public knew what they were doing—mortgaging the future to protect their buddies in the lucrative private equity world—there might have been an outcry. The people who traded bonds for a living, however, knew exactly what was going on. One such trader summarized it succinctly: "The Fed has made it clear that prudent investing will not be tolerated."[193]

And with that, the world of 1907 had been precisely turned on its head.

★ ★ ★

Post-Postscript: The financial world of 1907 was very different from the one we inhabit today. Inflation was low to non-existent, interest rates were high, and the creditor was King. In our more 'modern' world, it is still better to be a creditor than a debtor, but there can be little doubt that debtors are better off today than they were in 1907.

Creditors did not give up the privileged status they enjoyed in 1907 without a fight. In the ensuing years, they continued doling out credit on what we would today regard as stringent, difficult terms. This was true even of an institution that now must be considered the most openhanded creditor in the history of finance: the United States government. The U.S. government and its leaders were tight with their money for years after that Panic of 1907, even in dealing with loan applicants that the history books tell us were 'the good guys' who needed money to fight those that the same books tell us were 'the bad guys.'

---

193. *The Lords of Easy Money* by C. Leonard (New York, 2022), p. 282

"Operation Fish"[194]

Britain's Daring Top-Secret Shipment of Its Bank Deposits to North America in the Early Days of World War II

The rescue of the British Expeditionary Force from Dunkirk in the early days of World War II is well-known and dramatic enough to be the stuff of cinema. The evacuation of those men, the backbone of the British army, meant Britain could continue to defend her island nation.

At that same time, certain less dramatic yet important financial problems confronted the British.

The Germans had driven the British to the beaches at Dunkirk, and they now planned a land invasion of Britain. The British had every reason to believe the vast bank deposits in their possession were a prime target. German central bank reserves were low in the late-1930s, drained by German Chancellor Adolf Hitler's many military and infrastructure expenditures, and Germany needed gold and hard cash to pay for its imports of raw materials. Germany's annexation of the small and no longer wealthy country of Austria in March 1938 more than doubled Germany's bank reserves from these low levels.[195] "Whenever Hitler occupied a country," Third Reich historian William Shirer summarized, "his financial agents seized the gold and foreign holdings of its national bank."[196]

Yugoslavia bordered Austria in the 1930s. In early-May 1939 a Yugoslavian warship eased into Britain's Portsmouth harbor, bearing much of the country's gold reserves because at that point Britain was considered a safer spot for those reserves than Yugoslavia. [197]

---

194. "Operation Fish" appeared in the Spring 2024 issue of *Financial History* magazine.

195. *1938: Hitler's Gamble* by G. MacDonogh (London, 2009), p. 22

196. *The Rise and Fall of the Third Reich* by W. Shirer (Connecticut, 1960), p. 1230.

197. *Operation Fish* by A. Draper (London, 1979), p. 29

Britain had long been a haven for such stores of wealth, and its total stores were massive. Its reputation for conservative, discreet, and profitable banking practices combined with its well-defended perimeter to make it so. The Bank of England had been storing the wealth of people and combatant countries for hundreds of years. George and Martha Washington famously owned Bank of England stock during the Revolutionary War, and the Bank quietly paid the dividends to the Washingtons' London agent during the period of hostilities between Britain and the Colonies.[198]

The rest of Europe may have seen Britain as a haven, but the British knew their defenses were not impenetrable. Their island was protected by its navy—perhaps the best in the world—but the British knew that if the Germans got a toehold on the island, it could mean real trouble.

The British military was purchasing American war supplies on a "cash-and-carry" basis in 1939–1940 and needed to ship money to America to pay for them. In May 1939, shortly before the Yugoslavian gold arrived and before hostilities began, the Bank of England secretly sent gold on trucks—'lorries'—on three consecutive nights from London to Portsmouth harbor and aboard a military cruiser that then joined an entourage escorting King George VI on a Royal visit to Canada and the United States. The operation was kept completely secret, and it went off like clockwork.

The war began in September 1939 with Germany's invasion of Poland, and orders for American military supplies placed by Britain and France increased dramatically. Britain's Chancellor of the Exchequer notified his military leaders that such secret shipments of gold would also have to escalate. He estimated some 200 million British pounds worth of gold—800 tons of it, worth $44 billion today—would need to

---

198. The New York Times, Nov. 1, 1970, "Washington Note is Shown at Bank" by I. Shenker

be shipped over the next 12 months, all while German U-boats patrolled and sank ships in the North Atlantic.

In early October 1939, the first of the crossings was made, this time from Plymouth harbor bound for Halifax, Nova Scotia. Secrecy was paramount. The Royal Navy issued tropical gear to the sailors aboard the cruisers HMS Emerald and Enterprise to throw off any spies regarding their destination. The crossing weather was cold and rough, however, and the sailors' clothing proved completely inadequate. On arriving in Halifax, the captain of the Emerald casually requested warm clothing for the return trip, and the Canadian Red Cross rushed them horsehide gloves, woolen scarves, leather headgear, etc. The captain later called this act of generosity "unbelievable."[199]

Canada had declared war on Germany shortly after Britain did in early-September 1939, and their efforts on behalf of the British and the allied cause during those years before the United States entered the war are little remembered and nothing short of heroic. United States neutrality law prevented warships, such as those carrying gold, from docking at any of their many eastern ports, so the ships went to Canada, where Canadians transported, guarded, and brokered it.

The "Phony War" that followed the Polish surrender ended abruptly in April 1940 when Germany attacked Norway. Norwegian gold made it out of Norway to Scotland and then on to London as German para-troopers landed all around. German troops overpowered Holland and Belgium in May 1940, and Dutch gold made it across the Channel to England along with most of Holland's Royal Family. The Germans then steamrolled into France. Some French gold had been shipped to London in April, but the bulk of it left the harbor at Brest in northwest France bound for the Caribbean and West Africa mere hours before the Germans arrived.

---

199. Draper, p. 66.

Parliament had appointed a new Prime Minister, Winston Churchill, in mid-May. He had been First Lord of the Admiralty and was well-aware of the financial problem of paying cash for armaments. He wrote to American President Franklin Roosevelt, a man he did not know well at the time, on May 15: "We shall go on paying dollars for as long as we can," he wrote, "but I should like to feel reasonably sure that when we can pay no more you will give us the stuff all the same."[200]

Churchill tried to rally the French, but to no avail. The evacuation from Dunkirk and the French surrender in mid-June left Britain alone. British resolve stiffened behind Churchill, but Mr. Churchill was a realist. Britain's ability to buy weapons to defend itself was dependent on its wealth, which would be lost if the Germans were to reach London. That wealth had to be moved out of danger. The nation's bankers also knew that much of Britain's wealth was in securities owned by British citizens. The bankers determined that these private holdings, especially the highly marketable American and Canadian securities, could be moved as well under the provisions of the Emergency Powers Act.[201] Churchill told the cabinet of the plan as events were coming to a head at Dunkirk.

The operation would have to be kept secret for all sorts of reasons. U-boats would be expected to target ships known to contain such wealth, but the mere fact that the nation's wealth was leaving the country would look defeatist and be a blow to British morale. Communication was kept to an absolute minimum, and the word 'fish' was used to refer to the cargo.

The Bank of England work was supervised by Deputy Governor Basil Catterns, a highly discreet banker perfectly comfortable with secrecy. Catterns outlined the plan in a memo to the Deputy head of the

---

200. Draper, p. 179
201. "Operation Fish" by R. Low, Bank of Canada Museum Blog, May 8, 2018.

Treasury. "Our proposal in brief is that the Treasury should call in all restricted securities...and... [those should be] shipped to Canada by a vessel specially chartered for the purpose."[202]

Preparations began in late May 1940. The military situation was deteriorating and required quick changes in plan. The Channel ports— Portsmouth, Plymouth—were no longer considered safe, so the gold and securities would have to travel northwest to board ships. The Admiralty also sent the bankers an ominous warning: In the event of a German offensive, all battleships would have to be pulled back from convoy duty to defend the island, and ships carrying gold would have to cross the Atlantic without military protection.

The banks collected the gold and negotiable securities and sent them to the port of Greenock in western Scotland. Five Bank of England men were hastily sent to Greenock to board the HMS Emerald to travel with the gold and the securities. HMS Emerald left Greenock bound for Halifax on June 23.

The crossing would be windy and rough, especially on the bankers. The captain recalled that, "We left the Clyde that night with reports of really foul weather ahead." One of the bankers remembered hearing reports that U-boats were in their path, but, "I was too sick to even think of a submarine." The skill and professionalism and good cheer of the sailors, in the face of what seemed to the bankers to be almost impossible conditions, left an indelible impression on those five Bank of England men.

A small group of Bank of Canada and Canadian National Railway employees were notified that important cargo was headed their way, and they acted fast. One banker described the hectic trip from Ottawa. He was not informed of exactly what was being shipped but noticed

---

202. Draper, p. 188.

heavily armed Mounties guarding the train from Montreal to Halifax. On arriving he was introduced to five very tired Londoners. "We're Bank of England people," one of them told him disarmingly. "Hope you don't mind us dropping in unexpectedly like this, but we've brought along quite a large shipment of 'fish.'"

Large indeed. HMS Emerald carried 140 tons of gold and at least a billion dollars-worth (1940 dollars) of saleable securities.[203] The inventorying and valuing of the securities was done very quickly and somewhat conservatively. It was a shipment so flagrantly above the regulatory limits on gold per ship that the Risk Insurance Office was not even contacted, on the theory that the potential loss could not be covered anyway. Seven critical voyages conducted in late-June and July of 1940 carried roughly half of all the vast wealth moved from Britain to Canada during those two years.

The Canadians had formulated a plan. The securities would go to the commodious basement of the Sun Life Insurance building in Montreal, and the gold would go on to Ottawa, to the vault in the new Bank of Canada building just across Wellington Street from Parliament. The Ottawa vault was 60'x100' in area, 20' in height. In addition to the thousands of tons of gold heading there, some 50,000 sacks of rare coins—"Napoleons," and "spade guineas" from the reign of George III, French Louis-IV, -XV, and -XVI gold coins, etc.—were also sent and stored.[204] Summer heat made conditions below difficult: The workers moving the gold dripped with sweat; the white collar workers worked in shirt sleeves; and gallons of chilled fruit juice were brought down to combat dehydration.[205] The inventorying of the gold was exacting and time-consuming. Before being placed in the vault, the ownership of

---

203. Ibid, p. 256.

204. Ibid, p. 281.

205. Ibid, p. 296-297.

FISCAL FOLLIES

each bar and coin was recorded and each weighed with very accurate scales. The gold arrived so fast during that summer of 1940 that it was stacked in the halls outside the vault prior to weighing and recording.

The securities operation would be tricky and best done by people experienced in securities dealing, not just banking. Edward Hanna of Montreal had 13 years of experience as a Canadian securities dealer, and when war was declared, he quit to join the Air Force. It was as he was finishing his packing that Bank of Canada people called and asked him to work for them, but they wouldn't tell him exactly what the job entailed. He spoke with Alexander Craig, one of the five newly arrived Bank of England people, and after a few minutes of confusing conversation, he surmised that 'they have arrived,' meaning the British assets. When asked how he could possibly know this, he said that he kept up on the war news and knew Britain was in trouble, that "you [Craig] haven't been to Montreal or New York, yet have much experience in banking, and you speak with a transparently English accent."

Craig responded, "By Jove—how clever!"[206] Hanna was hired.

Gold and securities poured into the vaults in Ottawa and Montreal from Halifax after crossing the Atlantic. Miraculously few ships bearing gold bars were sunk. Filing cabinets—109 of them—were ordered to store the securities in Montreal, and Hanna and his colleagues set about organizing, valuing, and selling them to raise money. A special group did nothing but cut the coupons from the many stock and bond certificates. "I never saw so many coupons in my life," one of them remembered.[207] The organization was referred to as the United Kingdom Security Deposit, and it opened an office in New York to help with the brokering.

Britain's need for cash, however, was insatiable. After France

---

206. Ibid, p. 304.
207. Draper, p. 299

216

surrendered in June 1940, the British decided to take delivery of the orders the French no longer needed, thus doubling their spending rate.

The selling began in late-summer 1940. The need was for dollars—American or Canadian. Securities owned by British citizens would be sold for dollars, the citizen credited in sterling, a currency the Bank of England could print. Edward Hanna reflected that, "It was sad for me to see the wealth of the United Kingdom passing through my very hands."

The pool of assets was not bottomless, however. Churchill later reflected, "Up till November 1940 we had paid for everything...We had already sold $335 million worth of American shares...We had paid out 4,500 million dollars in cash. We had only 2,000 million left, the greater part in investments, many of which were not marketable."[208]

Many members of the American Congress—the "isolationists"—were opposed to getting involved in the war, and many were not convinced that the British were running out of money. Cash-and-Carry was still the policy, they insisted. President Roosevelt, an old Navy man, knew that American control of the Atlantic would be jeopardized if the British Navy fell into the hands of the Germans. During the Presidential election campaign of 1940, however, Roosevelt shrewdly avoided alienating the many isolationist voters by not advocating a change in policy.

Roosevelt won a third term in early November, and he began to lobby on behalf of a new policy. It would be called Lend-Lease, under which the British would be allowed to borrow the money to pay for their American-made armaments.

At a press conference in mid-December, the President made his case: "Suppose my neighbor's house catches fire and I have a length of garden hose four or five hundred feet away. If he can take my garden

---

208. *The Second World War—Volume II* by W. Churchill (Cambridge, 1949), p. 557.

hose and connect it up with his hydrant, I may help him to put out the fire…I don't say to him before that operation, 'Neighbor, my garden hose cost me $15; you have to pay me $15 for it.' No!… I don't want $15—I want my garden hose back after the fire is out."[209] On December 30, during one of his Fireside Chats, the President reasoned that "If Britain should go down, all of us in all the Americas would be living at the point of a gun…We must be the great arsenal of democracy."[210]

The wheels of Congress ground slowly towards a vote on the proposal. While Congress debated, the British were irked when the American arm of Courtaulds, the venerable British textile conglomerate, was sold to raise money for Britain. It was sold to a group of New York bankers at a highly discounted price, bankers who quickly re-sold it at a tidy profit.[211] In January 1941, some $500 million in stocks and bonds were sent from Montreal to Washington to secure an emergency loan of $375 million from the U.S. government.

The Congress finally passed Lend-Lease on March 9. Churchill had often privately expressed frustration with American politicians during these debates, but after passage he called Lend-Lease, "the most unsordid act in the history of any nation." The day after Senate passage, $7 billion in loans were approved to finance British war needs.

Britain's financial emergency was over. The war would be quite another matter: Victory over Germany was finally achieved in May 1945.

Winston Churchill is justifiably famous for his turns of phrase. He announced over the wireless on August 20, 1940, that, "Never in the field of human conflict was so much owed by so many to so few." He was referring to those few daring British pilots who held the German

---

209. Ibid, p. 568
210. Ibid, p. 573
211. Draper, p. 399-400

Luftwaffe at bay in the air war then raging over Britain. He might just as easily have been referring to those intrepid Royal Navy seamen and those tireless British and Canadian bank and brokerage employees who had secretly spirited all that wealth to Canada during that same summer of 1940, for it was they—just like those pilots—who allowed Britain to survive the German onslaught until the Americans could come to their financial and later their military rescue.

Chapter 13

IS IT ART?

It is a principle of copyright law that such a right extends not to knowledge or ideas but only to the specific expression of those ideas. The U.S. Supreme Court put it this way in 1879 in a case involving the copyright attached to an accounting ledger book: "The copyright of a work on mathematical science cannot give to the author an exclusive right to the methods of operation which he propounds...The very object of publishing a book on science or the useful arts is to communicate to the world the useful knowledge which it contains. But this object would be frustrated if the knowledge could not be used without incurring the guilt of piracy of the book."[212]

This same principle is easily extended by analogy to the law governing the copyright to dramatic works. The 'idea' in a dramatic work is the outline of the plot: a murder mystery in which the murder is committed by the butler, or a musical concerned with the lives of the members of a chorus line. The successful plaintiff must show more plagiarism than just these skeletal facts. For example, if William Shakespeare were in court today complaining that someone had stolen his idea for his play Romeo and Juliet, he would have to show more than that some defendant had written a story of two young lovers whose families disapprove of their attachment. That would merely be the 'idea,' the mathematical operation, of the story. Counsel for Mr. Shakespeare would have to show that the defendant had stolen particular parts of the story line: Feuding Italian families perhaps, the young

---

212. Baker v. Selden, 101 U.S. 99 (1879).

female who is in love looking out over her balcony and asking the night air of the whereabouts of a particular son of the other family, perhaps using the young man's name and a particular phrase such as, "Paulo, Paulo…Wherefore art thou, Paulo?"

This is a rare case where a legal principle is also aesthetically clarifying. Art truly is a matter of expression much more than it is of any underlying ideas. Ideas are abstractions, perhaps interesting to relate but never compelling and riveting in the way that a particular story or work of art can be. Artists are masters of expression and detail, not ideas.

The successful channeling of abstract ideas into beautiful artistic expression is illustrated nicely in the career and artistic work of the great Irish playwright George Bernard Shaw. Mr. Shaw enjoyed the world of ideas as much as anyone: Shaw was a Fabian socialist, a branch of socialism popular among English intellectuals who believed not in the revolutionary overthrow of the existing order but in positive change through incremental reform within the democratic system. More will be said of Fabian socialism a little later; suffice it to say that it was a very orderly, very reserved, very British form of socialism. Around the turn of the last century, Shaw and the Fabian socialists in and around London founded, among other things, the British Labour Party.

Shaw was artist enough, however, to know that people did not want to hear him spout his economic ideas when they went to the theater. His plays, many of which are classics, reflect his thinking on economic matters, but only when you stepped back a good distance. He knew that using some stick-figured character to mouth his economic ideas was fatal to good comedy or drama, and that the goal was to entertain, to create memorable characters who got the audience to laugh or cry.

Nevertheless, he realized that economic matters controlled his thinking. He wrote a friend in 1904 that "in all my plays my economic studies have played as important a part as knowledge of anatomy does in the works of Michael Angelo."[213] The mark of true artistry is thus struck: Mr. Shaw could channel his interest in economics and sociology into his plays without lecturing the audience, all the while using characters that were wonderful, dramatic, and comic creations in their own right.

Mr. Shaw's greatest theatrical work is perhaps Pygmalion, which was first performed in 1912. The title refers to the Greek poet Ovid's Metamorphoses, in which Pygmalion the sculptor falls in love with a statue he has carved. Shaw uses this germ of an idea to spoof the English caste system by having a wealthy Professor of Phonetics teach a young Cockney girl proper English pronunciation, thereby transforming her into a lady of flawless diction and fashion—and someone the Professor can then no longer live without. The young girl, Eliza Doolittle, has a Cockney father named Alfred, a character into whose mouth Mr. Shaw decides to place some ideas that are eerily similar to those of many of Shaw's economist friends—but in a way that will get the audience to laugh uproariously. It is only when the audience-member can stop laughing at Mr. Shaw's delightful comic creation that the economic ideas in Alfred P. Doolittle's dialogue can be recognized as such.

When you enjoy a production of Pygmalion or, more likely, the famous musical My Fair Lady that is based on Shaw's play, note that Shaw the artist is always in control, and that the economic ideas are subservient to the entertainment, yet still visible. This is possible only if you can tear yourself away from the fun of the story and regard the characters and the dialogue from a clinical distance. It is much more fun, however, to simply enjoy the show.

---

213. George Bernard Shaw to Archibald Henderson, 6/30/1904, appearing in print in *George Bernard Shaw: His Life and Works* by A. Henderson (1911) p. 287.

Doolittle Economics

First appeared in 2011.[214]

Unemployment benefits are in the news again. Congressional Republicans have proposed a bill that would allow states to redirect federal unemployment funds away from paying cash benefits and toward rebuilding depleted state unemployment-insurance funds.

Democrats object strenuously, saying the idea is neither fair nor effective. The White House lists such cash benefits as one "of the best measures for jump-starting growth and job creation." House Minority Leader Nancy Pelosi of California declares that curbing cash benefits "could destroy as many as 300,000 jobs over the next year," and that "every dollar invested in unemployment insurance yields a return of $1.60 in economic growth." The Economic Policy Institute says that such benefits put "cash in the hands of needy families that would spend it," and therefore, cash benefits have a high multiplier effect.

The economic reasoning of the Democrats has been consistent. Last year, then-Speaker Pelosi told us that extending unemployment cash benefits "injects demand into the economy" because the benefits are "spent quickly." Alternative policies that cut taxes for "wealthy people" are judged less effective by economist Paul Krugman because "they're not going to spend very much of it." Barron's readers who noticed probably chuckled. A few perhaps joked that the same sort of reasoning has put Greece and Zimbabwe on the sound fiscal footing they enjoy to this day.

Literary readers could trace such economic reasoning to Alfred P. Doolittle, George Bernard Shaw's delightful character in Pygmalion, one of London's "common dustmen." Doolittle held Keynesian economic views regarding spending and jobs and the proper rate for the creation of demand from any spare change he could scare up.

---

214. "Doolittle Economics" appeared in the July 4, 2011 issue of *Barron's Financial Weekly*.

In Pygmalion, and in the musical My Fair Lady that is based on the play, Doolittle learns that his daughter Eliza has moved in with Professor Henry Higgins to take elocution and grammar lessons. On the idea that this constitutes a loss to himself, he goes to see Higgins and his friend Pickering to try to get some 'benefits' out of them, specifically a five-pound note. He assures the two men that he understands that their intentions are honorable, for if they weren't he'd ask fifty. When asked whether he has any morals whatsoever, he tells the two gentlemen he "can't afford 'em."

Alfred P. Doolittle makes his case in
the 1938 movie Pygmalion.

Alfred Doolittle frames his final argument by focusing on the value of his daughter, "what he's brought up, he's fed, he's clothed by the sweat of his brow...until she growed big enough...to be interesting to you two gentlemen? Well, is five pounds unreasonable? I puts it to ya and I leaves it to ya."

Higgins: "Pickering, here. Shall we give him a fiver?"

Pickering: "He'll make bad use of it."

Doolittle: "No, no. So help me, guvnor. I shan't save it, spare it or live idle on it. There won't be a penny of it left on Monday. Just one good spree for myself and the missus...givin' pleasure to ourselves and employment to others."

Higgins: "This is irresistible. Let's give him ten."

Doolittle: "No. The missus wouldn't have the heart to spend ten. Ten pounds is a lot of money. Makes a man feel prudent-like. And then good-bye to happiness."

This is not to equate the spending of unemployment benefits with the particular spending that the bibulous Mr. Doolittle had in mind, but to point out that Alfred P. Doolittle was an economic theorist. Indeed, George Bernard Shaw was one of the founders of the London School of Economics.

Doolittle isn't merely bargaining with Higgins; he is advancing a broader, societal justification for a financial outlay. Doolittle assures Higgins he will inject those five pounds into the economy, and before Monday. He comments on the problem of prudence and thrift, and applies felicific calculus (without a nod to Jeremy Bentham[215]) in deciding to spend rather than save.

Doolittle also predicts the effect his outlay will have on employment, and although he does not estimate the multiplier effect, we must consider that he doesn't have the help of dozens of computer-trained dustmen at the Economic Policy Institute.

George Bernard Shaw arranges a grand ending for Alfred P. Doolittle. Shortly after his first encounter with Doolittle, Professor Higgins answers a letter from an American millionaire, one Ezra Wallingford, who is interested in starting moral-reform societies. Wallingford asks Higgins to recommend a moral instructor. Higgins writes back to suggest Alfred P. Doolittle, "one of the most original

---

215. Mr. Bentham developed the idea that all human economic behavior could be explained by the desire to maximize pleasure and minimize pain. This idea came to be known as the "felicific calculus."

moralists in England." Wallingford dies soon afterward, leaving a pot of money for Doolittle to use to lecture and live on.

Alfred tells Eliza that, is so doing, Henry Higgins has gotten his revenge and ruined his life, delivering him up "into the hands of middle-class morality." So situated, Alfred P. Doolittle's position is barely distinguishable from that of a tenured university economist, fatted by wealthy donors and contemptuous of the trappings of middle-class life.

The economic reasoning of the Democrats draws much from the same strain that animated Alfred P. Doolittle. They associate prudence and saving with idleness and unhappiness and the sterile image of money stacked up in bank vaults, while spirited spending leads to happiness and the employment of others.

The arguments in support of unemployment benefits are versatile, and can be used to support countless other programs as well: 'shovel-ready jobs,' a 'green economy' and 'infrastructure investments,' to name a few. They liberate capital from the capitalists and put some spending money in the hands of working folks, and thereby keep an ailing economy from producing more unemployment and unhappiness. The variations are many, limited only by the imaginations of public officials anxious to spend other peoples' money.

So the next time you hear another such official or economist trot out one of these arguments, think of Alfred P. Doolittle and his economic policy, and remember that the money will all be gone by Monday.

★ ★ ★

Postscript: The principles of Doolittle Economics—in the opinion of the High Priests of the Economics profession—were not followed closely enough in the response to the recession of 2008-2009. They complained that the federal spending was insufficient (at roughly

$1 trillion) and improperly targeted at people and institutions that "wouldn't spend much of it."

It was difficult to make the same complaint about the response to the decline in economic activity caused by the COVID 19-inspired shutdown of 2020-2021. The federal spending done in the United States in response to this downdraft in economic activity ran to $5 trillion over two years, and this time it was given directly to citizens who were often prevented from working due to health worries. Businesses were shut down, and federal spending was directed at compensating them with forgivable loans if they kept up their payrolls. The paperwork created to try to target the money was drafted such that billions in fraudulent claims were paid, but this money was also often spent in the sort of frenetic, fun-loving manner that Alfred P. Doolittle would endorse.[216] Even better from old Alfred P.'s perspective, the checks sent out to millions of Americans who were unemployed did not require its recipients to even bother to look for work.[217]

Practitioners of Doolittle Economics could hardly have asked for more. Consumer spending remained strong even as economic activity almost stopped. Amazon delivery trucks were kept very busy. Amazon had to resort to renting from other truck companies to keep their package deliveries going. Netflix rented millions and millions of videos. Food delivery services of all types flourished.

---

216. Examples abound here. Typical was the Oakland, California woman who claimed millions fraudulently and— according to court documents—spent $184,000 on private jet travel, other airfare, and hotel expenses; $124,000 on luxury purchases from Louis Vuitton, Neiman Marcus, and Nordstrom; $16,000 on boat and car rentals; and $14,000 on restaurants and entertainment. Another $150,000 was spent on Mercedes, Land Rover, and Nissan automobiles. Old Alfred P. would have been impressed by this show of "giving pleasure to ourselves and employment to others."

217. I refer here to musical version *My Fair Lady*, in which Alfred P. discusses his philosophy in the song "With a Little Bit of Luck," in which he sings "The Lord above gave Man an arm of iron, so he could do his job and never shirk; The Lord above gave Man an arm of iron but… with a little bit of luck, with a little bit of luck…someone else will do the blinkin' work.

Unemployment shot up with the mandatory business closures, but in percentage terms it quickly subsided with the re-openings, and nearly everyone who wanted to work could find a job. Total employment, however, was much slower to recover. Many businesses simply couldn't make it through—in some cases because they couldn't attract workers. This caused worry and concern in some quarters.

Then an odd thing happened, at least in the opinion of those Doolittle Economics practitioners. Prices started to shoot up for the seemingly unforeseeable reason that things requiring workers to assemble them were in short supply. It was seen at supermarkets: meat, spices, toilet paper, pet food were all in short supply and priced high. Then it was discovered that new cars were scarce because the auto assembly lines were difficult to keep supplied when the workforce of the parts manufacturers was being paid to stay home. People gradually began to do more driving and flying, which used crude oil that wasn't being re-supplied to refineries because the oil fields had been mothballed and the workers sent home in the early days of the pandemic when demand dropped to nearly zero. Workers willing to work were scarce, but the wage gains they were able to exact were cancelled out by these higher costs, and all others lost ground.

The inflation that began to gather momentum in early 2021 when "too many dollars" were clearly chasing "too few goods" had to be explained by the mandarins of the Doolittle Economics School. The President, the Treasury Secretary, the Chairman of the Federal Reserve Board—all members in good standing—formulated a one-word explanation, and they were quickly echoed by their acolytes. "Transitory," they all shouted, seemingly in unison. "This inflation will be transitory." As of the time of this writing, the transitory nature of this inflationary spiral is still of indeterminate length.

Chapter 14

THE ETERNAL DEBTOR

There are any number of wonderful characters in English literature that illuminate for the reader the essential nature of the hopeless debtor. Some enjoy the pathetic Mr. Micawber, Charles Dickens' sympathetic rogue in David Copperfield, who is "confidently expecting something to turn up." Others enjoy the quiet, respectable Bloomsbury desperation of Mr. Sedley in William Thackeray's Vanity Fair, a stockbroker who is convinced that but for Napoleon Bonaparte's escape from the island of Elbe—an event that caused Mr. Sedley's securities to collapse in price—all his financial plans would have worked out. There is something slightly pathetic, but at the same time wistful and beautifully human about the chronic debtor in literature—a confused, self-deluding hopefulness. From a literary perspective, such people are much more appealing than the hard-boiled financial types who try to get them to 'see sense.' Perhaps that is why they are such popular literary figures: The reader is sure to like them.

Literature supplies equally appealing sets of characters in the form of families of such people: the aging, often aristocratic family that gradually loses interest in accumulating wealth and opts instead to live off the wealth their ancestors left them. The decline doesn't usually involve descent of the family into complete penury; more often it becomes a state of collective impotence and inactivity.

Those who prefer such a 'family fall' from these greater heights, heights both social and economic, might enjoy the gradual dissipation and dissolution of the Flyte family in Evelyn Waugh's Brideshead

Revisited. This literature appears in other languages as well: Giuseppe di Lampedusa's The Leopard illustrates such a decline in an old aristocratic Sicilian Catholic family, and Thomas Mann's Buddenbrooks tells a similar story of the gradual decline in the work ethic among the members of a family of North German protestant merchants.

The Russian playwright Anton Chekhov also gave us a wonderful, somewhat more humorous portrait of such a family in The Cherry Orchard, first produced in 1904. Chekhov's play uses the family's vast cherry orchard as a sort of metaphor to illustrate this dissolution. The family obsesses over preservation of their magnificent orchard even as their finances are collapsing in a way that makes saving the orchard impossible anyway.

An eerily similar botanical backdrop is arranged near the seat of power of the United States government, a government that spurns any talk of aristocratic airs but that in matters of temperament and finance shares certain wistful, self-deceiving features with Chekhov's old aristocratic family.

Cutting Down the Cherry Trees

First appeared in the March 26, 2012.[218]

Madame Ranevskaya would feel at home in Washington. The 100th anniversary of the planting of Washington's cherry trees, alongside Washington's continuing fiscal imprudence, brings to mind the play by Chekhov.

Every spring, the citizens of the nation's capital and a horde of tourists celebrate with parades and cultural events the blooming of the cherry trees near the Jefferson Memorial. These trees were gifts from the mayor of Tokyo in 1912, and they blossom with beautiful pink-and-white flowers that reflect the spring sunlight to dazzling effect.

---

218. "Cutting Down the Cherry Trees" appeared in the March 26, 2012 issue of *Barron's Financial Weekly*. Since it appeared, federal debt has more than doubled, so the article is—if anything—more poignant now than it was then.

Cherry trees in DC: Life imitating art?

It is becoming difficult not to be reminded by Washington's Cherry Blossom Festival, and by the nearby government's precarious finances, of another grove of cherry trees that bloomed (in theatrical form) in Russia, surrounded—just as in Washington—by people of high social standing completely unable to deal with their debts.

Anton Chekhov wrote his great play, The Cherry Orchard, in 1904. The play portrays an aristocratic family returning to their vast Russian estate from Paris to find their finances in ruins and the ancient property and its huge cherry orchard in foreclosure.

"It's All So Vulgar"

The leader of this returning retinue is the owner of the estate, Madame Ranevskaya. She and the others look at the blooming cherry trees and, oblivious of the looming foreclosure proceedings, they reminisce about the idyllic childhoods they spent there. A rich, local merchant who grew up as a serf on the estate remembers kindnesses shown him by Madame and the family, and he offers them financial advice. He suggests ways they might raise money and save the estate from foreclosure, but his suggestions fall on deaf ears.

"Forgive me," he says finally in exasperation, "but such frivolous people as you are, so queer and un-businesslike—I never met in my life." He is a sort of czarist Pete Peterson.[219]

The merchant assures the family that it could raise the money needed by cutting down the cherry trees and leasing the land for summer cottages, but the family won't hear of it. "This orchard is even mentioned in the encyclopedia," Madame's brother, Gayev, claims. Madame can't bring herself to consider the idea. " Cottages—summer people—forgive me, but it's all so vulgar."

Similar suggestions are made to the debt-laden government in Washington, with similar results. Raising money by leasing land for oil or mineral development, or by selling unneeded government land or buildings? These are all unacceptable ideas. The new land use may threaten historic sites or aquifers or certain species of flora or fauna or government jobs. There is also the blight that oil derricks and commercial activity wreak on the landscape—it's all so vulgar.

Madame's daughters understand the family's financial trouble, but one tells the other on returning that "Mama wouldn't understand. When we had dinner at the stations, she always ordered the most expensive dishes."

The particular fiscal genius of the financially troubled federal

---

219. Peter G. Peterson, Secretary of Commerce during the Nixon Administration and later co-founder of financial-services firm The Blackstone Group, later set up a charitable foundation dedicated to "addressing America's long-term fiscal challenges."

government lies in making whatever it orders, from solar cells to corn muffins, more expensive than it should be.

A Lack of Attention

Madame and the group are visiting an abandoned chapel on the estate one evening when a tramp emerges from the darkness. He asks directions, and then asks for "30 kopecks for a hungry Russian." Madame searches her purse before absentmindedly handing him a gold piece. Her daughter, annoyed, exclaims that, "at home, the servants have nothing to eat, and you gave him a gold piece."

Our government is subject to similar criticism—from all sides. One 'progressive' group, appalled by recent school-budget cuts, noted on its website that there is no shortage of money for schools elsewhere. "Let's start calling Wisconsin Iraq!" they counseled their followers. As a number of politicians on both sides of the aisle have asked: "Why do we give money to people who hate us, when they'll hate us for free?"

Gayev is unable to focus on the family's debt problem. As finances are discussed, he withdraws, and daydreams of playing billiards. "Bank shot in the corner!" he says to himself. "Three cushions in the side pocket!"

With expenditures running at over 160 percent of revenues, are those who run the government in Washington paying any more attention than Gayev?

Madame hopes her wealthy aunt will pay her debts, but the money her aunt sends isn't enough. Madame decides to use the money to return to Paris. "Long live auntie!" she exclaims.

Debt reduction is no more popular in Washington than it was with Madame. PayGo ('pay as you go'), Balanced Budget Amendments, Budget Enforcement Acts, Gramm-Rudman—there have been countless enactments to reduce deficits and retire debt. They have all run aground when our elected officials happen upon a new expenditure that they judge to be more popular with their constituents than debt reduction.

Is Anything Left?

We can't know how things will turn out near the cherry trees along the Potomac, but we do know how things turn out near the cherry trees in Chekhov's play. The estate is sold at auction (to the rich former serf), and the family prepares to leave its ancient home. They share hugs and tears. Madame asks after the family's loyal old manservant, and is told that he is in the hospital, but in fact he's still in the house. Quiet descends after they leave, broken by the mournful sound of an axe striking a cherry tree outside. We see the old, feeble manservant walk in, sit among the ancient furnishings, and wonder out loud at his lost strength and that of the family he served. "Nothing is left," he mumbles, "nothing."

Washington's cherry trees are not about to be cut down; Treasury debt is not collateralized. The situation in Washington is different, although exactly how much different is hard to say. The federal government, like Madame, is given huge amounts of money that it did not have to earn and occupies itself with spending it unwisely. But our earnest, highly educated government officials appear to worry about their debt problem, while Madame did not. Our government can also print dollars, while Madame could not print rubles. Different, yes–but by how much?

★ ★ ★

A recurring theme in these pages is the idea that economics is not a science, at least not in the same sense that the physical sciences are science. The physical sciences concern themselves with studying forces and matter, and when confronted with an interesting question, its practitioners can run carefully controlled experiments. Those 'social scientists' who study the behavior of humans aren't nearly so fortunate. They must infer their conclusions from maddening piles of statistics—piles of such statistics often derived from surveys—and the experiments they run cannot be so elegantly controlled.

The preface to this book mentions the ground-breaking scientific paper published in 1915 in which Albert Einstein laid out his fascinating yet mystifying General Theory of Relativity. Einstein knew that the theory he was advancing was at variance with some of the time-tested laws first advanced by Isaac Newton some 200+ years earlier. Newton's laws had been exhaustively tested and verified, and Einstein knew it. As mentioned, Mr. Einstein therefore set out a series of three tests by which his theory could be confirmed by showing that his predictions would work better than Newton's. These were very specific tests, one of which – the most famous one, the one of legend—involved traveling to the part of the globe where there would be a complete solar eclipse in May 1919. If by photographing the position of certain stars, it could be shown that during the eclipse, the position of those stars was shifted slightly from the Newtonian prediction, Einstein's theory could be confirmed. Einstein reasoned that the light from these specific stars that would be near the Sun on this particular day in May would be shifted in 'apparent' position by more than that predicted by Newton's math. The difference between Einstein's prediction and Newton's well-tested rule was very slight: less than 1/1000th of a degree of arc. The position of these specific stars near the Sun is not visible to those of us on Earth without the benefit of the solar eclipse. Einstein offered that if his theory did not improve on Newton's prediction of the position of those stars during that eclipse, his theory could be discarded.

In formulating these tests of his own theory, Einstein was fully demonstrating a fact that scientists had always taken for granted: the idea of falsification. Mundane scientific advancements, like laws governing mechanical motion or chemical behavior, are very easy to test, and if they do not pass those tests, they are quickly discarded. Einstein was doing what physical scientists have always done in offering up a theory, but he was going one step further: Because his new theory and the implications of his new theory were not that easy to understand let alone test, he offered his own tests.

The rule regarding true scientific theory is thus set: If it can't be shown to be wrong, it can't be right either. This rule is rigorously enforced in the physical sciences, and keeps its practitioners from advancing nonsense. Such a rule is seldom discussed in the social sciences. Social scientists often run 'controls' in which two populations are subjected to the same treatment and differences between the groups observed and quantified, but this is not quite the same thing because the groups are somewhat small and composed of humans who are never exactly the same. The drive to publish and discuss results is so central to the job of a social or a biological scientist that there simply isn't time or money available to test their results and theories thoroughly before publishing.

The differences between the physical and the social sciences can also be seen in the statistical methods they employ in their research, as well as the repeatability of their results and conclusions. Statisticians have seen an explosion of interest in some of their more arcane methods of data analysis in recent decades as social scientists have begun to give their work some statistical patina. Grim experience has taught that one source of the lack of repeatability in the social and biological sciences is in these statistical methods used and the lack of strength of the correlations and dependencies thus developed. Most physical science experimentation involves the systematic study of three, four, maybe five variables that can be well controlled and that might 'plausibly' influence the physical response, with the hope that the experimentation will allow the researcher to develop an equation or a model that will involve only two or three that can be shown to explain at least 95 percent of the variability in the response studied. This information is then summarized in what such scientists call 'equations.' Social scientists routinely screen many more variables, turning their data set analysis into a 'fishing expedition' of sorts that might hope to explain maybe 50, or perhaps as much as 60 or 70 percent of the variability. Such work often results in something such researchers call a 'model,' which in specificity and precision has little in common with an equation. A study looking at a dozen variables hoping to explain a little more than half of the variability in the response is a study that will be difficult to reproduce.

This same sort of 'fishing expedition' approach is the basis of the current fascination with 'big data.' An example, one that might be familiar to the reader, might be instructive: I bought a very specific part for the automatic garage door opener installed at my house, using—of course—the searching and shopping power available on the internet. For months afterwards, I was confronted with pop-up ads extolling the merits of other garage door opener deals and sites that could be used to look for more garage door opener parts. The information sent into the computer system by ordering a somewhat obscure part for a garage door opener was causing me to be identified, with an associated degree of statistical certainty, as a garage door repairman, someone who would undoubtedly need to order more such parts in the future.

This is harmless, and somewhat commercially useful in that those persons who are in fact repairing garage door openers for a living are getting good offers for parts they will need to buy. The statistical methods employed, however, are only attempting to improve a little bit on the normal 'shooting in the dark' approach of advertising, and merely trying to improve the odds that their ad campaigns will rise above that of mere randomness. Mathematical algorithms are employed to do this, but their goal is hardly to arrive at some demonstrable, eternal truth.

There is yet another source of error and imprecision. It is one many that social scientists and data analysts are barely aware of. In the physical sciences, equations expressing the dependencies between variables are often checked to make sure they are 'dimensionally homogeneous.' This means that, in the parlance of scientists and engineers, "the units cancel." For example, Einstein's famous equation $E=mc^2$ equates energy with a mass times a velocity times a velocity. The velocity "c" in this equation is the speed of light, which is a big number. Mass multiplied by acceleration is force, and force times distance is energy. Einstein's equation involves mass times a velocity times a velocity, and an acceleration times a distance involves the same physical units as a velocity times a velocity, so mc^2 expresses energy, and the equation is 'dimensionally homogeneous.' The ideal gas law that is so ubiquitous in chemistry and physics, $PV=nRT$, involves a constant "R", the 'gas constant,' which varies in nominal value depending on the units of pressure, volume, temperature, and the number of molecules involved. The gas constant is actually a constant value; the number merely changes as the units in which it is expressed change.[220] When done properly by choosing the correct gas constant with the correct combination of units of measure, the units on both sides of the equal sign, when multiplied, are the same, and then the units 'cancel' and then—and only then—will the equation yield the correct answer. Such dimensional analysis also keeps the physical scientist from mouthing nonsense, from explaining pressure changes using units of distance or energy or volume, for

---

220. A common way to express the gas constant is 0.0821 liter*atmospheres per mole per degree Kelvin.

example. There is nothing, and I mean absolutely nothing, like this elegant dimensional analysis done in the social sciences.

Units of measure are extremely important in the physical sciences. They are scarcely discussed by data analysts and social scientists. A nice example of how this can lead to misunderstanding and confusion is the idea of the economic 'multiplier,' an idea that sounds very scientific. On closer examination, however, it could use a little dimensional analysis. The connection with debt? This misunderstanding is useful to those who wish to propose spending a little government money on a project they have in mind, and who feel they need a scientific justification for doing so.

'Multiplier' Mischief, OR How to Try to Spend One's Way to Prosperity

The standoff in Washington D.C. has reached almost comic levels. The two sides of the aisle now talk past one another. On almost any issue, Democrats insist we cannot "turn our backs" on the vulnerable, and Republicans insist that we're saddling the young with impossible bills. The two sides have developed their own partisan shtick to justify their positions, like an old Vaudeville "Who's On First?" routine.

The yearly food stamp debate is a case in point. Each side comes armed with facts to spout. Democrats tout the 'multiplier' effect of food stamp spending. Republicans complain about debt and the growth of the program.

Citizens might ponder: If food stamp spending 'multiplies' so effectively, does it really add to the debt at all? Economists could help answer this important question, but most are too busy choosing sides in the debate and arguing past one another to be of much help.

The 'economic multiplier' attempts to predict the change in some measure of economic activity, usually 'total national income' or GDP, connected with the spending of money—government money in most cases. The math behind the 'multiplier' is blessedly simple:

($-amount of government spending) X (the "multiplier") = (Increase in GDP)

As an example, a lump sum of government money spent on an 'infrastructure' project—re-paving a road, for example—results in income to the road crew and to the gas stations that sell them fuel to get them to the job site and to the sandwich shops that sell them lunches. The total income related to the project should therefore exceed the original sum spent on the crew and supplies, so the 'multiplier' might be greater than 1.0.

The first problem is the units of measure: Spending and GDP are not the same. Although both are measured in currency, money spent is single-counted, and it is appropriated and spent quickly. GDP involves double and triple counting—spending and the resulting income and re-spending of that income to create still more income—measured over a longer period of time. They are apples and oranges. The mathematical relationship between the two should therefore involve a number best described as a conversion factor between one unit of measure (cash spending) and the other (GDP). "Multipliers," as the term is used in the hard sciences, are normally unit-less numbers—'scalars,' or 'coefficients'—defining the amplification or attenuation of a quantity or the weightings in an equation, so that the units of the quantity being multiplied don't change when they are multiplied.

Economists explain that they use 'multipliers' when equating 'exogenous' and 'endogenous' variables, verbiage that hints at their interest in being clearly understood.

The more serious problem with such usage is that the term 'multiplier' implies the money spent is multiplying like rabbits. When rabbits multiply they do not change form; they simply multiply into more and more rabbits. They do not multiply themselves into orangutans, or egrets. This is how 'multiplying' is normally understood. Economists must know that their use of the term 'multiplier' in this context is misleading. They must know that politicians love using the term because it makes the careless spending of large sums of government money sound vaguely constructive. At least one prominent politician, a Speaker of the U.S. House of Representatives, was quoted extolling the "bang for the buck" that the 'multiplier effect' of certain spending can have on the economy.

Economists associate different 'multipliers' with different sorts of spending: There is one for unemployment benefits, for food assistance, tax refunds, tax cuts. The multiplier associated with food assistance is thought to be larger than others and greater than 1.0, for the simple reason that nearly all such spending will quickly become income to grocery stores. A 'multiplier' greater than 1.0, however, implies that something is increasing as a result of the process of spending. This is so clearly not the case that the outsider is left to wonder if economists are as interested in conveying information as they are in directing those lump sums.

Let's do the math surrounding the food stamp 'multiplier' using some science.

The multiplier associated with government spending on food assistance is generally thought to be about 1.7 or so, meaning that for every billion dollars spent on such benefits, there is a corresponding positive effect on "national income," or "GDP," of about $1.7 billion dollars. This 'food assistance multiplier' is estimated by different public policy groups at between 1.0 and 2.0. We're not talking here about the precision associated with estimates of, say, the speed of light.

Spending and GDP are not equivalent measures. A more useful metric to compare with government spending—one for which the term 'multiplier' might make sense to technicians and scientists and voters—would be resulting government revenue. Spending and revenue are identical in that both are measured in currency, with no double counting. Tracking revenue has the added benefit of determining the extent to which the government can actually sustain such spending—i.e., whether certain forms of spending might create a true multiplier effect that could then fund and actually grow more such spending, as the term 'multiplier' implies.

Federal government tax revenue is consistently around 20 percent of GDP in the U.S., with little variation.[221] A billion dollars of food assistance therefore generates—if we assume a 'multiplier' of 1.7—about $1.7 billion in GDP, which then produces around $340 million in government tax revenue.

In comparing like quantities, roughly 34 percent of spending on any single lump sum of food assistance will be re-captured in additional revenue. If that 34 percent in revenue is in turn spent on more such benefits and the resulting revenues spent yet again, only five such cycles of spending will reduce the original billion-dollar outlay to roughly $4.5 million dollars in revenue. This means that after five spending cycles, 99.55 percent of the original outlay—199 parts in 200—has been lost to the government. Some multiplier!

Economists should clear things up. Why not clarify that different forms of spending simply 'convert' the spending into general economic activity at different rates, or that different types of spending 'cascade' or 'diffuse' through the economy differently? Issuing food stamps

---

221. This empirical observation – based on six decades of grim experience – is called "Hauser's Law," after Stanford economist W. Kurt Hauser. Mr. Hauser observed that U.S. federal tax revenues as a percentage of GDP averaged roughly 19% of GDP, whether the top tax rate was 92% (as it was in 1952-1953) or 28% (as in 1988-1990). The slight variations from 19% observed over time had more to do with the health of the economy (healthier economies generated higher percentages) than with the particular income tax rates imposed at the time. This is a grim reality for planners who wish to propose higher tax rates to "pay" for new programs.

will increase national income and therefore government revenue, but shouldn't economists point out that the cost of the assistance will always vastly exceed the resulting revenue? Shouldn't they tell the public that most government spending is not remotely 'self-financing'? The use by economists of the term 'multiplier' obscures these important facts and allows the two sides to continue to talk past one another.

Chapter 15

MONEY MISMANAGEMENT

"We Have Met the Enemy, and He is Us."[222]

Seventeenth century scientist and mathematician Blaise Pascal of France was one of the brightest lights in a century of real incandescence: Shakespeare, Galileo, Kepler, Milton, Bacon, Newton, Leibnitz, Descartes, etc. The seventeenth century world he lived in was still quite primitive, however, and he could hardly help noticing some of the folly of his contemporaries: the thirty-year religious war that was waged over most of his short life, the tulip bulb financial mania that consumed nearby Holland, etc. At one point, he was moved to observe that, "All men's miseries derive from not being able to sit in a quiet room alone."

The problem of managing money with an eye toward a comfortable retirement was not one that appears to have concerned Pascal, even though his insights about misery seem to have been inspired by the problem.

Modern twentieth century money management 'science' has finally caught up with Pascal.

The systematic study of investor psychology has revealed specific truths that might have caused Pascal to smile knowingly. It has been conventional wisdom in recent decades among investors that you want to be very wary of 'popular' stocks, those whose popularity is often traceable to the fact that they have been shooting upward recently.[223]

---

222. Pogo.

223. This was expressed best in the delightful 1940 book "Where are the Customers' Yachts?" by Fred Schwed. Mr. Schwed describes the movement of two securities: The much discussed and actively traded "American Popularity" and the thinly traded "United Chamber Music."

The idea stems from the observation that when the stock movement progresses to the point where it has captured the attention of large numbers of investors, the price has usually exceeded its rational price, and that to buy at the now higher price is a bad bet, and one more than likely destined to decline than to continue increasing. The systematic studies done on this have indeed confirmed this bit of conventional wisdom, and more: Not only are popular stocks best avoided, but—conversely—stocks that have been doing very poorly of late are often good bets to do better than average in the future.

Is human nature hopeless? From these studies of investor psychology, it appears so. The problems created by humanity's tendency to act on immediate impulse have always been legion, but it had been felt that finance was more rational than the humans who comprised its moving parts. Not so. The field of study has been given a name—behavioral finance—and some big financial firms have gone so far as to employ its experts.

These experts have isolated particular problems that rhyme with other distinctive human failings. For instance, such experts have determined that 'inertia'—the tendency of humans to do nothing when faced with a decision that must be made—is an investor problem. If this doesn't sound like a problem that infests most humans you know, you must live in a higher-functioning bit of the planet than your author. How about "bounded self-control"? This is the name they've given to the problem of having the correct intentions but not the willpower required to change one's behavior to conform to those intentions. The multi-billion-dollar dieting industry is utterly dependent on this little flaw in human nature. Then there is 'myopia,' which these experts call

---

Schwed concludes "The pathetic fallacy is that what are thought to be the best are in truth only the most popular – the most active, the most talked of, the most boosted, and consequently, the highest in price at that time."

the inability to see or imagine 20 or 30 years into the future—hardly a rare shortcoming among most of the adults I know.

Behavioral scientists have also identified the simple problem of 'attachment,' or 'loss aversion.' We all make some bad decisions, and when we do, we have a little trouble acknowledging the fact. We develop a fondness for the problems we've chosen and the approach we've taken to solve them, and perhaps we rebel at the thought of hazarding another decision that might be still more disastrous. The rational creature buried deep inside us might be able to get us to fess up and discard the burdens caused by these bad decisions if we could just find that creature and listen to him or her.

Pascal knew all this as well. He also gave us the pithy insight that, "The heart has its reasons of which reason knows nothing." In the allocating of financial assets, it is this heart that—for most of us—should probably not be consulted, but—alas—probably will be.

Our Bad Behavior

The new study of behavioral finance, which seeks to root out the sources of investor behavior that grow in the fertile field of human error, certainly has plenty of work it can do. I can see its practitioners busying themselves with the study of certain commonly encountered 'chart' patterns that technicians have observed for years: tops, straddles, shoulders. They'll surely attempt to explain why 'momentum' investing works so well, at least right up to the point when it doesn't. These price patterns reflect the immediate reactions that the investing public has to fast-changing securities prices. Some of these reactions are less than perfectly rational, of course, and many of them are distinctly unprofitable. The field's experts can't help but eventually conclude that most investors would be better off ignoring these daily gyrations and simply buying and holding, that most investors make mistakes when they let their emotions dictate their trading.

In the interest of helping the field along, then, I would like to offer an insight from my investing experience that might help its practitioners to understand why such a conclusion will not increase dramatically the legions of buy-and-hold investors. To put it simply: 10 percent-per-year is boring.

We have all been taught to expect certain returns from certain asset classes: a couple percent over inflation for bonds, perhaps 8-10 percent for stocks, etc. These returns seem so adequate when we start out, and when—as we are all so tempted to do—we extrapolate these returns for a few dozen years or so. What we are not quite so prepared for is exactly how it feels to earn these rates of return on a daily basis, and how with only the slightest bit of imagination these returns can appear capable of improvement.

Fred Schwed, the author of the invaluable 1940 investing guide-book *Where are the Customers' Yachts?*, was fascinated by the pro-fessional speculators he knew who willingly put millions at risk in taking progressively larger and more precarious financial bets when they already had a pile big enough to live comfortably. "They seem to believe with Mother Goose," he wrote, "that a treetop is the proper place for a cradle."

Mr. Schwed suggested such persons were "incurable romantic(s)," often "egotistical." It was the nature of the business, he claimed, "a business of dreams."

It is also possible that what is at work is a simpler, more general human failing, one you might call Perpetual Discontent with One's Immediate Circumstances, or more prosaically, Impatience. This fail-ing stems from the fact that the speed at which reasonably profitable public companies can compound our capital is glacial when compared to the rate at which we would like to see our material future take shape. There is a little of the Jay Gatsby in most of us, if we were to be honest, and the erratic 8-10 percent per annum we are taught to expect from common stocks eventually tends to dismay us with "its ferocious indifference to the drums of [our] destiny."[224]

Individual investors who buy and sell individual stocks can confirm this for themselves. They can go back through their brokerage statements and find securities that, over a particular year, generated an 8-10 percent return. They should try to recall how they felt about the performance of that stock at the end of that year. Chances are good that they did not regard it as having generated much of a return at all. A $20 stock with a 3 percent dividend need increase in price to only $21 to generate this 'average' market return, a change in price so small as to be hardly noticeable, especially if the price usually changes 25-50 cents during an average trading day. No wonder we find ourselves attracted to gizmo stocks with little in the way of sales or earnings: At least they'll move decisively in one direction or another in the very near future and stop this middling, mediocre performance!

Most market participants have discussed the tremendous increases and declines in price of certain 'tech' stocks. Seldom does the discussion end without mention of the silver lining of price action: "Sure it went from 100 to 2," you'll hear, "but if a guy had bought at 2 he could have made a quick double!" In this way a stock with the recently demonstrated potential for falling in value by 98 percent can still be spoken of favorably because at the bottom, it was capable of a quick 100 percent snap back. It leaves one to consider if the only truly unforgivable sin a security can commit is to simply sit still and throw off profits in the form of dividends.

---

224. *The Great Gatsby* by F. Scott Fitzgerald (New York, 1925).

Traders and individual investors are hardly alone in their interest in near-term price action and the potential it has for goosing returns. Mutual Fund and Hedge Fund managers have home remodeling projects on hold and 'upgrade-able' vacation plans, too. Most of them are paid based on the assets they have under management, and most know that actually growing these assets through capital appreciation is a pitifully inadequate way to realize their true income potential. Far more lucrative is a few months or even a quarter or two of hot performance that can draw a slug of new money to manage, and hot performance can hardly be realized without taking a few chances.

The new high priests of behavioral finance should therefore go easy on their subjects. Sure, mistakes are being made, often with depressing regularity, and these mistakes can seem very obvious and preventable if investors just understood more fully how their "fear and greed" impulses lead them to commit trading errors. When these high priests feel like getting a bit critical, however, or when it seems to them that the old saw "the masses are asses" can also be applied to the capitalists, they should pause. They should recall that there are hot new sports cars in the showroom windows, and private school tuition fees are being discussed in the evenings, and vacation homes that would be so much easier to swing if only a certain little security could continue heading north just a little while longer.

Chapter 16

THE SOCIALIST ORPHANAGE

First appeared in 2020.[225]

"Success has many fathers and failure is an orphan."[226]

The merits of socialism are again a hot topic of political debate and discussion—debates often more heated than enlightening. Politics is properly concerned with the future, but debates over socialism often focus on whether history can teach us anything. In the case of socialism, the answer is: quite a lot.

Collective ownership of productive assets is the textbook definition of 'socialism.' Such collectivizing can be accomplished in different ways. The pooling of assets can be voluntary, so that the members of the group are self-selected. If not voluntary, confiscation of the assets from those who built or bought or otherwise own them is necessary, something eventually requiring force. Less violently, wages and assets can be taxed at very high rates so that the benefits of owning those assets are transferred from the owner to the group. All of these methods have been tried with results that have led not to any real effort to understand them but instead to intellectual contortions on the part of socialist thinkers to disown or ignore them. One popular approach is to dismiss earlier forms as not the 'true' socialism

---

225. "The Socialist Orphanage" appeared in the Fall 2020 issue of *Financial History* magazine.

226. The original idea behind this phrase dates from the writings of Roman historian Cornelius Tacitus around the year 100AD. It was later used by Italian politician Galezzo Ciano in 1942, and most recently by U.S. president John Kennedy following the failed invasion of the Bay of Pigs in Cuba in 1961.

they envision, one that—they insist—has yet to be tried.[227]

An early and eloquent spokesman for this idea of collective ownership was an eighteenth century Swiss, Jean-Jacques Rousseau. Born to an upper-middle class family in Geneva, Rousseau led a directionless life until about the age of 37, when the announcement of an essay contest in a Parisian literary magazine got him thinking:

Rousseau rests under a tree: Socialism as fever dream?

"Crowds of vivid ideas thronged into my mind with a force and confusion that threw me into unspeakable agitation. I felt my head

---

227. This line of reasoning was very recently offered by Professor Cornel West, a well-known and outspoken American advocate of socialism. When asked about these many failures of socialism in a nationally televised interview in 2018, West said "I don't think democratic socialism as an ideal has been able to be embodied in a larger social context."

whirling in a giddiness like that of intoxication. A violent palpitation oppressed me. Unable to walk for difficulty of breathing, I sank down under one of the trees by the road, and passed half an hour there in such a condition of excitement that when I rose I saw that the front of my waistcoat was all wet with tears…Ah, if ever I could have written a quarter of what I saw and felt under that tree, with what clarity I should have brought out all the contradictions of our social system! With what simplicity I should have demonstrated that man is by nature good, and that only our institutions have made him bad!"[228]

Rousseau got around to writing essays, discourses, even novels. His underlying premise, however, remained: "Man was born free and is everywhere in chains." He saw in advanced civilization—its property laws, science, art, 'modern' Christianity—decadence, hierarchy, inequality, greed, moral decay: i.e., the chains. He traced the source, the wellspring of this immoral civilization: "The first man who, having enclosed a piece of ground, bethought himself of saying 'This is mine.'"[229]

Rousseau's ideal was a rustic village of simple yeoman farmers, a rural collective, a charming notion, and one that appealed to the utopian mind. After all, if our civilizing institutions have made us bad, replacing them with better ones would result in a better humanity—and who isn't in favor of a better humanity? If the reader can put this riveting book down for a moment, they might agree that there is some humanity within eyeshot that could stand some improving. Rousseau was also offering his followers a form of absolution, erasing guilt they might feel for past misdeeds and placing blame squarely on some flawed institution.

---

228. "Citizen of Geneva — Selections from the Letters of Jean Jacques Rousseau", translated by C.W. Hendel (1937, Oxford) p. 208.

229. *Discourse on the Origin and Basis of Inequality Among Men* by J.J. Rousseau (1754)

If private property is the root cause of greed and civilization's resulting decay, then the institutions responsible for protecting such property—the courts, the deed registrars—should be changed. Reflective persons might observe that there are many types of greed—sexual greed, the grasping for power, the drive for adulation and attention—but Rousseau and his followers focused on the one dealing with property, the one protected by those institutions, the one they could do something about.

Voluntary sharing of property was one obvious solution. It was first tried in the utopian communes of the early nineteenth century: secluded, rural communities organized by wealthy, influential leaders like Robert Owen of Scotland and Charles Fourier of France. Such communes banned the arms-length transactions involving labor and goods that were thought to be based on greed. Members worked the property for the benefit of all the commune's members.

By the mid-nineteenth century, however, it was clear such communes could not sustain themselves and were failing due to inefficiency. Robert Owen's son worked alongside his father in their failed commune in southern Indiana, and later wrote that, "I do not believe that any industrial experiment can succeed which proposes equal remuneration to all men, the diligent and the dilatory."[230] Such communes were in this way like many family businesses, where the drive and ambition of the founder(s) is not necessarily shared by other family members.

A broader and more sustaining mandate was needed, one that could extend the reach of the theorist to everyone and exist in perpetuity—i.e., one involving government. German philosophy was ideally suited to provide one, a strain of which had a love-affair of sorts with government.

---

230. *Threading My Way* by R. D. Owen (London, 1874)

The cronyism and corruption that generally plagued government action in practice didn't seem to trouble them, and they saw the possibility of bringing about a governmentally mandated utopia. Prominent Prussian philosopher Georg Hegel was enchanted by the idea of unified state action to direct seemingly chaotic individual behavior. "The modern State, proving the reality of political community, when comprehended philosophically, could therefore be seen as the highest articulation of Spirit, or God in the contemporary world," he wrote, concluding "The State is God's will."[231]

First, however, such thinkers had to explain the flaws in these earlier utopian forms. Young Karl Marx of Trier, Germany cut his intellectual teeth critiquing these utopian communes.[232] He argued that organizers made their error in appealing to all members of society, ignoring the fact that society is comprised of classes whose interests are at odds with one another. Marx reasoned that the working class—he called "the proletariat"—was developing around the machinery of the dawning industrial age, and it had to take control from the capitalists—"the bourgeoisie"—by force, and impose a new governmental order that would collectivize all productive property and eventually rid society of classes and greed. In deference to these early utopian experiments, he called this final, blissful, classless and greedless world "communism."

The idea had a certain appeal when it was floated in Marx's 1848 work The Communist Manifesto. Industrialism did seem to be changing everything, and it was definitely creating some losers. Early industrial machines were not very productive and required little skill to operate. Then as now, supply drives down price, and industrial wages

231. *Hegel* by R. Plant (Indiana, 1973), p. 122-123, 181.

232. *Manifesto of the Communist Party* by K. Marx (London, 1848). In a section entitled "Critical-Utopian Socialism and Communism," Marx writes that "The undeveloped state of the class struggle [in these utopian communes] causes Socialists of this kind to consider themselves far superior to all class antagonisms."

were low.[233] Marx exhorted low wage workers to "unite" in revolution against the capitalists, telling them they "have nothing to lose but their chains!"[234]

Marx set about working on his magnum opus, what would become Das Kapital. Marx wrote for English-language newspapers but preferred to write in German. He worked on it at the British Museum in London, where his place of study later became a shrine of sorts. It took him until 1867 to come up with Volume I. In it he concluded that the divide between industrial workers and management was unbridgeable, that capitalists would maximize profits at the expense of workers, whose wages would inevitably decline as their numbers increased.[235]

Karl Marx was not the first nor the last person to effectively analyze a particular point in history just as conditions began to change. Alongside the path he walked to the British Museum, the world was changing in ways his theories could not explain. During the 1850s, `60s, and `70s, faster and more powerful machines used in London and elsewhere empowered those tradesmen with the skills to use them effectively, and as they became more productive, their wages tended to increase rather than decline as Marx predicted. The prices of goods that could be purchased with those wages also declined as goods of all

---

233. "But the price of a commodity, and therefore also of labor is equal to its cost of production. In proportion, therefore, as the repulsiveness of the work increases, the wage decreases." *Manifesto of the Communist Party* by K. Marx and F. Engels (1848).

234. Ibid

235. Marx put it this way in his chapter on Time-Wages: "If one man does the work of 1-1/2 or 2 men, the supply of labor increases, although the supply of labor-power [i.e., hours worked] on the market remains constant. The competition thus created between the workers allows the capitalist to force down the price of labor, while the fall in price allows him, on the other hand, to force up the hours of work even further." *Capital- Volume I* by K.Marx (1867, London 1990), p. 869.

types became more plentiful.[236] A perfectly good theory was being shot down by the dreadful specter of reality.

German philosophers may have been entranced by these socialist plans, but other, pragmatic Germans could see problems. Prussian politician Eugen Richter composed a little novel entitled Pictures of the Socialistic Future, published in 1891, a first person account imagining the effects of Marxist socialism on a modest German family that is initially enthusiastic for the proposed changes.[237] Family members begin to grumble as their bank balances are confiscated to achieve financial equality; their children are placed in state-run orphanages promoting formative equality; and their "unnecessary" furnishings are taken and re-purposed. The family is temporarily heartened by the government's plan to allow citizens to choose their own occupations. When the citizenry registers its job preferences, however, it is discovered that there are "a greater number of persons registered … as gamekeepers than there are hares within forty miles' circumference of Berlin," and that "The number of young women who have put their names down as waitresses and public singers is very considerable." At the same time "The entries for the more arduous labors of the road paver, the stoker, the smelter are more sparse," and "Those who have manifested a desire to become cleansers of sewers are, numerically, not a strong body." The idea is abandoned, and people are assigned jobs and relocated, with predictable effects on morale. The young and ambitious begin to leave. Fences are erected to halt the exodus. Armed sentries are ordered to shoot those attempting to flee. 1891.

Karl Marx died in 1883, still largely deaf to the incredible material

---

236. See "Prices" by G. Warren and F. Pearson (New York, 1933), p. 201. Table 38 displays average wages in England over this period and show no decline. From the publication of "Capital" in 1867 until Marx's death in 1883, average nominal wages in England increased 14%, and average purchasing power wages increased 40%.

237. *Pictures of the Socialistic Future* by E. Richter (London, 1907)

progress of the late nineteenth century—railroads, the telegraph and telephone, the automobile—that was occurring all around him. Most other economic thinkers around Marx couldn't help but notice. Many had to concede that the institutions protecting private property and the capital markets had so quickly and ambitiously commercialized that these advances were in some way responsible for this progress.

Socialism had to adjust. In London, just down the road from where Marx did his theorizing, a group of economically minded social thinkers coalesced, a group that could acknowledge what Marx could not. They called themselves "Fabian" socialists after Roman general Fabius Maximus–Fabius the Delayer[238]—and they believed not in revolution but in gradual change, and in private property, and in taxing the rich rather than overthrowing the institutions that produced the rich. They knew Marx, and they understood his limited vision. The most famous of them was Irish playwright George Bernard Shaw, who wrote that Marx was "without administrative ability," and his theories "generalized the human race under the two heads of bourgeoisie and proletariat apparently without ever having come into business contact with a living human being."[239]

Marx's ideas were impractical, but they were too appealing to some, and events furnished these ambitious acolytes the opportunity to impose Marxist order on large masses of people. They took control of governments throughout the world in the twentieth century: Russia and China most visibly, but other places like Cuba, Vietnam, Cambodia, Tanzania, Uganda, Venezuela, and throughout Eastern Europe. These were places where industrialism was less advanced, and Marx's 1848 ideas could still resonate. In more advanced places like Germany and Italy, the collectivist

---

238. Fabius the Delayer became famous in military history during the Second Punic War for choosing his battles carefully, avoiding direct confrontation with Hannibal's superior troop strength, opting instead for guerilla attacks on Carthaginian supply lines.

239. *The Truth about Soviet Russia* by Sidney and Beatrice Webb (1942). Mr. Shaw contributed an introductory chapter to the book entitled "The Webbs" in which he discusses Karl Marx.

impulse channeled high tax revenues into garish, cruel, aggressive regimes that rejected the Marxian goal of an international workers' paradise in favor of an ethno-centric, "nationalistic" socialism.[240] [241]

Looking back on the century, Oxford historian Paul Johnson diagnosed the problem as a fascination with abstract social science which, alas, wasn't science at all. He wrote that "by the year 1900 politics was already replacing religion as the chief form of zealotry."[242]

The experience of the ordinary citizen in these Marxist states followed Eugen Richter's novel, although the killing of the non-compliant began even more quickly than Richter predicted. It was horrific. Modern-day socialists now busy themselves with re-interpretation of these dreadful places. The killings, the slave laboring, the vast spending on munitions, the industrial pollution and nuclear meltdowns are cleverly dismissed as 'state capitalism,'[243] despite the fact that these

---

240. Nazi Germany's corporate tax policies accomplished the goal of de facto government ownership without confiscation of the assets. Nazi tax law dictated that corporate profits earned by German corporations in excess of 6% on their corporate equity had to be re-invested not in their business but in German government bonds, which — not coincidentally — were being issued in great profusion by the Third Reich to re-arm and re-invest in the country's infrastructure. The profits in excess of 6% were thus effectively taxed at 100% in the short-term, and the corporations holding those Reich bonds were made investors and partners with the Nazi regime in the longer-term

241. Herr Hitler himself was not ambiguous on this point regarding the socialist roots of the Nazi Party. In a May 1, 1927 (May Day) speech before about five thousand people in Berlin laying out the tenets of the Nazi Party, he announced "We are Socialists. We are enemies of the capitalistic economic system for the exploitation of the economically weak, with its unfair salaries, with its unseemly evaluation of a human being according to wealth and property instead of responsibility and performance and we are all determined to destroy this system under all conditions." *Adolf Hitler*, J. Toland (New York, 1976), p. 224-225. Some of Hitler's rivals within the Nazi Party also advocated socialism, and some of these people Hitler later had killed. The idea that he had them killed for their socialist beliefs is the thin reed used to try to catapult him and his party from the socialist ranks.

242. *Modern Times* by P. Johnson (1991), p. 784

243. Linguistics professor Noam Chomsky gave this line of reasoning an airing in an interview with the Detroit Metro Times in 1991: "Every industrial society is one form or another of *state* capitalism...Now in the Second World of the Soviet Union's dominance, there was also economic collapse [beginning around 1980]... a stagnation of the command economy system, which has even less to do with socialism than our system has to do with capitalism."

countries had no commercial banks or capital markets.

The Fabian Socialists, meanwhile, achieved some political success at the ballot box, notably in Britain and Scandinavia. The post-World War II British Labour governments of Clement Attlee, Harold Wilson, and James Callaghan nationalized industries, expanded public services, and pushed marginal tax rates to over 80 percent on upper middle-class incomes and to over 90 percent on high incomes. Similar initiatives were taken by governments in Scandinavia.

The freedoms the Fabians preserved, however, became a problem. Fabian socialism involved no border restrictions, no limitations on free expression. These freedoms produced a backlash among an odd new group the theorists could never have anticipated: The young, self-made rich, creatures our modern age has spawned and endowed with much social significance.

The fabulously successful British rock band The Beatles wrote lyrics in the mid-1960s descrying Harold Wilson's Fabian state. In "Taxman," the song opens with the taxman explaining to them. "Let me tell you how it will be, There's one for you, nineteen for me." This is not hyperbole. One for you and nineteen for the taxman is simply a tax rate of 95 percent.

Another British rock star, Mick Jagger of the group The Rolling Stones, explained in a television interview the band's move from Britain to France at about the same time: "In those days, in England, the high tax rate was 90 percent, so that's very hard...You made 100 pounds, they took 90. So it was very difficult to pay any debts back. So when we left the country, we would get more than the 10 pounds out of 100. You know, we might get 50 or something."

Swedes watched their famous movie director, Ingmar Bergman, move

---

Chomsky's talent for re-naming these societies should probably be classed as another of his linguistic achievements to Munich and their star tennis player, Bjorn Borg, move to Monaco to avoid Swedish tax collectors. The popular Swedish rock band ABBA wore ridiculous, sequined outfits on stage, because the high cost of such outfits was tax deductible, but only if the outfits were too outrageous to be of use as street clothing. "Nobody can have been as badly dressed on stage as we were,"[244] commented one band member years later.

The young rich were more notorious than numerous, so the harsh taxes paid by those who remained were inadequate to support vast spending. Britain tried to control the resulting inflation by limiting pay raises. Workers responded by going on strike, because Fabians also preserved the freedom to strike. In 1978, Britain's truck drivers and garbage collectors struck to protest the Labour government's proposed pay limits. Shortages resulted: food, petrol, heating oil–during the bitterly cold winter of 1978-1979.[245] Alongside the piles of uncollected garbage, conditions were thought positively Shakespearean: Prime Minister Callaghan himself called it Britain's "winter of discontent."

These unintended consequences caused a political backlash. The Tories wrested control of Parliament from the Fabians in May 1979 and reduced union control over workplaces. Top marginal rates were gradually reduced in Britain and Scandinavia from those 80-90 percent levels to around 50 percent today.

Time has healed the chilblains of the 1970s, though. The sting gone, some of today's politicians ignore the unintended consequences of those earlier policies. They offer new benefits—proposing new revenue through higher tax rates on "the few"—and ask voters to consider, "Why not?"

History, unlike politics, has no recuperative power. Ignoring or disowning historical events cannot heal them of their plain meaning.

---

244. *ABBA: The Official Photo Book* by P. Karlsson and J. Gradvall (2014).

245. The final indignity foisted on the British citizenry might have been the strike convened by a loosely affiliated group of grave diggers.

★ ★ ★

Postscript: There are those who feel no need for any re-interpretation of the historical record, even some for whom age and education should prevent the defense of ignorance. In 2016 and again in 2020, a long-time American social activist from the small state of Vermont, who had spent his long life in and around electoral politics, came close to winning the Presidential nomination of the Democratic Party. He had never been a member of the Democratic Party. He was an avowed, unapologetic socialist. He had honeymooned in Soviet Russia in the late 1980s. His 2016 campaign called for a political 'revolution'[246] of the established order, and he insisted that American business decisions be scrutinized and regulated and business assets re-directed, as they were improperly deployed in producing too many varieties of deodorants and sports shoes.[247] No mere Fabian socialist, he!

Senator Bernie Sanders' 2016 and 2020 presidential campaigns were surprisingly successful. He nearly won the nomination of a political party that he had never really joined. Imitation is indeed the sincerest form of flattery, and other candidates for the 2020 Democratic Party nomination rushed to embrace Mr. Sanders' policy prescriptions: free college, free health care, etc. all of it to be paid for with higher taxes on upper incomes.

Many of the enthusiastic supporters of these ideas are young, and perhaps they can be excused for believing that such ideas have never been tried and found wanting before. Many of these young people have been raised in a world in which the most powerful ideas are generated

---

246. "…What began last week in Iowa, what voters here in New Hampshire confirm tonight, is nothing short of the beginning of a political revolution." Senator Sanders' acceptance speech following his win in the New Hampshire Democratic Primary election in February 2016.

247. "You don't necessarily need a choice of 23 underarm spray deodorants or of 18 different pairs of sneakers when children are hungry in this country." This quote is from a television interview Senator Sanders gave CNBC television's John Harwood on Feb. 19, 2016.

by television programs and movies rather than by dry, black-letter history. "Ignorance is like a delicate exotic fruit," Oscar Wilde's Lady Bracknell says in The Importance of Being Earnest, "touch it and the bloom is gone." The ignorance of such young people might be 'touched' most successfully not with the historical facts recited earlier but with video images. Some of the best of these, alas, are somewhat old, black-and-white images. Nevertheless, it may be worth a try...

SOCIAL INJUSTICE? IT DEPENDS ON THE TIP

*Ninotchka, a 1939 movie starring Greta Garbo,
remains Hollywood's most vivid, humorous,
and accurate portrayal of socialism*

First appeared in 2016[248]

Economists who study markets, and others who believe that you pay for what you get, were appalled by how close Sen. Bernie Sanders came to winning the nomination of the Democratic Party. Some apparently imagined that the struggle against U.S. socialism had been won. Now they should see that it must be fought in every generation.

As one economist muttered recently, "For people 30 years of age and younger, saying 'Bernie Sanders is a socialist' cuts exactly no ice. It's useless. It doesn't persuade anyone."

Sanders' candidacy is now over, but his young supporters rattled their cages at the Democratic National Convention, and they intend to influence Democratic Party politics and platforms for years. They are energetic, and Sanders' "democratic socialism" feels to them like a fresh idea full of promise.

The benefits of socialism are appealing. Certain goods and services are 'free' to the citizenry. The costs of socialism are more subtle. Books

---

248. "Social Injustice? It Depends on the Tip" appeared in the September 5, 2016 issue of *Barron's Financial Weekly*.

have been written detailing these problems, but reading them takes time away from Facebook postings. So, for young readers who want to learn a little about socialism while having a few laughs, Hollywood offers the brilliant 1939 movie Ninotchka, the wittiest and most popular movie send up of socialism ever done.

Ninotchka is a romantic comedy starring Greta Garbo. The story opens on three members of the Russian Board of Trade, who have been sent to Paris to sell a 14-piece set of court jewels that until the Russian Revolution of 1917 belonged to the Russian Grand Duchess Swana, part of the 'billionaire class' that ruled the country. The Soviets are selling the jewels to raise money because they fear another poor harvest back in Russia.

Poor harvests were a Soviet specialty. Farmers lose interest in sowing and harvesting crops when the crops are confiscated and sent to Moscow.

The Grand Duchess escaped the revolution and is living in Paris. When she hears of the jewelry sale through her émigré network, she has a dashing young male friend file a petition to enjoin the sale pending clarification of title by a French court. Moscow hears of this legal difficulty, and sends its no-nonsense envoy extraordinaire—Greta Garbo's Ninotchka—to Paris to remove the injunction, sell the jewels, and bring the badly needed money back to Moscow. The young friend of the Grand Duchess, Count Leon (Melvyn Douglas), falls in love with Ninotchka, and there we have our romantic comedy.

The portrait of socialism under the Soviets in Ninotchka is devastatingly funny. Western audiences in 1939 still could laugh at the jokes about mass trials leading to "fewer but better Russians," even though it actually was brutal. Russia was far away.

Director Ernst Lubitsch, story writer Melchior Lengyel, and screenwriters Billy Wilder, Walter Reisch, and Charles Brackett knew their subject. Except for Brackett, these men were immigrants from central

Europe, and an illusion-free group where socialism was concerned. Lubitsch was born in Berlin in 1892 to a Russian father and German mother. Lengyel was born in what is now Hungary in 1880, Reisch in Vienna in 1903, and Wilder in Poland in 1906. These men grew up in the time and place that produced both socialism and communism. They knew their movie subjects well, including Russian aristocrats living in Paris.

Loyal Soviet emissary Ninotchka arrives in Paris by train and is approached by a porter. "Why should you carry other people's bags?" she asks him. When told that this is his business, she exclaims "That's no business…that's social injustice." The porter replies, "That depends on the tip."

Ninotchka informs her Board of Trade comrades of the importance of their mission: "Why are we peddling our precious possessions to the world at this time? Our next year's crop is in danger, and you know it. Unless we can get foreign currency to buy tractors, there will not be enough bread for our people."

The filmmakers knew socialist planners were good only at producing social plans. Russia in the 1930s was always just one good long-range plan away from turning bad harvests and bread shortages into abundance. Count Leon tells Ninotchka, "I have been fascinated by your Five Year Plan for the last 15 years."

Sanders voters should know that most of the Senator's diagnoses of today's ills were yesterday's diagnoses, too. Ninotchka spots Count Leon's income and social status instantly. "I have heard of the arrogant male in capitalist society," she says. "It is having a superior earning power that makes you like that."

Sanders supporters might applaud Ninotchka's keen sense for income inequality, and perhaps also Ninotchka's next line. "Your type will soon be extinct," she tells Count Leon. If Count Leon were a Wall

Street banker, the encounter would be up-to-date.

Count Leon is fascinated by Ninotchka nonetheless. He meets her before he learns that she is the new envoy, and he offers to show her the sights of Paris. Ninotchka decides Leon is "an interesting subject for study." She notes the square footage of his apartment and his relationship with his butler. She assumes Leon takes mean advantage of his social status and privilege, and on being introduced to the butler, she asks Leon, "Do you whip him?"

Lubitsch, Wilder, and Lengyel knew that the rights of the working class have limits under socialism. In the screenplay, Ninotchka calls for room service at her Parisian hotel and learns that the kitchen workers are on strike. "Will you assure the strikers of my hearty sympathy in their cause," she says. "I hope they will not weaken in their demands, and tell them to put no dressing whatsoever on my vegetables...What? You won't serve me either? Now look here, Comrade, I think it is a fine thing to let the capitalists go without luncheon, but when you keep food away from me, you are weakening the People!"

However poor the socialist harvests become, the people's leaders will always eat first.

Chapter 17

MUGGED BY HISTORY

It is not a bad idea in life to keep your eyes open.

My parents enjoyed very good health into their 70s and 80s, and they especially enjoyed bicycling as a form of exercise. Some years ago, the family discovered that a bicycle trail that passes very near my house in suburban St. Paul ends up near Oakland Cemetery. Many of our ancestors on Dad's side of the family are buried there. Oakland Cemetery, the oldest cemetery in Minnesota, is a mile north of the state capitol building, and reading the more prominent headstones and learning the stories of some of the people buried there can be a good way to learn the history of the state.

Dad liked to take his children and grandchildren around to the various family grave sites. They are all over the cemetery, which had the effect of making us somewhat familiar with the entire place. The oldest of these sites is that of Dad's great grandpa, the Reverend Wilhelm Rotert, a man who arrived in St. Paul from St. Louis in 1857 and who was one of the first Methodist ministers in the state. The Reverend Rotert and his immediate family are buried alongside a small, tree-covered hill that faces the east entrance to the cemetery.

If you follow the path westward and up that hill and away from the Rotert site, as you near the top of the hill, you come to a small clearing where on a beautiful Memorial Day weekend morning a few of the stones along the path are lit up by the morning sun. Right where the path merges with another path that runs north and south along the top of the hill there is such a sun-lit stone. The family name is Kochendorfer, and three people are buried there: a father Johan, a mother Catherine, and a three-year old daughter Sarah. The inscription below reads: "Victims of Redwood Falls Massacre Aug. 1862."

More Minnesota history. These three unfortunates were clearly victims of perhaps the most difficult event in the state's history, the Dakota War, or alternatively, the "Sioux Uprising," of 1862. The Dakota, the indigenous people living in this area when the Europeans arrived beginning in the seventeenth century, were coerced in the 1850s into living on a reservation along the south side of the Minnesota River at about the time Minnesota was made the 32nd state. Once there, the Dakota were kept at arm's length and some-times treated very unfairly by the U.S. government and the traders who dealt with them. In August 1862 many of the warrior men had had enough. They attacked in all directions: the traders, the govern-ment soldiers at nearby Fort Ridgely, and the settlers who had begun farming on the north side of the Minnesota River Valley. It was some of these Dakota warriors who had attacked and killed these three unfortunate Kochendorfers.

Still, the gravestone was intriguing. Redwood Falls is a small city along the Minnesota River, about 100 miles from Oakland Cemetery. How would these three unfortunate Kochendorfers have ended up in St. Paul? Nobody would have taken three dead bodies 100 miles in 1862 just to bury them at Oakland Cemetery. What was the story?

The "Find a Grave" web site that contained a photograph of the grave-stone also contained a paragraph describing how the Kochendorfers of 1862 had been a family of seven, and that four of the five children survived. Their parents and younger sister who died in 1862 had been hastily buried near their farmstead; their remains were uncovered and then re-interred at Oakland Cemetery in 1891.

What was the family story, though? What was the story of those four children who somehow survived and later reclaimed the bodies of their family members and brought them to St. Paul?

I went down to the Minnesota History Center one Saturday morning and asked a research assistants if there wasn't anything there on the Kochendorfer family. She sent down for a privately published booklet entitled Johan Kochendorfer and the Sioux Uprising of 1862. The family story is captured most vividly in a few family letters that appear in the booklet, letters that had been translated into English and that were written by the mother and father who died. They were evidently translated from the German by someone. Who? How? The letters were written in the late 1850s and early 1860s from St. Paul and are addressed to a relative in Illinois. How did the letters survive? How did the family retrieve and retain them, and who translated them?

The story told in the booklet was riveting. On that fateful day, August 18 1862, when the Dakota warriors attacked their farm, the father was quickly killed, the mother and youngest daughter soon after. The father was able to motion to his children to run for the woods as he lay dying, and the four other children ran down into a creek ravine very near the family's log cabin. The four children were 11-, 9-, 7-, and 5-years old. They were initially very confused and did not understand what was happening. They ran from their own cabin and towards the nearby farmstead, only to discover that the Indians were attacking there as well. The oldest was the only boy, and he remembered what his father had told him about the way to Fort Ridgely, the military outpost set up to supervise the reservation lands, but it was 25 miles away. The children made it, walking roughly 11 miles before catching an ox cart ride the remaining distance. Fort Ridgely was attacked twice in the next three days by the Indians, but the children survived and then were shipped back to St. Paul a week later. What a story.

I still had more questions though: The letters, the story, the church that was so pivotal in placing the Kochendorfer children with families, the four children orphaned by those events. The booklet was written by a man named Robert Tegeder, whose initial interest in the family story derived from the fact that his wife's last name had been Kochendorfer. He discovered through his research that his wife was not a member of the family, but he found the story fascinating nonetheless. Mr. Tegeder had died a dozen years before. He credits a woman in Hampton, Minnesota, a small farming community just south of St. Paul, for helping with the family story and records, including the assembling of a very impressive family genealogy. There were over 700 names in that genealogy that was put together in the late 1980s, all descendants of those four children who survived. I looked in the genealogy for the woman's name, Marilyn Hoffman, the woman in tiny Hampton, Minnesota. Sure enough, she was a granddaughter of the second daughter orphaned by those August 1862 events, Katherine Kochendorfer.

I looked her up. There she was, still listed in Hampton. I called her one Saturday. She remembered helping Mr. Tegeder all those years before, and she said she had many family records dating back to those four children who survived the Dakota War back in 1862.

I asked about the letters, those somewhat mysterious letters that appear in English in the Tegeder booklet.

"I have those letters," she said, matter-of-factly.

"What do you mean you 'have those letters'"? You mean you have the translations of the letters, right?"

"No. No," she said, in the perfect, patient, well-mannered Minnesotan of the pre-mass media age that I had heard my elders speak since childhood. "I have the original letters."

"The original letters? You mean you have those original handwritten letters, written by the woman who died in the Uprising? In German?"

"Yes. Yes, I do," she said. "I have many letters that she wrote."

I made the half-hour drive down to Hampton a few weeks later and met with her and one of her nephews. She pulled out the old records, and I spent an hour or two trying to digest them while listening to their family stories. There was pervading all these records and family stories a sort of peace, a deep understanding of the tragedy that had occurred all those years ago, a tragedy that the family understood was larger than their own family tragedy.

Marilyn Hoffman and the author and some
of her Kochendorfer family records.

I knew that two of the Kochendorfer children, the boy and his youngest sister, had been placed with a farm family in the St. Paul area, a husband and wife who had adopted a Sioux Indian child ten years before, a boy who would have been about the same age as the Kochendorfer son. There, amid those records, was an original 3" x 4" metal tintype photograph of the two of them when they were about twenty years old around 1870. The two 'brothers' posed in suitcoats and ties and stared somewhat jauntily at the cameraman. It was stunning.

I would discover soon enough that although these many hundreds of descendants of the four Dakota War surviving siblings are all sorts of people—quiet and gregarious and everything in between—they are not the sort of people who were going to bend your ear about their 'great' family story. They simply could not, or would not, do it. I could, though.

This was a story that deserved to be told, and by someone who could tell it in a way that the family could not. Rather than a story confined to the events of 1862, it was a story of an ordinary American family that suffered a severe blow in the wrenching process of turning a wilderness into a civilization, a family who forgave and forgot, but who kept their memories, and their records, not out of antipathy but simply to remember ...

The book appeared in July 2014, and the next month the Renville County Historical Society[249] helped organize a large gathering of descendants of those Dakota War survivors, people whose ancestors were both European and American Indian. The society was going to dedicate a series of plaques commemorating those who acted heroically during that Dakota War. They invited this 'non-descendant' to speak to them after lunch.

We convened in a covered picnic area in a park in little Morton, Minnesota. Reckoning from a photo I took of them, there were four generations of Kochendorfer descendants, a total of 31 of them (counting spouses), in attendance. Central Park in Morton is just a mile or so east of Beaver Creek, where almost exactly 152 years before, those four Kochendorfer children—their ancestors—were rescued by a group of adults with an ox cart bound for the relative safety of Fort Ridgely.

---

249. Renville County is where the Kochendorfers had been homesteading in 1862.

Four generations of Kochendorfer descendants
gather about a mile from where their ancestors—those four children—were rescued.

The story goes that the youngest, little 5-year-old Margaret Kochendorfer, fell fast asleep on reaching Beaver Creek after walking those 11 miles, and she had to be lifted up and set in the ox cart. It was this same Margaret Kochendorfer who, years later, would ask her Aunt in Illinois for her mother's letters and translate them from the German, those same fading letters I was shown in that farmhouse in Hampton.

Renville County Plaque Dedication Ceremony August 23, 2014

Luncheon Talk

My name is Dan Munson, and I've written a book about a Minnesota family and four of their children—the Kochendorfer children, ages 11-, 9-, 7- and 5-years of age at the time—who lived alongside Middle Creek in August 1862 and who escaped the attacks and, after watching their parents and younger sister killed, then made it 25 miles to Fort Ridgely, and went on to live very admirable lives. Their descendants now live throughout the country. Quite a number of them are here today. I'm not one of those descendants. I came upon their family name and their story quite by accident, but it's a good story, and I'll be glad to sell you a copy of the book I've written about them.[250] Today, however, I would like to talk about all the folks who were farming alongside the Kochendorfers here in the Minnesota River Valley those 152 years ago.

That was a long time ago: 1862. It's important to consider just how long ago it was, and how different the world was then, and how different were the prospects of each of those folks living here back then.

It had been only sixty years before that a somewhat obscure English pastor named Thomas Malthus had published a pamphlet entitled, Essay on the Principle of Population. Malthus fancied himself a bit of a mathematician, and he set out to make a mathematical argument. He stated in his pamphlet that human populations in a world of plenty would tend to increase in numbers in a geometric, or "exponential" manner: 2, 4, 8, 16, 32, 64, etc. He argued that the food supply, however, would only tend to grow in an "arithmetical manner: 2, 3, 4, 5, 6, 7, etc. The conclusion he drew was obvious: Humans would tend to

---

250. *Malice Toward None: Abraham Lincoln, the Civil War, the Homestead Act, and the Massacre – and Inspiring Survival – of the Kochendorfers* by D.C. Munson (Minnesota, 2014).

find themselves short of food because the food supply would always grow more slowly than the mouths it would have to feed.

Here was a happy thought: Humans will always tend to live on the verge of starvation—Have a nice day! Ever since that time, theories that are very pessimistic concerning the prospects for humanity have been labeled "Malthusian," in tribute to that great demographic pessimist, Thomas Malthus.

When Malthus published his pamphlet in around the year 1800, it was difficult to show him that he was clearly wrong. Humans had been routinely on the verge of starvation, and even in a place with as much good farmland as England, hunger and starvation were not uncommon. There was a sense in which Malthus appeared to be correctly diagnosing a problem, and his pamphlet was very popular. All the well-educated people read it. In one of her letters, the great English novelist Jane Austen—the woman who gave us Pride and Prejudice and Sense and Sensibility—commented that in her literary circle "everyone was reading 'the pamphlet.'"

Thomas Malthus would be much better known today if his theory had been correct, but he is now a largely forgotten figure to all but college humanities students. He had both good and bad luck in the timing of the publication of his pamphlet. Good luck in the sense that he seemed to correctly diagnose much of the plight of humanity up to that time and to find a large audience for his diagnosis. Bad luck in that he published at the dawn of the nineteenth century, the century that would change everything.

The nineteenth century was the century that took all the scientific knowledge that had been slowly growing and percolating in the seventeenth and eighteenth centuries and suddenly extended it into the lives of the ordinary citizen: steam power, electricity, the railroad, the automobile, and very early in the twentieth century—the airplane.

This 'progress' set powerful gears in motion, and in those gears certain people and their institutions got caught. Here in the Minnesota River Valley, Native Americans and their way of life got caught in those gears. The ideas of private property and land development and trading were foreign to them, and they struggled to adapt their ways, but many could not. Europeans had developed and adapted to these institutions over centuries, but the Indians were asked to adjust to them almost overnight. They were being asked to change much faster than the Europeans had, and all the difficulties this created were a source of anger and frustration for many of them.

Superior farming techniques were developed in Western Europe over hundreds of years, and the steamboat power of the nineteenth century allowed that farm produce to be shipped quickly to wherever it was needed. Governments suddenly realized that all these new modes of transportation made it possible to put far-flung farmlands into production, and to transport that farm produce hundreds of miles from where it was grown to where it was wanted.

That is what those immigrant farmers were doing down here in this Minnesota River Valley in 1862. They were here, most of them, because of the Homestead Act that was signed by President Lincoln on May 20 of that year. Lincoln and the Republicans were 'progressives' in the sense that they championed this new technological future of steam power, and railroads, and spreading farmland and cash crops far and wide. Those Minnesota River Valley farmers of 1862 knew that here in this rich soil underneath our feet they could generate 'bounty'—food in amounts far greater than that required for their own needs—and get it to markets hundreds of miles away, something that even fifty years before would have been impossible.

Progress, material progress, was a much more intoxicating concept then than it is perhaps nowadays when we have so much. We're occasionally bored, perhaps even jaded, by the flood of products and options we have today. I mean, do we really need another internet search engine? Or another drug to combat arthritis pain? Or a faster, quicker car engine when there is a clearly posted speed limit, and traffic often slows to a crawl? It is important to try to remember what 'progress' meant then, not what it means now. For them, progress was not another internet search engine—it was indoor plumbing! For them, progress wasn't a new turbo-charged engine (slightly better than last year's model), but a railroad that could allow them to travel overland without bouncing up and down in wagons being pulled very slowly by work horses! The story of the Kochendorfers involves a mother's letter that describes the trek the family made from central Illinois to St. Paul in 1857 by covered wagon. It was not easy!

In the process, those farmers here in the Minnesota River Valley and others like them throughout the world were taking that clever little pamphlet of Thomas Malthus' with all its clever arithmetical reasoning and politely throwing it in the trash can! (Not literally, of course.) Their descendants can be proud of the effort they were making.

I would like to say a word or two about the Kochendorfers and the book I've written about them.[251] The Kochendorfers were like so many others living here back in August 1862, with one small but very important exception. Mother Catherine Kochendorfer was a dedicated letter writer. Some others here in August 1862 undoubtedly wrote lots of letters, but Catherine's descendants can prove it, because the folks who received some of her letters saved them. Those same people were often told in those letters that they should sit right down and write a good long letter back to Catherine. Catherine liked writing 'em, and Catherine liked getting 'em.

---

251. *Malice Toward None: Abraham Lincoln, the Civil War, the Homestead Act, and the Massacre –and Inspiring Survival—of the Kochendorfers* by D.C. Munson (Minnesota, 2014)

Her sister Rosina Ebert back in Illinois saved quite a few of the letters she got from Catherine. Catherine Kochendorfer's first letter written from here in Renville County to her sister back in Illinois is dated May 21, the day after President Lincoln signed the Homestead Act. Those letters are very interesting, and in them we hear a little of the loneliness that must have been a part of pioneer life. We also learn all about that family, the Kochendorfer family that was living alongside Middle Creek on August 18, 1862. There were five Kochendorfer children: ages 11-, 9-, 7-, 5-, and 3-years of age. Seven people in all. Like I mentioned, four of the children made it to Fort Ridgely. At intervals, the oldest son carried his 5-year-old sister, probably on his back, when she could walk no further. They survived the two Dakota Indian attacks on the Fort, and then were sent from Fort Ridgely back to St. Paul around September 1.

Consider those four children arriving in September 1862, following the death of their parents and younger sister. Those four children were about as vulnerable as it is possible to be. The three girls were less than ten years old, and their nearest relatives, their only relatives in all of North America, were a single family farming near Peoria, Illinois—hundreds of miles away. They are orphans living in the center of a large continent, a continent on which they have only one set of relatives. Such a thing is actually quite impossible in human history up to that point: to be so young, and to have so few relatives on the same continent on which you are living, the only continent on which you have ever lived! All their other relatives were back in Germany, people the children did not know. These four children were not unique here in the Minnesota River Valley in September 1862, of course. I'm making the point that the situation faced by the remaining adults throughout this area back in 1862 was in some ways unique in human history.

Not only did those four Kochendorfer children survive. They thrived. There is no other way to put it. The church their parents had joined on arriving in Minnesota in 1857, the St. Paul Evangelical Church community, found homes for them. The children went on to have families of their own. Boy did they ever! Between the four of them, they had 26 children. The descendants of those four very vulnerable orphans who stepped onto the St. Paul landing in September 1862, with nothing but the clothes on their back, now number over one thousand. This story, the Kochendorfer story, is a tribute to the resilience and good sense and charity—and tolerance—of those early Minnesotans.

Postscript: When you publish a history book, you discover that your relatives want to congratulate you on your achievement by palming off on you some of the big dusty tomes they've been looking to get rid of for years on the theory that, "Well, you're the historian." I inherited a big old Luther Bible—"die Heilige Schrift"—that had served as a sort of Family Bible for our family for generations. My parents didn't want to move it to their new apartment. When I got it home I set it on the shelf and promptly forgot about it. One day, time perhaps weighing too heavily on my hands, I opened it. There, just inside the big imposing cover, were some loose-leaf papers containing, among many other things, a very detailed obituary of the Reverend Rotert, in both German and English. I learned that he arrived in St. Paul from St. Louis in 1857—the same year the Kochendorfers arrived, and from the same general direction—and that he and his wife joined the very same small German Methodist congregation the Kochendorfers joined that same year. It was a very small congregation—only a couple dozen families. They simply must have known one another!

★ ★ ★

This series of articles concludes with a detailed review of a particular instance in history where these abstract and somewhat arcane monetary matters had very concrete, and very unfortunate, effects. The Dakota War that occurred in Minnesota in 1862 had a number of causes, but one of them was monetary. Although historians often discuss the causes of the Dakota War, the monetary angle is seldom explored. This is understandable, given that these monetary decisions occurred many miles away from Minnesota in Washington D.C.

The monetary issue that did so much to trigger the Dakota War is one discussed earlier: the gold standard. The argument as to whether to use a gold-backed currency and all the constraints it creates or opt for an easily expandable currency backed only by the full faith and credit of the government always comes down to a question of convenience. This convenience, or more specifically the lack of it, was a reason that the Dakota War began.

Those focused on a permanent, long-term solution—one monetary policy for all time—are naturally drawn to the 'flexibility' of the unbacked version. This long-term analysis is the one economists drone on about, the one drenched in theory. In this one, the economy is seen as a wild, impetuous beast requiring taming. Its various dramatic ups and downs create desperate conditions that routinely require government intervention. The banking panic of 1907 might be the model, when the aggressive plunging done by certain investors caused such wreckage that at the very moment when large amounts of banking credit was most sorely needed, little credit was available. A government obligated to redeem its bonds and currency in gold would be hamstrung by the lack of gold in the quantity necessary to meet the shortage in banking credit. A government without such obligations, one free to create credit with the stroke of a pen, was a government that 'in theory' was equipped with the tools needed to meet any-and-all emergencies.

The difficulties and confusions created by a credit shortage, is best illustrated by the one that makes the Panic of 1907 look like a hangnail. The classic test case was provided by perhaps the greatest single 'emergency' in the country's history: The Civil War that began in 1861.

The magnitude of the emergency was not immediately apparent in mid-year 1861, but as the year wore on, it was clear that the U.S. government simply did not have the money—that is to say, the gold or the credit line—to finance the war effort required to combat the determined Confederate forces. The U.S. Treasury began to print 'greenbacks,' legal currency backed not by gold but only by the green ink used to print the bills, to pay and transport and outfit Union soldiers.

Certain of the contracts the U.S. government had entered into in the years preceding 1861 stipulated payment in gold or gold-backed currency, however. Those owed money under these pre-1861 contracts were left to wonder exactly how they would be paid ...

The Gold Standard and The Dakota War of 1862

Appeared in the Spring 2023. [252]

The Dakota War, or Sioux Uprising of 1862, was the bloodiest event in the long and bloody history of warfare between the U.S. government and Native Americans. Although much has been written about that very unfortunate event, its connection to the monetary and financial history of the country is seldom mentioned or analyzed.

In the spring and early summer of 1862, the Dakota tribes of Minnesota were living on a reservation along the southwest side of

---

252. "The Gold Standard and the Dakota War of 1862" appeared in the Spring 2023 issue of *Financial History* magazine.

a 150-mile-long stretch of the Minnesota River. The north side of the river was being settled by white farmers who were taking advantage of the provisions of the Homestead Act that was signed into law by President Lincoln on May 20, 1862. In August of that year, many events conspired to cause a large group of Dakota men to begin attacking the whites in the area: those farming the north side of the Minnesota River, the traders with the Dakota near the Indian Agencies on the south side of the river, and the U.S Army installation at Fort Ridgely near the little village of New Ulm. The attacks went on for a few weeks; hundreds died, and 38 Dakota men were found guilty of having killed defense-less settlers—many of them women and children—and were hung in a large public mass execution in Mankato, Minnesota on December 26, 1862.[253]

Historians have since busied themselves with showing how those terrible events of August 1862 might be seen as part of a long chain. A popular narrative is to review the entire 200+ year series of conflicts between white Europeans and the Indians of North America. This huge span of time, if compressed sufficiently, takes on the feel of inevitabil-ity and what some historians have called "Manifest Destiny."[254] While a phrase summarizing events far apart in time and space can be useful, a close study of these individual conflicts—the special circumstances, chance occurrences, different governments, different weaponry, etc.— is often much more interesting than such a bland, summary judgment.

The Dakota War of 1862 is a case in point. Certain facts are dif-ferent in 1862 than they were in the seventeenth, eighteenth and early

---

253. For more detail on the events of the U.S.-Dakota War, see *The Sioux Uprising of 1862* by Kenneth Carley (St. Paul: Minnesota Historical Society Press, 1976).

254. Evidence of such a plan among high officials of the U.S. government is openly stated in the U.S. government's opposition to a British proposal at the Treaty of Ghent talks in 1814 to set up a state within the United States for the American Indians. C.M. Gates (1940), *Mississippi Valley Historical Review* 26.

nineteenth century clashes between Native Americans and the British or the U.S. government or white settlers. Differences included industrial development and fearsome government artillery power. Some of the historical factors that are known to have influenced those 1862 events are well documented: the Treaties of 1851 that moved the Dakota Indians to that reservation along the Minnesota River, the corruption and petty thievery surrounding the implementation and operation of the treaties, and the Civil War itself with its commandeering of so many able-bodied men, etc.

An interesting financial issue at the heart of those events in Minnesota in 1862 is seldom discussed, and it looks to have been a precipitating factor, namely, the gold standard of money and the precarious state of U.S. government finances.

Financial historians regard the Civil War as an important event in U.S. financial history for reasons that escape most other historians. Lincoln's government was the first to issue paper currency and U.S. Treasury notes and bonds that were not exchangeable for gold. Such historians like to trace the effects of these changes wrought by the Civil War into many other financial matters, but their gaze seldom wanders too far from the corner of Broad and Wall Streets in lower Manhattan. Your author seeks to trace these financial effects out west to the comparative wilderness of the Minnesota River Valley in 1862.

The history of attempts to issue paper currency is one that is littered with failures from the eighteenth century South Sea bubble to the hyperinflations of the present century in Zimbabwe and Venezuela. There is always a strong temptation to print more of the stuff than is prudent to pay soldiers, to build palaces, etc. The result is often rampant "inflation"—or, more pointedly, devaluation—of the paper currency.

Those currencies that have held their value for centuries, currencies like the old British pound sterling and the Swiss franc, have had a common feature: They were exchangeable for gold. There is nothing special about gold as such, but its beauty, rarity, and its extreme density make it easy to store and difficult to counterfeit, features appreciated by bankers centuries ago. Such gold-backed currencies therefore have an intrinsic value while the gold backing prevents the government issuing such currency from printing more of it than it has gold to exchange for it.

The United States dollar in 1860 was considered such a currency. A person in possession of $20.67 of U.S. currency could, at his/her option, go down to a certain government office or a certain bank and exchange the $20.67 in currency for precisely one troy ounce of gold. As a result, the price of a pair of good quality boots in 1860 was basically the same as it had been in 1790 when the U.S. treasury began operations. The U.S. dollar was said to be a 'sound' currency.

The Civil War changed all this. In early-July 1861, when Abraham Lincoln asked the U.S. Congress for $400 million dollars to combat what he then called an 'insurrection' in the states of the Confederacy,[255] the U.S. government did not have the gold to back it. The Union was in danger of dissolution, of course, and the fact that there wasn't the gold to continue to issue gold-backed money to pay for the war was a somewhat minor point to the politicians in Washington D.C.

It took a few months for the government to fully realize the implications of this fact. Shortly after President Lincoln got his authorization of money from the Congress on July 5, 1861, the U.S. government issued fifty million dollars in debt notes, payable—as usual—on demand and, at the holder's option, in either paper currency or in gold.

The folks working at the Treasury department were the first to perceive the government's looming financial problem. On the outflow side

---

255. Address to the U.S. Congress in Special Session – July 5, 1861.

of things, Treasury secretary Salmon Chase observed in October 1861 that, "the expenditures everywhere are frightful."[256] On the other side of the ledger, one veteran Treasury official recalled that although tariffs—the main source of federal revenue in those days—could be paid either with Treasury notes or with gold, tariff payers in late-1861 began paying almost exclusively with notes. "There were demand notes out to the amount of sixty millions of dollars," he recalled, "and as these were receivable at the Custom-House the same as gold, and did not command so high a premium, duties on imports were almost exclusively paid in them, and little or no specie [i.e., gold] was received."[257]

Gold was fleeing the government coffers.

The investing public took a little longer to adjust to the government's fiscal problems. Confidence in the federal government's finances was pinned on the hope of a quick Union victory, but the Union defeats at the first Battle of Bull Run and at Wilson's Creek in late-summer 1861 began to shake that confidence. The state-chartered banks, initially willing to buy federal notes in large amounts to do their part for the war effort, began to lose their faith in those U.S. government notes as their depositors began to redeem their bank notes for gold.[258] By late December 1861 these state banks had lost half their gold reserves and such reserves were daily dwindling further.[259] The banks suspended gold exchange on December 30, 1861.[260]

---

256. *Sovereignty and an Empty Purse: Banks and Politics in the Civil War* by B. Hammond (Princeton, 1970), p. 125.

257. *Memories of Many Men and Some Women* by M.R. Field (New York, 1874), p. 257-258.

258. "The banks could neither pay coin to the government for bonds, nor dispose of them to their customers for specie." *Abraham Lincoln: A History* by J.G Nicolay and J. Hay, Volume VI (1890), p. 230.

259. *A Financial History of the United States* by M.G. Myers (New York, 1970), p. 152

260. *Recollections of Forty Years in the House, Senate, and Cabinet* by J. Sherman (London, 1895), p. 216-219. Sherman was a member of the Senate Finance Committee during the Civil War.

It is one of the recurring themes in financial history: War causes gold to disappear into private hands as prospects of a quick military victory dim, and as the costs of the war effort mount.

The federal government was out of options, and it began printing new, unsecured paper currency in February 1862. This new federal currency that was no longer exchangeable for gold was called a 'greenback,' and it became a derogatory term as the war dragged on and the greenbacks printed to pay for the war declined in purchasing power.[261]

These financial events in Washington D.C. were of considerable interest out in Minnesota. Those 1851 treaties between the government and the Dakota Indians were negotiated around that stable, gold-backed dollar. The Indians and their leaders would naturally wonder as to the government's ability, during time of war, to meet the treaty terms. They could be understandably concerned as to whether they would be paid at all.

These fiscal problems of the federal government would have been of considerable interest to the agents and traders at the Indian agencies along the Minnesota River. Their trading with the Indians was dependent on the U.S. government coming through with the yearly treaty payments. Perhaps, the traders might speculate, the annuity payment would be made in greenbacks rather than in gold. Perhaps it would be smaller than usual due to senior government claims. Or perhaps payment would simply be delayed or suspended until the war was over.

This uncertainty these traders would probably have communicated to the Indians who lived nearby, and the Indians would have understood. The Indians would understand the situation somewhat differently, however. The traders might see most clearly the financial uncertainty; the Indians perhaps saw the military uncertainty most clearly. Once war commenced, tribal leaders knew the outcome could never be certain. If

---

261. *A Monetary History of the United States*, by M. Friedman and A. Jacobson Schwartz (1963), see Chart 6, p. 68.

their treaty was with a government that could be defeated in battle and fail, then did they not have a potentially unenforceable treaty?

The Indians had little in the way of stored provisions—their crop yields had been poor in 1861 due to a generally poor growing season. The crops of 1862 were looking very good, but they were not ready just yet, and the Indians were hungry and increasingly impatient.[262]

The federal government initially answered the question as to how the Dakota would be paid by treating the Dakota like everyone else. Thomas Riggs was working with his father at his father's mission to the Dakota along the Minnesota River in 1862. He recalled that, "Currency had been sent out first instead of [gold] coin, but it had to be returned because the Indians would not accept currency."[263]

Bishop Henry Whipple, cousin of Union General Henry Hallock and the head of the Episcopal diocese in Minnesota, was a great friend of the Dakota Indians of his state. He described the cluster of Indians that began to gather about the Lower Agency in late-July 1862, demanding food for their tribes.

"I had never seen the Indians so restless," he wrote. "The Indians had heard that they were not to receive their payment [in gold]," Bishop Whipple recalled, and he tried to assure them they would. The bishop addressed one of the clerks and told the clerk that "Major Galbraith [the U.S. government's agent], is coming down to enroll the Indians for payment."

The clerk tried to impress upon the bishop that he knew better. "Galbraith is a fool," the clerk told the bishop. "Why does he lie to them? I have heard from Washington that most of the appropriation has been used to pay claims against the Indians. The payment will not be made. I have told the Indians this and have refused to trust them."

---

262. *Through Dakota Eyes* by G.C. Anderson and A.R. Wentworth (St. Paul, 1988), p. 27.

263. *Sunset to Sunset: A Lifetime with My Brothers, the Dakotas by Thomas Lawrence Riggs* (1847-1940), p. 30.

Bishop Whipple was taken aback. "I was astounded that a trader's clerk should claim to know more about the payment than the government agent," he wrote later.[264]

This trader's clerk, for better or worse, was the representative, the front face, of the U.S. government—at least as far as the Lower Sioux tribes were concerned. It was easy for the Indians to not much like what they saw.

Benjamin G. Armstrong was another Minnesotan caught in the middle of this confusion. A southerner who had traveled north in 1840 to try roughing it in the Minnesota wilderness, Armstrong quickly learned to live with the Ojibwe Indians, and he became fluent in the Ojibwe and Dakota languages. By 1862 he was a trusted intermediary between the U.S. government's Interior Department and the Indians of Minnesota. He wrote of a meeting in August 1862 between Superintendent of Indian Affairs Thompson and the Dakota chiefs: "The superintendent called the chiefs together and told them that he would give them their goods annuities at once, as they were then on the ground, and ... as soon as the money came, he would notify them and they could come for it.

"They asked what kind of money it would be, to which he answered, he did not know, but whichever kind it was he would pay it to them. He could not tell what kind of money the great father had on hand, but thought it would be currency. They then demanded coin [i.e., gold] and said they would not take greenbacks."[265]

This uncertainty surrounding the payment is also confirmed by one of the Dakota chiefs who survived the war and related his memory of those events to a reporter years later. "Big Eagle" enumerated five causes of the conflict and remembered distinctly that, "The government

---

264. *Light and Shadow of a Long Episcopate* by H.B. Whipple (1899), Chapter 10.

265. *Early Life Among the Indians* by Benjamin G. Armstrong (Wisconsin, 1892), p. 75-76

was in a great war, and gold was scarce, and paper money had taken its place, and it was said the gold could not be had to pay us."[266]

The combustible situation along the Minnesota River Valley that July–August of 1862 was of little moment back in Washington D.C. The demands made by the Indians of Minnesota reached Washington as the Union Army, President Lincoln's army, was stalemated at best in its battles with the Confederacy. Confederate troops, specifically General Robert E. Lee's Army of Northern Virginia, were camped within 50 miles of the U.S. capital that summer of 1862, a capital that seemed to its residents to be woefully under-protected. These problems were of much more pressing concern to the residents of Washington D.C. than any news reports from those distant Minnesota lands, lands that had only become part of the Union four years earlier.

The escalation of events in mid-August 1862 are well known to Minnesota historians—the refusal of the Agency traders to release food stores for the Indians living nearby. There was precipitous behavior by some young Dakota men on August 17 who attacked and killed some clerks and farmers near Acton, Minnesota after those Dakota men may have been denied service at the general store there.[267]

The early hours of August 18 were chaos. The Indians, perhaps fearing government retribution for the events the day before at Acton, attacked in all directions: They attacked the defenseless farmers and their families just across the river, and they attacked those Lower Agency traders. Those near the Lower Agency were the first killed, and those who resided near the Lower Agency and escaped those attacks were the first to reach Fort Ridgely and sound the alarm.

Meanwhile, as those events were occurring, a well-guarded wagon

---

266. *Through Dakota Eyes*, edited by G.C. Anderson and A.R. Woolworth (1988). Big Eagle's Narrative 1, p. 26.

267. Carley, p. 6-9

was cantering down the road between St. Paul and Fort Ridgely. The ambush of a detachment of Fort Ridgely soldiers left the fort temporarily under the command of a 20-year-old lieutenant, Thomas Gere. Gere later described those hectic events and mentioned almost parenthetically that, "At about noon [on August 18, 1862] there arrived at the fort in charge of C.G. Wykoff, clerk of the Indian superintendent, and his party of four, the long-expected annuity money, $71,000 [~235 pounds, $7 million today] in gold."[268]

The U.S. government was late, but it was making good on its treaty promises. The gold had arrived in St. Paul on August 16, but with no telegraph lines between St. Paul and Fort Ridgely, the people most interested in this development had no idea the yearly annuity payment was on the way.

The gold arrived at Fort Ridgely four short hours after those calamitous events began.

268. *Minnesota in the Civil and Indian Wars*, St. Paul Pioneer Press Co.—Account of Lt. Gere, p. 250

Chapter 18

A CHASTENED CRITIC

The job of the dramatic critic, as far as most artists are concerned, is easy—at least when compared to the job of the artist. Worse yet from the artist's perspective, the profession seems to attract rather sour-faced, splenetic, contemptible people who often lack even the hint of artistic talent. "I'd like to see them try to sing-write-dance-paint-act," the artists of the world no doubt find themselves muttering daily.

The great comic writer P.G. Wodehouse, who generally received good press, nevertheless harbored similar views. In a private letter to a friend late in his long life, Wodehouse wrote of a book he had been reading that consisted of Max Beerbohm columns of criticism. "What lice these dramatic critics are,"[269] he wrote his friend.

This critic of economic planners and government officials is left to consider whether he is not a similarly wingless and parasitic insect. After all, it is very easy to point out the many errors made by modern economic theorists. In addition, he must concede that these theoreticians and officials—most of them, anyway—were well-intentioned. Human affairs are a tricky business; humans are all too fallible.

When I talk with the many descendants of the Kochendorfer children who survived the Dakota War, there is little or no discussion of economic matters. They tell me about their latest adventures and the various goings-on of their many family members, and the many stories they were told about their four orphaned ancestors. It is impossible for their family biographer not to reflect on the arc of their family's

---

269. "P.G. Wodehouse: A Life in Letters" by S. Ratcliffe (London, 2011), p. 490.

dramatic story, though, and to consider the grain of economic wisdom that it may contain.

If government justifications for economic action are pseudo-scientific and often counter-productive, then something like a gold standard that keeps government officials from committing too much folly might be a good idea. The Kochendorfer story, however, and the larger story of the Dakota War of 1862, requires this ink-stained critic to think a second time.

It was the gold standard and the limits it placed on government action that had, in no small measure, caused the disaster that descended on that young family homesteading along the Minnesota River in August 1862. A more modern system such as those that have come in for criticism in these pages would have made the required payments to the Dakota tribes on time because it could print the money and would never have agreed to make payment in gold or gold-backed currency in the first place. It was impossible to avoid this uncomfortable fact. It needed to be made sense of, somehow.

Government's time-honored activities, of course, do not require clever rules and provisions. Mensa-level insight, such as that prescribed by Woodrow Wilson in his 1887 scholarly paper, is not required to keep order, register property ownership, pave roads and build bridges. Furthermore, Mr. Wilson's mandarins seem no more able to apply their superior cognitive ability to successfully anticipate and plan for the improbable than is the great voting public.

Should government officials therefore be limited to doing nothing but those narrow, circumscribed tasks? Should legal knots be tied to prevent them from attempting anything more? Of course not. A practical reading of history shows that improbable events often require the government to be empowered to do more than those narrow, dependable tasks.

The mistake the critic makes is perhaps of the same variety as that made by the mandarin: to ignore the chaos and mayhem of unplannable events. The mandarins may pass off their policy guesswork as 'scientific' and fail to consider the irrationality of human affairs, but the critic may make his error in ignoring the floods, fires, earthquakes, epidemics, and strife that call for a government strong enough to combat their adverse consequences.

The implications of the Kochendorfer story are clear: Government is properly concerned and must be equipped to respond to the chaos and mayhem of an unplannable world.

This book concerns itself with only certain kinds of snafus, namely the economic or financial sort. They are less common than others, and on close inspection, they are sometimes difficult to categorize. The Panic of 1907, for example, was an odd one that didn't occur again for another hundred years. It gave us that dubious creation, the Federal Reserve Bank, which stood at the ready for years afterwards waiting for a similar panic.

What sort of financial emergency should trigger a governmental response? What lessons can be drawn from all these mistakes, from practical experience, to place limits on institutions while at the same time keeping them flexible enough to address the unexpected event? The limits, the trip wires, must be set as low as practically possible when the emergency is a fire or a flood or a war, where the lives of citizens are at stake. The limits are a little more difficult to set when the problem is economic, or financial.

What should trip the wire at the Federal Reserve Bank or the Treasury? What sort of fiscal fire should cause its officials to ride to the rescue of the financial system? Set the limit too low, with the government rushing to paper over the smallest problems, and the country's fiduciaries grow lazy and inattentive, and the resulting currency devaluation causes the citizenry to gradually lose faith in that currency and later in the government itself. Set it too high and government waits and waits until things have pretty much descended into chaos and lives are lost, as they were along the Minnesota River Valley in the late summer of 1862. If a fast response is required, a gold-backed currency is probably impractical, given the time required for a big, lumbering government to decide to suspend such a monetary standard.

Much of the difficulty is with the nature of government power. A government empowered to act with the force necessary to combat dire emergencies like the Civil War is a government that can use that same grant to swat with tremendous power what are actually small problems, often with disastrous longer-term results. The difficulty is, as it often is, with self-control. The need is to somehow restrain officials to control the use of a vast grant of potential power and resort to its use to combat only those dire emergencies for which that power was reserved, and not to employ it to address the small matters the citizenry can handle on its own.

The news business does not help. Every day brings with it what they describe as such emergencies: bankruptcies, plant closures, 'cataclysmic' 3 percent market declines. How does one sort through these daily disasters and decide which of them require government to ride to the rescue?

The Civil War was certainly such an emergency, and the federal government did suspend gold convertibility in favor of greenbacks, but not quickly and powerfully enough to save the Kochendorfer family. On the other end of the scale, a 10 percent downdraft in the market for common stocks probably should not be considered dire.

Ours is an age of specialization. The critic does not want to wander too far from his area of expertise. The job of criticizing government and its economic planners, while perhaps louse-like, is taxing enough without adding to it the job of providing detailed policy suggestions as well. Those reading this book for meticulously crafted policy suggestions will have to be satisfied with these few but simple guidelines: The wire triggering government action should be tripped by civil war, and it should not be tripped by a 10 percent decline in stock prices. This sort of guidance is perhaps not of much help to policymakers, but the critic is willing to go only so far. Those interested in more specificity will have to be satisfied with the observation that the critic has framed the issue and has conceded that criticism alone is insufficient.

About the Author

Daniel C. Munson is a graduate of the University of Minnesota and worked for many years as a chemical engineer. He lives in St. Paul, Minnesota with his wife and in retirement he enjoys writing technological and financial history.

Other Books by this Writer

Malice Toward None: Abraham Lincoln, the Civil War, the Homestead Act, and the Massacre—and Inspiring Survival—of the Kochendorfers (Minnesota, 2014)

Index